Getting Russia Right

GETTING RUSSIA RIGHT

Thomas Graham

A Council on Foreign Relations Book

polity

First published in 2023 by Polity Press

Polity Press
65 Bridge Street
Cambridge CB2 1UR, UK

Polity Press
111 River Street
Hoboken, NJ 07030, USA

ISBN-13: 978-1-5095-5689-2

A catalogue record for this book is available from the British Library.

Library of Congress Control Number: 2022948488

Typeset in 11.5 on 14 pt Adobe Garamond
by Cheshire Typesetting Ltd, Cuddington, Cheshire
Printed and bound in the United States of America

For further information on Polity, visit our website:
politybooks.com

Contents

For Ro

Acknowledgments

This book would never have been written if not for Louise Knight, Publisher for Politics and International Relations at Polity Press. She approached me in March 2022, shortly after Russia had launched its brutal assault on Ukraine, to gauge my interest in writing a short book to explain what the West got wrong about Russia. I needed little persuasion. I was working on a much longer history of US–Russian relations, but Louise offered me an opportunity to articulate my ideas in a more concentrated form and to release them into the public debate at a time when people would be inclined to pay attention. Since then, it has been a pleasure to work with her and her colleague and editorial assistant Inès Boxman, from the initial drafts to the final book. Two anonymous reviewers engaged by Polity provided trenchant critiques of the manuscript, which helped me refine my argument and its presentation.

The Council on Foreign Relations has been my professional home while I worked on this book. Richard Haass, the president, James Lindsay, the Director of Studies, and Shannon O'Neil, the Deputy Director of Studies, all read the entire manuscript and offered invaluable advice on how to improve it. My research associate, Anya Konstantinovsky, provided much appreciated research support and editorial assistance. Samuel Farbman and Julian Gonzales-Poirier, while interning at the Council, verified dates for events cited in the text and saved me from some embarrassing errors. Drew Guff and the Friedman Family Foundation Strategic Innovation Fund offered generous support for my research program at the Council, for which I am deeply grateful.

In addition, while I was writing this book, I was a research scholar and lecturer in the Program on Russian, East European, and Eurasian Studies of the MacMillan Center at Yale University. I want to thank the Center's director, Steven Wilkinson, for the appointment, which enabled me to test drive many of my ideas with dozens of bright and demanding graduate and undergraduate students in seminars on US–Russian relations since the end of the Cold War. Their questions and comments made for a better book.

My ideas about Russia and US–Russian relations have evolved over the past thirty-five years over hundreds of conversations with Americans, Europeans, and Russians too numerous to mention, many of whom have become valued friends. Some deserve special recognition. Bob Otto read the entire manuscript – more than once – and shared numerous insights and counter arguments that challenged me to sharpen my own. Peter Charow, Ivan Kurilla, Bob Legvold, Rajan Menon, Ivan Safranchuk, and Ray Smith reviewed one or more chapters. I am grateful for their probing questions and comments.

I also want to thank the *Polis* Non-Profit Partnership for permission to freely re-use parts of my article "Russia and the USA on the World Stage," originally published in Russian translation in *Polis*, issues 1–3, 2022. The article served as the basis for Chapter 2.

I am of course solely responsible for the views expressed in this book and the perhaps naive hope that, if the United States gets Russia right, constructive relations are possible in the future, despite the disappointments of the past and the horrors of the present.

Preface

Russia's massive invasion of Ukraine on February 24, 2022, was a day of reckoning – for Russia, Ukraine, and the West, to be sure, but also at a less exalted level for all Russia experts, especially those like me who, up to the last moment, believed Russian President Vladimir Putin would take a less fateful route. Diplomatic talks had not run their course. A small-scale intervention, as in 2014, could have underscored his seriousness of purpose, tested Ukrainian and Western resolve, and helped assess the risks of further military action. Such steps seemed to be more in line with the pragmatic approach Putin had taken to most issues since he assumed power a generation ago. Alas, he decided to roll the dice.

Why did so many experts get it wrong? Were their assumptions about Putin and Russia fatally flawed, or did they overlook a significant event that set Russia on an unlikely path? Beyond those immediate concerns loomed the larger question of how Russia and the United States had arrived at this point some thirty years after the Cold War's end, which had given birth to grand visions of enduring US–Russian partnership in building a more peaceful, secure, and prosperous world.

That question was of particular salience for someone like me who had been studying Russia for most of his life – the Sputnik moment in 1957 that convinced the United States to radically elevate its response to the Soviet challenge also sparked my life-long fascination with Russia. Finding the answer was a matter of professional pride for someone whose career as a Russia expert began during the dying days of the Cold War.

I entered US government service in 1983 and spent twenty years working on Soviet and then Russian affairs at the American Embassy in Moscow, in the Departments of State and Defense, and on the National Security Council staff, including three years as the senior director for Russia. Since I left government in February 2007, I have continued to work on Russian matters, as a consultant, teacher, and researcher. For the last 35 years I have either lived in Moscow or traveled to Russia regularly for meetings with senior Russian government officials, businesspeople, media representatives, experts, students, and others.

My positions and travels have provided various perches from which to observe the evolution of US–Russian relations since the last years of the Cold War. During the George W. Bush administration I was directly involved in the formulation of US Russia policy, although I was never more than a second-tier player, who will not merit even a footnote in the history books.

With Russia's invasion of Ukraine, it was time to take a critical look at the post-Cold War history of US–Russian relations and the quality of US policymaking, with the hope that the lessons learned would help the United States better deal with the Russia challenge in the future. Thus, this book.

Despite my government service, this book is not a brief in defense of any administration's policy. To the contrary, I turn a critical eye to all post-Cold War administrations, with a focus more on the shortcomings than the successes. Nor is this book a lament that administrations did not take my advice on the overall approach to Russia or on specific matters. Nowhere do I argue that relations would have turned out better if senior officials had done so. I have suffered from my own share of misperceptions, blind spots, and illusions, which become all the more stark in retrospect. Rather, my goal throughout has been to understand what I have witnessed during the past three to four decades, with a particular focus on US policy.

Policy is always made in a situation of imperfect knowledge. As a rule, policymakers are compelled to act before they have a full understanding of the issue at hand. This is always the case during a crisis. To a lesser extent, it is true of strategic planning, as well – policymakers have blind spots; they lack critical information about the target country of the policymaking. No outsider can fully appreciate the often subterranean forces that shape a country's destiny – and, truth be told, few natives do, although their intuition is usually more acute. This is the natural state of things; the policymaker has no reason to complain.

As Henry Kissinger has noted, there is an inverse relationship between influence and certainty. The policymaker often has the greatest opportunity to shape events when much is uncertain. Waiting for more information can diminish influence. This is not a plea for hasty judgments and actions. It is rather to note that the art of statesmanship requires a keen sense for the moment when the statesman has sufficient knowledge to act decisively, and when waiting for its further accumulation begins to erode his influence.

That intuition comes from experience and the study of history. It requires distilling out of a complex situation the essence that enables purposeful action. In this sense, essentialism – so suspect in academic circles – is a necessary aspect of policymaking. Complexity paralyzes the will, which is one reason why few academics adjust well to the policy world. Policymakers need to simplify reality to a manageable degree, and they necessarily operate on the basis of what they consider to be a few essential truths about world affairs, the country they serve, and the foreign lands they deal with. As Bismarck eloquently put it, "The statesman's task is to hear God's footsteps marching through history, and to try and catch on to His coattails as He marches past." Success depends on whether he hears those footsteps clearly through the noise of a turbulent world.

Critics will object that I have painted with too broad a brush in the following pages. That I have left out nuance. This is indeed the case. But my goal was not to provide an exhaustive examination of US policy, Russian national interests, and US–Russian relations. It was to distill the few key ideas that have shaped policy and the critical forces that have driven events, to provide a framework for understanding Russia, which it is hoped will help future policymakers advance US interests in relations with that country. Cold War containment, widely praised as an historic triumph, the critics should remember, was grounded in a few essential truths about Russia and the United States, first articulated by the American diplomat George F. Kennan in his Long Telegram from the Embassy in Moscow to the Department of State in 1946.

In the end, policymaking is always haunted by regrets. In retrospect, policymakers could always have done better, if they had known then what they know now. But "the owl of Minerva takes flight only at dusk," the great German philosopher Hegel observed. Understanding comes only when it is too late to act. The best one can do is to pass that belated understanding on to the next generation of policymakers in the hope that they will know how to use it.

Introduction

The United States and Russia are once again adversaries. This is not where either country wanted to be some thirty years ago at the end of the Cold War. Back then, both countries harbored visions of partnership, although they sought it for different reasons. The United States hoped to integrate Russia into the Euro-Atlantic Community of free-market democracies. That would seal the American victory in the Cold War and vindicate its system, much as the emergence of liberal democracy in Germany and Japan under American tutelage had after their defeats in the Second World War. Russia, meanwhile, sought to use partnership to restore its status as the second leading global power, if not exactly the other superpower. Whether it was democratic or authoritarian was of little intrinsic interest as long as it was powerful. So the destinations were distant from one another, and yet both Washington and Moscow believed the path to their respective goals lay through partnership.

After a quarter century of failed efforts to build a lasting partnership, followed by several years of mounting tensions, Putin's invasion of Ukraine on February 24, 2022, crystalized a profound alienation between Russia and the United States. Relations today are scraping the depths of Cold War antagonisms. Indeed, they have probably not been so hostile since 1983, the darkest year of the second half of the Cold War. Then President Ronald Reagan denounced the Soviet Union as the "evil empire" and launched his Strategic Defense Initiative (SDI, or Star Wars as it was quickly dubbed), which questioned the principles that undergirded strategic stability, much to Moscow's alarm. The Soviets shot down a South Korean commercial airliner in the Far East, killing all on board. When the United States protested in the strongest terms, Moscow broke off arms control negotiations. On at least two occasions in the Fall, the world came close to nuclear war, once because of a technical glitch in the Soviet early warning system, then because the Soviet leaders feared that a regular NATO nuclear-launch exercise was merely cover for a decapitating strike against the Soviet Union.

No Cold War Redux but Dangers Abound

Against this background, it is easy to see the current situation as Cold War 2.0 and to turn to that era for insight into the current US–Russian dynamic and guidance on the appropriate response. That the United States won the original Cold War makes the analogy all the more appealing to policy-makers, experts, and the public alike. But the Cold War frame obscures as much as it illuminates, and it favors policies that are out of sync with current circumstances – containment, for example, cannot describe an adequate policy in a multipolar, interconnected world when key countries, notably China and India, are unwilling to follow the US lead.

The original Cold War was of different dimensions. It was a global existential struggle between the world's two superpowers, which espoused diametrically opposed views of the state, society, and individual. Each ultimately built nuclear arsenals capable of devastating its rival several times over. Each headed its own bloc, with major allies or satellites in Europe and East Asia. Soviet–American relations were the central axis of global politics around which other countries oriented their foreign policies. Not surprisingly in this light, the Soviet Union lay at the core of American foreign policy – all major foreign-policy challenges were assessed through the prism of Soviet–American relations.

Nothing close to those conditions obtains today. US–Russian rivalry is not truly global in scope – it is focused on Europe. It is not existential, except in the nuclear realm; the two countries do not espouse diametri-cally opposed worldviews, despite President Joseph Biden's defining the current era as a struggle between democracy and autocracy, or President Vladimir Putin's claiming to be the champion of traditional Christian values against Western decadence. A vast asymmetry in power robs the relationship of the centrality it once enjoyed in world affairs and on the American foreign-policy agenda. China now occupies the place the Soviet Union once did in Washington's imagination as the sole peer strategic competitor for global leadership. Russia is dismissed as an "immediate and persistent threat." It is hard to conduct a cold war against a country you do not respect or fear.

To be sure, as Robert Legvold, a leading Russia watcher, argues, the current US–Russian confrontation bears attributes of the Cold War. As during that earlier period, each side regards the confrontation as the exclusive fault of the other side. Since the battle is over conflicting purposes, neither side is looking for common ground and each believes that the contest can only end with radical change on the other side, or its collapse. Moreover, agreements do not have a positive effect on other areas of relations, while conflict tends to spread poison elsewhere.[1] The Biden administration's *National Security Strategy*, released in October 2022, exhibits all those attributes in its discussion of Russia. It makes clear that Russia spurned American offers of more constructive relations and holds out little hope for improvement as long as Putin is in power.[2]

Yet the Biden administration – rightly – refuses to talk of a cold war, even if its policy of hard-edged containment draws inspiration from that earlier time. It prefers to speak of great-power competition, as did the Trump administration previously. But the US–Russian rivalry is more than just normal great-power competition, largely because of the way in which the United States deals with major competitors. In general, it does not recognize geopolitical rivalry that is not grounded in diverging systems of values. The Ukraine conflict provides an apt illustration. For the Russian elite, it is fundamentally geopolitical – at its core lies the question of Russia's security and power – even if Putin entertains some curious ideas about making Russia whole again by reabsorbing Ukraine. Washington, however, rejects the security dimension out of hand, insisting that neither Ukraine nor NATO could be reasonably seen as threatening Russia. Rather, it frames the conflict as a manifestation of aggressive Russian imperialism, grounded in its autocratic political system. Moscow believes that the United States is out to crush it because it cannot abide Russian power, while Washington is seeking to contain what it sees as Russia's malign ideas and impulses by eroding its power. Moscow's geopolitical contest is ultimately an ideological one for Washington. There is no common ground between those two positions, no room for compromise.

To say that the United States and Russia are not engaged in a new cold war does not mean that the situation is not dangerous or without far-reaching consequences. Russia may be much weaker than the Soviet

Union was – and its unexpectedly dismal performance in the initial months of the Ukraine conflict only underscores that point – but it still has considerable power. Its nuclear arsenal is the world's largest; it can still destroy the United States as a functioning society in as little as thirty minutes. It has the largest reserves of fossil fuels, which will power the world for years to come, even as the West and others press ahead in the development of green technologies. Its location in the heart of Eurasia enables it to project power and pathologies into the world's major strategic regions outside of North America.

The risk of nuclear war once again focuses minds in Washington as Moscow rattles its nuclear saber in the face of deteriorating battlefield conditions in Ukraine. Global energy markets are in the midst of dramatic change as Europe seeks to end its excessive reliance on Russia and accelerates its move to renewables, while the United States steps in, in hopes of becoming a major supplier of both gas and oil to European markets. Sweden and Finland, with Washington's encouragement, have broken with their longstanding tradition of neutrality to join NATO, as concerns about Russian aggression mount. US policy is driving Russia into an even closer embrace of China. The US-led rules-based world order is breaking under the strain of a shifting strategic landscape. No new global equilibrium is apparent on the horizon. The world is a dangerous place, and it is so in part because of the breakdown in US–Russian relations.

The Plan of the Book

How did we get to this point? Where do we go from here? Those are the two questions that animate this book. The subject is US–Russian relations since the end of the Cold War. This book is not a history. Rather, it is a critique of America's post-Cold War Russia policy through six administrations, beginning with George H.W. Bush's and ending with Joseph Biden's, with a particular focus on the grand strategy of integrating Russia into the West, which began in the dying days of the Cold War and ended abruptly in March 2014, when Putin's Russia seized and annexed Crimea illegally. The book ends with an appeal to think about relations beyond the current conflict in Ukraine, to consider ways in which the United States could construct relations with Russia to best advance its interests long term, as a period of historic change gives rise to a new world order.

The book makes two core claims: That, to defend its long-term strategic interests, the United States must treat Russia as a great power, which entails, as all great-power relationships do, making trade-offs and compromises to manage the inevitable competition responsibly, and that the integration model, the premise that Russia could join the West, ultimately failed because it was, and remains, incompatible with the deeply held national aspirations and policy imperatives of both the United States and Russia.

To expand slightly, the initial American post-Cold War goal of integrating Russia into the Euro-Atlantic Community as a free-market democracy and building an enduring partnership was doomed from the start. Clashing worldviews and national missions, grounded in geography, geopolitical circumstances, and historical experience, which could never be fully reconciled, inevitably injected a lasting element of tension in relations, which was exacerbated by US actions and Russian reactions. But there was nothing foreordained about the depths of antagonism that divide the two countries today. There was another pathway forward, toward, if not strategic partnership, then more constructive relations of mutual benefit, which would have required the United States to respect Russia as a great power. Taking it would have, however, required greater clarity of vision, imagination, and political will than successive American administrations could muster at the time.

Now Russia's unjustifiable invasion of Ukraine has radically altered the context of US–Russian relations, as have the dramatic geopolitical, technological, and other changes underway across the globe. Looking forward, the United States faces a two-fold challenge: Defeating the Russian assault on the European order in the short term, while preparing the ground for relations that will enable the United States to interact with Russia as a major pole of power in the emerging polycentric world, to construct and sustain a long-term complex global equilibrium and to deal with transnational threats.

The argument unfolds across seven chapters. Chapter 1 begins with an examination of the foundations of US–Russia policy. Why did the United States decide to focus on Russia's integration at the end of the Cold War? Why did it believe that a country with a long autocratic tradition could successfully make a transition to free-market democracy in a relatively short historical period? Why did it believe that a country that prided itself on being a great power would willingly become a junior partner in supporting a US-led world order? How did it hedge against the failure of its preferred course? And did the hedges ironically increase the risk of failure? The answers are found in the euphoria that swept over the American political class after the triumph in the Cold War, which was a vindication of the American system and a confirmation of its universal applicability.

An historical exegesis follows in Chapter 2 to identify the sources of the inherent tension in US–Russian relations that has repeatedly bedeviled efforts to build an enduring partnership. In brief, geography and geopolitical setting shaped over time competing American and Russian concepts of security requirements and national purpose. Russia expanded in search of security on a vast territory with few formidable physical barriers against foreign invasion; the United States expanded from its most secure position in North America to spread its "universal" values and nourish its prosperity. Russia was determined to maintain its own unique identity as a great power; the United States hoped to transform the world in its image. Those opposing goals inevitably produced friction as these two expansionary powers came into ever more frequent contact on the Eurasian supercontinent from the end of the nineteenth century onwards.

Chapter 3 explores the question of Russian power. It lays out the reasons why the United States has considered Russia to be a country in decline, destined to lose its status as a great power, if it had not already done so, and to play an ever lesser role in world affairs. That attitude has led American administrations to conclude that they need not pay much heed to Russian interests. The chapter then assesses the state of Russian power today with a focus on the economic, technological, demographic, and political challenges the country faces in coming years as it seeks to sustain itself as a world power. The paradoxical conclusion is that even a Russia in decline will long retain the capacity to act as a major power, to advance or thwart American interests in critical areas, and, therefore, remains a country that Washington cannot afford to ignore.

Two chapters follow on Russia's views of its national interests and foreign-policy challenges. Chapter 4 identifies the preservation of the state and Russia as a great power, as the historically grounded core national interest. It traces the steps Russia has taken at home and abroad since the end of the Cold War to validate its great-power status. It highlights the challenges posed by Russia's geopolitical position and analyzes the changing ways in which Russia has sought to meet them. In particular, it looks at the developments that led the Kremlin to abandon the effort to build a partnership with the United States in favor of seeking strategic alignment with China, as the best way to bolster its claim to be a great power.

Chapter 5 is devoted to the Ukraine crisis, providing a brief overview of the historical background that has convinced Russia of the importance of Ukraine to Russian identity and security as a leading power. It also takes a close look at Putin's own views and the calculations that led him to launch a massive invasion of Ukraine. The argument is that, while any Russian ruler would have been alarmed by developments in and around Ukraine, few would have run the risk of war at this time, as Putin has. In short, it is more Putin's war than Russia's. That is an important conclusion that should affect the way the United States approaches the war in Ukraine and long-term relations with Russia.

Chapters 1 to 5 lay the groundwork for assessing the quality of US Russia policy since the end of the Cold War in Chapter 6. It shows why certain US policies discredited the very idea of integration in Russian eyes and how a lack of imagination led the United States to hedge against Russia's failure to integrate in ways that increased the likelihood of failure. Indeed, the chapter concludes that excessively vigorous hedging against the reassertion of Russian influence in the former Soviet space caused relations to break down in 2014, when Putin pushed back by seizing Crimea and destabilizing eastern Ukraine. Thereafter, however, it was not US policy but Putin's aggressive conduct, culminating in the massive invasion of Ukraine in 2022, that produced the complete rupture that characterizes relations today.

As for lessons learned, Chapter 6 focuses on those that arise from Russia's insistence that it is, and must be respected as, a great power: it will reject any interference in its domestic affairs; it will always be tough in negotiations, presenting its own unique views on global issues; and it will be tenacious in the defense of its interests in the former Soviet space, where it views its preeminence as critical to its security and prosperity.

It also underscores the importance of strategic patience, of managing relations with Russia so as to advance American interests incrementally over time.

The final Chapter 7 deals with the inevitable question: What is to be done? On the basis of an analysis of global trends and Russian developments, as well as the lessons of the past thirty years, it underscores why the United States benefits from a Russia strong enough to play a major role in world affairs, with a focus on three critical issues – strategic stability, European security, and China. It ends with a proposal on how to approach the conflict in Ukraine that supports the long-term strategy, while building toward an enduring, and just, settlement.

Understanding Russia in its Own Terms

To get Russia policy right it is critical that the United States has a clear understanding of that country, of its fears and ambitions. This is not an easy task. Russian writers have reveled in the mystery of their country, its ability to play a large role in human affairs, despite the seemingly debilitating contradictions of Russian life – the opulence of the court and the grinding poverty elsewhere, economic backwardness and spectacular military victories, harsh external conditions and extraordinary resilience. The nineteenth-century Russian poet, Fedor Tyutchev, avowed that Russia defied reason; one had no choice but to "believe in Russia," whatever that might mean. Churchill famously called Russia "a riddle wrapped in a mystery inside an enigma."

Washington policymakers cannot, however, avoid using reason to penetrate the riddle of Russia. The typical way of doing that in the West has been to seek answers to the question of why Russia has not become Western. That issue was in the forefront as the United States sought to bring Russia into the Western world. The answer is generally found in what Russia is lacking. Western observers are quick to point out that it missed the Renaissance, Reformation, and Roman Law; its engagement with the Enlightenment was superficial. Western ideas and values therefore had to be imported into Russia and used to re-form the character of basic Russian political and economic institutions and habits to Western standards.

A more fruitful approach, however, is to ask why Russia became what it is, as the historian Edward Keenan suggests in his seminal work on

Russian political culture. How did a great empire emerge in such adverse climatic and geopolitical conditions? How did a small number of men exercise control over such a vast territory? How did they manage to tax a population that was sparsely settled and remote? How did they mobilize the resources of far-flung territories for their own purposes?[3] Such an approach highlights Russia's successes more than its shortcomings. Given the prevailing view in the United States that Russia is in decline, it is worth remembering that Russia has been among the most successful countries in world history, at least in terms of what it values, geopolitical advance and international sway. Pride in that success, and commitment to the values and institutions that produced it, has meant that there will always be tremendous resistance to Western attempts to re-form Russia.

The latter approach is the one I have taken in the following pages, as I seek to explain why Russia has conducted itself the way it has in the post-Soviet period. It is an effort to understand Russia on its own terms, to see the world as Russian leaders do, to uncover the forces and considerations that have driven decision-making, to engage in what is called "strategic empathy," without casting moral judgments.

This effort to understand Russia should not be taken as a justification for Russia's actions during the past thirty years, and certainly not its invasion of Ukraine. Knowing how that country figures in Russia's worldview, or what considerations drove Putin's decision to invade, is essential if Washington is to formulate a response that advances American interests. But it in no way justifies the invasion or the brutality with which Russia has prosecuted the war. That conduct has fueled moral outrage in the West, and rightly so. But moral outrage makes for poor policy, even if morality should always have a place in policymaking.

Seeking the Enduring in the Temporal Flux

There are obvious perils in writing a book about US–Russian relations while a war is raging, which Putin defines as a proxy war with the "collective West," led by the United States. The drafting began shortly after Russia's invasion in February 2022; the final chapter was drafted nine months later, shortly after Ukraine regained Kherson, the only provincial center that Russia had seized during the war. At that time, Western commentators were in thrall of an impressive Ukrainian counteroffensive that had driven Russian forces out of Kharkiv and Kherson, regaining over half the territory Russia had seized during the campaign. Russian forces were widely depicted as inadequately trained and provisioned and utterly demoralized. Many pundits predicted a Russian defeat, Putin's demise, and dire consequences for the fate of Russia itself, up to and including its collapse. Nevertheless, most Western governments operated on the assumption that Ukraine and Russia were engaged in a war of attrition that could last for months, if not years.

Much will have probably changed by the time this book is published. The war could have taken a decisive turn in favor of Russia or Ukraine. It could have spread beyond Ukraine into Eastern Europe, sparking a direct confrontation between NATO and Russia. A nuclear weapon could have been used in anger. Putin could have left or been removed from power. Political disarray could have engulfed Europe as it deals with ever more onerous socio-economic challenges arising from the war – inflation, energy crises, refugees, and so on. If the situation changes radically, what will be the value of this book?

I have tried to situate US–Russian relations in the broad historical sweep. Putin, of course, figures large in the discussion of Russian national interests and the path to war in Ukraine. It could not be otherwise. He came to power after a decade of systemic crisis and national humiliation, and dominated Russian politics for the next twenty-plus years, as Russia regained some of its lost stature and played an active role in world affairs.

But this book is not about Putin. It is about Russia – about the geopolitical conditions and historical experience that have shaped rulers' worldview, about the nature of the political system that constrains what a ruler, even Putin, can do – and American relations with that country. And the argument is that Putin's Russia is only the current concrete manifestation of a larger Russia problem that will test American policy-makers well into the future, even if his recent messianic impulses strain Russia's long tradition of realpolitik in foreign policy. The evolution of the conflict in and around Ukraine will shape the specific challenges the United States faces in the years ahead, but it will not alter the basic contours. That, at least, is the premise on which this book rests. But, as the Russians like to say in the midst of uncertainty, time will tell.

1

The Foundations of America's Russia Policy

On January 28, 1992, before a joint session of Congress, President George H.W. Bush triumphantly declared victory in the Cold War. "A world once divided into two armed camps," he said, "now recognizes one sole and preeminent power, the United States of America." And it trusted that power to do "what's right."[1]

Earlier, the president had avoided any note of jubilation, concerned that he might alienate or undermine the Soviet leader, Mikhail Gorbachev, whose actions had greatly benefited American interests. Gorbachev had refused to use force to crush the anti-communist, anti-Soviet revolutions in Eastern Europe in 1989; he had pursued major arms control agreements with the United States; he had wound down Soviet involvement in regional conflicts across what was then known as the Third World of developing nations. And he had been slowly, if haphazardly, dismantling the Soviet totalitarian system in favor of a more open, democratic political system and a market-based economy.

But Gorbachev was no longer the Soviet leader. By the end of December, the Soviet Union had dissolved into fifteen new states, the unintended consequence of Gorbachev's ill-fashioned reforms. Bush could now say publicly what he deeply believed without fear of doing harm.

But, if the Soviet Union had collapsed, a new Russia had emerged from the wreckage. It was in crisis – the government was in disarray, the economy was imploding, inflation was surging, food shortages loomed. Russia nevertheless remained a potentially powerful presence on the global stage. It was still by far the largest country in the world, spanning eleven time zones, with the world's richest endowment of natural resources. It had inherited the lion's share of the Soviets' fearsome nuclear arsenal, as well as the Soviet Union's permanent seat – and accompanying veto – on the United Nation's Security Council. What happened in Russia would impact developments all along its long periphery stretching from Europe

11

through the Middle East and South and Central Asia to Northeast Asia and the Arctic. What's more, this Russia aspired to play a large role on the world stage. No matter what its current plight, Russian leaders could conceive of their country as nothing other than a great power. They were determined to reassert Russia's prerogatives and compel others to respect them as soon as possible.

What this new Russia would become was uncertain. The Russian president, Boris Yeltsin, had played the leading role in breaking up the Soviet Union. For the past two years he had criticized Gorbachev's political and economic reforms as much too timid. He stressed his commitment to democracy. He surrounded himself with young, aggressive reformers who were laying the basis for what they hoped would be the rapid erection of a free-market economy on the ruins of a planned economy. Western leaders fervently wished Russia success. But Russia's imperialist past weighed heavily in their calculations, and the prominence of vengeful communists and rabid nationalists in the legislature, the Congress of Peoples' Deputies, did little to ease anxieties.

Bush may not have said so in his address, but this new, inchoate Russia still loomed large in American foreign policy. How should the United States approach it to prolong America's period of preeminence as far as possible into the future? How should the United States balance its hope for a democratic Russia and its fear of revanchism? Was productive partnership possible, or was the return of dangerous confrontation inevitable?

Anchoring Russia

The beginnings of an answer came four days later, when Bush met with Yeltsin at Camp David for three-and-a-half hours to discuss Russia's reform program and arms control. The two leaders issued a short declaration that laid out principles to guide relations. The first and most important was that the two countries no longer viewed each other as potential adversaries; rather, relations were to be "characterized by friendship and partnership, founded on mutual trust and respect and a common commitment to democracy and economic freedom."[2] When Yeltsin traveled to Washington in June for a formal summit, the two presidents issued "A Charter for American–Russian Partnership and Friendship," which stressed the two countries' commitment to democracy, their determination to promote a democratic peace, and their intended cooperation in advancing market-based economic reform in Russia.[3]

In broad terms, the administration's goal was to anchor Russia (and the other former Soviet states) in the Euro-Atlantic Community as a free-market democracy. Success would go a long way toward building the Europe "whole and free" that Bush sought, sharply reducing the risk of another great European war, hot or cold, like those that had plagued the twentieth century and devoured so much American blood and treasure. Advancing that goal entailed most immediately working closely with Russia's popularly elected leader and his government to consolidate democracy. A critical step would be to assist Russia in revitalizing the economy on the basis of free markets, in alleviating the hardship for vast numbers of Russians, so as to help to expand and deepen support for the country's democratic leaders. In response to Yeltsin's urgent plea, the administration took the lead in forging a $24-billion multilateral assistance package ($18 billion in loans, debt deferral, and other financial assistance, and a $6 billion stabilization fund),[4] and pushed the Freedom Support Act through Congress to back democratic and economic reform in Russia and the other post-Soviet states.[5]

Nevertheless, Bush and his colleagues knew that a bet on integration and Russian democracy was far from a sure thing. Two threats loomed large: anarchy and Russia's reversion to its expansionist traditions. Either would resurrect ominous threats to European peace and stability and undo America's triumph in the Cold War. Bush needed to hedge against both.

One hedge was to ensure that the Soviet Union's vast nuclear arsenal, now split among four states (Russia, Ukraine, Belarus, and Kazakhstan), remained under firm, reliable control and did not create an acute proliferation risk. The preferred option was to bring all the weapons under Russia's control and then sign an arms control agreement with Russia that would reduce the size of the arsenal. After tough negotiations – the Ukrainians proved especially recalcitrant – the United States persuaded the three non-Russian states to commit to relinquishing their nuclear weapons and joining the Non-Proliferation Treaty as non-nuclear weapons states. Washington and Moscow then negotiated the START II agreement, which would lead to only a small reduction in arsenals after the massive reductions achieved under START I (signed in July 1991) but, more importantly, would ban intercontinental ballistic missiles (ICBMs) with multiple reentry vehicles (MIRVs), one of the most destabilizing systems.[6]

While pursued primarily to limit the dangers of possible anarchy, the nuclear agreements also acted as something of a hedge against the reversal of reform – if Russia turned hostile, it would be better if it had fewer weapons. But we should not exaggerate their significance in this regard. Both sides had an interest in maintaining strategic stability. In the past two decades, treaties had been negotiated with the Soviet Union, and a Russia that abandoned reform would undoubtedly have engaged in arms control talks, even if reaching agreement would have proved to be much more arduous. The United States needed a more formidable hedge against Russian recidivism to prevent the reemergence of a threat of Soviet dimensions in Eurasia.

The critical geopolitical task – the second hedge – was to block Russia from reasserting its dominance over the states that had emerged from the Soviet empire. The United States was already working closely with former Soviet bloc countries in Eastern Europe to bolster their independence after the revolutions of 1989; with the demise of the Soviet Union, it moved quickly to recognize the independence of the new post-Soviet states. Shortly after Yeltsin's February visit, Secretary of State James Baker embarked on a ten-day trip to those states to reinforce the American commitment to their sovereignty, independence, and territorial integrity.[7]

Oddly, however, the Bush administration did not put much effort into building relations with the new Russia, to consolidate what the president saw as a hard-won victory in the Cold War. With that war over, he turned his attention to his reelection campaign, which compelled him to focus on his domestic agenda amid mounting economic anxiety. Rhetorical support for Yeltsin and his reformist government was never matched with vigorous concrete action, except in the area of strategic arms control. Tellingly, the president and his national security adviser, Brent Scowcroft, end their joint memoir with the demise of the Soviet Union at the end of 1991 – there simply wasn't much to write about their effort to engage the new Russia.[8]

Nevertheless, the Bush administration created a broad framework for relations with Russia that was to endure a quarter century, until

Russian invaded and illegally annexed Crimea in 2014. Euro-Atlantic integration, equal partnership, shared democratic values, and free-market economies were declared to be the foundation of relations between the two countries. Arms control, especially symmetrical cuts in strategic nuclear weapons, would be both a symbol of equality and partnership in preserving strategic stability and, in the American view, a hedge against chaos in Russia and the surrounding region. Geopolitical pluralism in the former Soviet space and the advancement of Western institutions, as well as the American presence, in the former Soviet bloc would serve as a hedge against Russian recidivism. All the while, Russia's glaring strategic weakness and the absence of any other great-power competitor would enable Washington to overcome any Russian resistance to its grand design. It was one part idealism, one part realism in the name of advancing American interests in the world.

The three succeeding administrations – under Presidents Bill Clinton, George W. Bush, and Barack Obama – all operated within this framework, albeit with waning enthusiasm and confidence, and greater cynicism and disregard for Russia, from administration to administration. Even though each administration began with great expectations, only to leave office with relations in worse shape than it found them, the Bush and Obama administrations continued to use this framework, confident that they could succeed where their predecessor had failed. And each wanted to succeed because Russian cooperation remained critical to its broader goals. Clinton had the largest ambitions, hoping to turn Russia into a junior partner in support of American aims across the globe. Bush initially sought Russian cooperation in preventing the spread of nuclear weapons and, after 9/11, more broadly, in prosecuting the global war on terror, his top foreign-policy priority. And Obama could not do without Russia if he hoped to realize his grand vision of a world without nuclear weapons.

Grand Strategy: Integration and Partnership

Clinton Allies with Russian Reform

Clinton thought that his predecessor had been woefully remiss in not seizing the historic opportunity presented by the emergence of a democratic Russia. He would make that his top foreign-policy priority. To underscore that intention, he appointed an old friend and Russia expert, Strobe Talbott, as the special advisor to the Secretary of State on the states of the former Soviet Union, charged with overseeing the formulation and execution of his Russia policy. A few months later, he devoted his first major foreign-policy address as president to Russia, a seminal speech that remains to date the most comprehensive presidential explication of an administration's Russia policy in the post-Soviet period. Thereafter, he remained so actively engaged on Russia matters that Talbott dubbed him the administration's main "Russia hand."

The US goal, in Talbott's words, was to help Russia become "a normal, modern state – democratic in its governance, abiding by its own constitution and by its own laws, market-oriented and prosperous in its economic development, at peace with itself and with the rest of the world."[9] To that end, Russia would be integrated into the Euro-Atlantic community through a wide-ranging effort to assist Russia in its internal transformation in what Clinton billed as a "strategic alliance with Russian reform."[10]

For Clinton, Yeltsin personified reform, and this alliance translated in the real world into nearly unconditional support for him. His senior advisers may have had doubts about the erratic Russian president, but Clinton was convinced that Yeltsin was on the right side of history in the struggle between democracy and dictatorship. More to the point, he saw no leader capable of replacing him.[11] That support was not to waver through a series of challenges, and Yeltsin's less than fully democratic maneuvers, which began as soon as the administration took office: the bitter struggle between Yeltsin and the Congress of People's Deputies that ended with Yeltsin's shelling the Russian White House, the seat of the Congress, in October 1993; Yeltsin's brutal war against Chechen separatists, starting in 1994; and a bitter, nasty, but victorious reelection campaign against a communist foe in 1996. For Clinton, Yeltsin's transgressions represented merely the growing pains within democracy, not a retreat from it.[12]

The core problem that Yeltsin needed to tackle, Clinton decided, was the economy – hardly surprising for a man who had made overcoming the American economic malaise the winning plank in his own campaign for the presidency. As in the United States, economic revival was critical to building popular support for government policies. More important in the Russian context, it would foster a middle class, which would sustain the transition to a full-blooded democracy.[13] This was a daunting challenge – the task was not the restoration of what had been lost, but rather the construction of an entirely new socio-economic system on the ruins of the Soviet planned economy.

To meet the challenge, the Clinton administration developed a bilateral assistance program for Russia in the amount of $1.6 billion and coordinated a multilateral assistance package worth some $43 billion, both of which Clinton unveiled at his first meeting with Yeltsin in Vancouver, Canada, in April 1993.[14] Clinton and Yeltsin also launched a joint commission on economic and technological cooperation, called the Gore–Chernomyrdin Commission after its co-heads, US Vice President Albert Gore and Russian Prime Minister Viktor Chernomyrdin. This was a massive US assistance effort, in the guise of cooperation to make it more palatable to the Russians, that brought US cabinet-level officials together with their Russian counterparts on critical matters such as space, energy, science and technology, defense conversion, business development, agriculture, environment, and health.[15] The administration subsequently flooded Russia with aid workers, technical advisors, and volunteers, to instruct Russians in the ways of free markets and, to a lesser degree, democratic politics.[16]

Thus, in its first three months, the Clinton administration had set the course of its Russia policy. In the years ahead, it would repeatedly underscore the progress Russia was making in its transition and the mounting strength of US–Russian partnership. It did so even though Russia's precipitous economic decline continued, rapacious entrepreneurs and regional barons seized lucrative state assets for a pittance and privatized parts of the state for their own parochial interests, and Yeltsin and his allies undermined democratic norms in the name of defending democracy against communist and nationalist foes and Chechen rebels.

In September 1997, Talbott surveyed the landscape. Yeltsin's victory in the 1996 presidential elections had thwarted a communist comeback. The Russian economy had just produced its first year of growth. Yeltsin had brought the Chechnya conflict to an end. Final success still lay in the future, but Russia, Talbott declared, was at the end of the beginning of its transition to free-market democracy.[17]

He spoke too soon. Less than a year later, Russia suffered a devastating financial collapse. Mounting debt, capital flight, and the contagion of an Asian financial crisis undermined Russia's solvency. In mid August 1998, the Russian government devalued the ruble by 50 percent and defaulted on its outstanding debt. Yeltsin dismissed the reformist government and appointed a new prime minister, Yevgeny Primakov, who enjoyed strong backing from the communists and selected one of their leaders, a former head of the Soviet economic planning agency, Gosplan, to serve as his first deputy in charge of the economy. So much for Clinton's grand ambition to turn Russia into a free-market democracy.

Shortly thereafter, US–Russian foreign-policy cooperation approached a breaking point in the dispute over Serbia's effort to cleanse its autonomous region of Kosovo of its Muslim population. The United States and its NATO allies were determined to end Belgrade's ethnic cleansing, through the use of force, if necessary. Russia was vehemently opposed to any military interference in a country that was a traditional ally. Nevertheless, NATO launched a massive air bombardment campaign against Serbia – bypassing the UN Security Council to avoid a Russian veto.

Three months later, facing the unpalatable need to introduce ground forces to subdue the Serbs, the United States turned to Russia for help in negotiating an end to the conflict. Despite Russia's assistance, the United States then sought to deny it a role in the peacekeeping force to be set up in Kosovo. Although it remains unclear who gave the order in Moscow, Russian troops from a peacekeeping force in Bosnia raced to occupy the airfield in Pristina, Kosovo's capital, before NATO forces could arrive. After a brief, but tense, NATO–Russia standoff was defused, Moscow got the role in the peacekeeping operation it sought. But the damage to US–Russian relations was done.[18] And Clinton left office with Russia less democratic, and relations with Russia worse, than he found them.

Bush's Lesser Ambitions

Despite Clinton's failure and his own team's sharp criticism of Clinton's policies during the election campaign,[19] once in office George W. Bush pursued a similar course. To be sure, he abandoned large-scale direct intervention to transform Russia internally: there would be no strategic alliance with Russian reform and no need for a follow-on to the Gore–Chernomyrdin Commission; assistance programs would wind down as a matter of policy or at Russia's request. And he would not make Russia his top foreign-policy priority. Indeed, his administration restructured the national security bureaucracy deliberately to downgrade Russia's overall standing and to signal that it would not view the former Soviet space through the prism of relations with Russia, as its predecessor had.[20]

But Bush's Russia policy was not without ambition. Early on, he stated his goal as building a qualitatively new relationship that moved beyond Cold War antagonism to cooperation on a number of pressing security challenges, non-proliferation first of all.[21] Like Clinton, Bush would seek to ground that cooperation in a shared commitment to democratic values. The emergence of a new Russian leader, Vladimir Putin, who replaced the discredited, decrepit Yeltsin, and was elected in a more or less free election in 2000, made such an endeavor sound reasonable, despite Putin's KGB past.

The devastating terrorist attacks on New York and Washington on September 11, 2001, transformed a presidency with modest goals into a crusade to eliminate international terrorism and advance freedom world-wide. The attacks also raised the standing of Russia in the administration's eye: Here was a country that, because of its own experience in Afghanistan in the 1980s, could help the United States in the initial phase of the campaign to oust the Taliban and drive al-Qaida out of Afghanistan. And it did – facilitating the opening of military bases in Central Asia to US forces, permitting the US military to fly through Russia airspace to provide loosely defined "humanitarian" aid to Afghanistan, and sharing sensitive intelligence that accelerated the overthrow of the Taliban.[22] But, given the way the administration framed the war on terror, the defense of freedom against "evil-doers," broad-based counterterrorist cooperation with Russia, not to speak of an alliance, could only be sustained if the administration could plausibly argue that Russia was moving toward democracy.

To make such a claim, Bush and his team suppressed qualms about Putin's authoritarian instincts; from the moment he assumed power, he began to rein in the media and limit the space for competing centers of power, formal and informal. But Bush believed that Putin could not long resist the powerful secular forces that were moving the world, and Russia, toward "a single sustainable model for national success: freedom, democracy, and free enterprise," as he would write in his first *National Security Strategy*.[23] The American president could thus, without undue cynicism, declare in a joint statement with his Russian counterpart in November 2001 that "our countries are embarked on a new relationship for the twenty-first century, founded on a commitment to the values of democracy, the free market, and rule of law."[24] That statement might not have reflected the current reality, but it did arguably describe the trajectory of relations, at least in Bush's mind. The two leaders would use a similar formula in their May 2002 Joint Declaration, which laid out a framework for US–Russian strategic partnership.[25]

For the next six years, the administration was to talk as if its partnership with Russia was grounded in a common commitment to democracy, even as the gap between American pronouncements and Russian reality widened into a chasm. It had little choice, if it wanted Russia's cooperation. The Freedom Agenda, Bush's commitment to spreading democratic values, had become not only the guide for prosecuting the war on terror but also the core of the administration's entire foreign policy.[26] As Bush declared in his second inaugural address, "It is the policy of the United States to seek and support the growth of democratic movements and institutions in every nation and culture, with the ultimate goal of ending tyranny in our world."[27] Moreover, the administration had some success to point to: the Moscow Strategic Offensive Reductions Treaty, which would reduce the number of deployed strategic nuclear weapons by nearly two-thirds; joint sponsorship of a global effort to combat nuclear terrorism; and enhanced security of Russian nuclear weapons and infrastructure.

Yet all the while Putin was cracking down on independent media and civil society organizations, especially those with ties to the West. He was squeezing competition out of the political system and stripping elections of any genuine choice. He was pursuing more aggressive policies toward Russia's neighbors and increasingly challenging the US presence in the former Soviet space. At the 2007 Munich Security Conference, he launched a scathing attack on the United States' allegedly global hegemonic designs, unilateral and illegal use of military force, and refusal to respect Russian interests.

And yet Bush and his senior officials remained reluctant to criticize Putin, or Russia, publicly for backsliding on democracy, despite growing public pressure to do so. When they did, starting with a Bush–Putin summit in Bratislava, Slovakia, in February 2005, the criticism was muted, articulated more out of regret than anger. And yet, in a last effort to salvage a deteriorating relationship, the two leaders met in Sochi, Russia, in April 2008 and unveiled a new strategic framework for US–Russian partnership that reiterated their joint commitment "to respect the rule of law, international law, human rights, tolerance of diversity, political freedom, and a free market approach to economic policy and practice."[28] Appearances to the contrary notwithstanding, it was still a democratic partnership.

Russia invaded Georgia four months later, derailing its aspirations to join NATO. The qualitatively new relationship that moved beyond Cold War antagonisms had met the same fate as the strategic alliance with Russian reform.

Obama Resets

It was left to Obama to pick up the pieces. He needed Russian coopera-tion on many matters critical to the United States, including his signature goal of a world without nuclear weapons. But he could not overlook Russia's aggression against Georgia and other acts that ran contrary to American interests and principles. He reconciled those imperatives in a policy that was christened the "reset." The United States would engage actively with Russia on key matters where interests overlapped – primarily security matters, such as strategic arms control, nonproliferation, and counterterrorism – without ceasing to criticize and push back against Russia where interests were opposed, for instance, on the question of Georgia's territorial integrity or human rights.

For those purposes, Obama did not need democratic partnership; shared interests would suffice. That philosophy was reflected in the first joint statement he released with the new Russian president, Dmitry Medvedev, in April 2009. It laid out an agenda for relations focused on security-related matters, but did not invoke shared democratic values as the basis for relations. It merely noted, almost as an afterthought, that the two countries would "seek to be guided by the rule of law, respect for fundamental freedoms and human rights, and tolerance for different views."[29]

Nevertheless, the new administration did not abandon the effort to integrate Russia into the Euro-Atlantic community as a free-market democracy. But Obama would not repeat Clinton's extensive direct intervention in Russian domestic affairs to push reform along. He had little regard for America's ability to engineer other societies. Nor would he follow Bush's hands-off approach (at least with regard to Russia; in Iraq, Afghanistan, and elsewhere, Bush resorted to military force in an effort to impose democratic practices). Rather, Obama saw public and private-sector American engagement with Russian business and civil society as the most promising way to nurture pro-democracy and free-market ideas inside Russia. That would form the second track of the administration's "dual-track engagement," the first being government-to-government talks.

To facilitate closer working relations and to encourage private-sector engagement, at their first meeting the two presidents set up the Bilateral Presidential Commission. With more than a dozen working groups, this body brought senior officials together on a regular basis to work on traditional hard security issues, as well as a range of political and socio-economic matters, including health, education, sport, environment, and the media. One working group was expressly set up to bolster civil-society ties, and, in the spirit of dual-track engagement, all groups were encouraged to liaise with the business community and non-governmental organizations.[30]

Whether Obama needed it or not, Medvedev turned the relationship into a democratic partnership, which the administration was pleased to foster. In sharp contrast to Putin, the new Russian president was an avid modernizer, eager to embrace new communications technology, and a seeming democratizer. Six months after his meeting with Obama, he published a political manifesto, Go Russia!,[31] which detailed his commitment to innovation and democratic reform, including the development of civil society, the encouragement of genuine political competition, and the construction of a fair judicial system. The two matters – innovation and democracy – were inextricably linked in Medvedev's mind, and progress in both was needed if Russia was to flourish in the twenty-first century.

Of the same generation, both lawyers by training and forward-looking as political leaders, Obama and Medvedev worked together productively for two-and-a-half years. They signed the New START agreement further limiting nuclear arsenals, jointly pressured Iran to abandon its nuclear-weapons ambitions, cooperated in supplying American and NATO forces fighting in Afghanistan, and advanced Russia's effort to join the World Trade Organization. Meanwhile, Russian society gradually opened up after the last years of Putin's authoritarian policies.

This promising trajectory in US–Russian relations came to an abrupt halt in September 2011, when Putin unveiled his intention to reclaim the presidency, much to Obama's chagrin. His administration had made no effort to conceal its desire to see Medvedev reelected for a second term – Vice President Joseph Biden told opposition leaders in Moscow in March 2011 that he was opposed to Putin's seeking a third term, a remark that was immediately leaked to the press.[32]

The next two-and-a-half years witnessed a steady deterioration in relations, beginning with the Russian leader's vehement accusation that the United States had organized the Russian protests against rigged Duma elections in December 2011 in an effort to effect regime change in Russia itself. There followed growing discord over the civil war in Syria, Putin's granting of asylum to Edward Snowden, the renegade NSA employee who had exposed some of the United States' most sensitive operations in cyberspace, and the near total breakdown in relations after Russia's annexation of Crimea and instigation of rebellion in eastern Ukraine in 2014.

Like his predecessors, Obama left office with relations in worse shape than he found them. But he went a step further. In the wake of Russia's aggression against Ukraine, he brought to an end the United States' post-Cold War effort to integrate Russia into the Euro-Atlantic community in favor of containing Russia. An era in US–Russian relations had ended.

Why Integration?

We will leave the question of why this effort failed for later. The question now is why three American administrations made it. And why two presidents – George W. Bush and Obama – continued, despite the obvious failure of their predecessors.

On one level, the answer is simple and straightforward. The United States has been promoting democracy since its founding, initially by the power of its example and subsequently during the Cold War by direct support for democratic forces overseas, as well. But the Cold War triumph lent a certain exuberance and hubris to the effort. In the titanic ideological struggle of the twentieth century, liberal democracy, the American system, had vanquished communism less than a half century after crushing fascism, granted with communism's support, in the Second World War. This marked the end of history, in the provocative thesis of the American political scientist Francis Fukuyama. Liberal democracy had demonstrated that it was the only viable form of political and economic organization in the long run; no new ideological challengers were imaginable. States might resist that conclusion in the short run – and consequently geopolitical conflict would not disappear – but they could only endure and thrive over time by yielding to the verdict of history.[33]

The rising tide of globalization reinforced that judgment. The interconnectedness of global markets, a consequence of rapid innovation in communications and information technologies, was spreading universal norms and practices necessary for economic success – and these were largely American norms and practices because of the leading role the United States had played in fostering globalization. Moreover, a wave of democratic revolutions, beginning with Greece, Portugal, and Spain in the 1970s, had swept through Latin America and then reached Eastern Europe and undid the Soviet bloc in 1989. Previous waves had been reversed, but this one appeared to have momentum,[34] as it penetrated into Russia and much of the former Soviet space.

Beyond American tradition and the spirit of the times, there was a profound psychological need to seek Russia's transformation. The Cold War victory, the vindication of the American system, would not be complete until liberal democracy was consolidated in Russia. For wars are won not when the enemy's armies are defeated and it surrenders, but when it acknowledges the superiority of your system by adopting it. That was the great lesson of the Second World War. Then, American drive and persistence had transformed the vanquished Nazi Germany and Imperial Japan into liberal democracies. Now, the United States was called to replicate the task with an erstwhile Soviet Russia. Success would underscore the worth of each president in the broad sweep of American history.

Admittedly, this was a formidable challenge in a country that lacked a substantial democratic tradition and where old-time communists and ardent nationalists commanded considerable elite and popular support. But American leaders had sufficient reason to believe they could meet the challenge. To begin with, the United States had powerful intellectual tools to guide policy. "Transitologists," scholars who studied how countries transition from totalitarian or authoritarian systems to liberal democracies, produced volumes of guidelines and best practices for democratic reform.[35] In the economic realm, policies developed to deal with the Latin American debt crises in the 1980s were packaged as the so-called Washington Consensus on how to pursue economic reform and promote macroeconomic stability.[36]

Moreover, the United States had material to work with in Russia. Clinton seized on the avowed commitment of the Russian leadership and, first of all, Yeltsin, to democratic and free-market reform. Yeltsin had immense credibility. He had broken with the Communist Party in 1990. He had trounced rivals in more or less democratic elections to become a deputy to the first Soviet Congress of People's Deputies in 1989 and to the first Russian Congress of People's Deputies in 1990, and then president of Russia in 1991. He had defied the putsch leaders and then crushed them in August 1991. Yeltsin could be erratic, but his sense of direction was flawless, or so Clinton thought.

Putin posed a more difficult challenge for George W. Bush. But one could rationalize his initial authoritarian steps as necessary to bring some order to the chaos he had inherited from Yeltsin. Central state power did indeed need to be restored to create the foundation on which a well-ordered democratic polity could be built. Bush thought he had a reasonable chance of convincing Putin to take a democratic path by embracing him. As for Obama, Medvedev was a leader in the right mold; he too appeared committed to democratic reform. The problem was that he was not the key decision-maker; Putin was. But Obama appeared to wager that if he treated Medvedev as a leader, and produced some successes for both countries, he could turn him into the real leader.

In this light, the three administrations' bet on integrating Russia into the Euro-Atlantic community does not appear to be outlandish, at least early in each one's first term. But why did they continue to speak of a democratic partnership as the evidence mounted of Russia's backsliding on democratic reform? The answer lies in each administration's need to build and sustain public support for its Russia policy. It is a fundamental truth of American foreign policy that the American public, with rare exception, will not long support a durable alliance with a major power not grounded in shared values; shared interests will not suffice. Nor, again with rare exception, will it support even a limited partnership with an authoritarian regime absent an overwhelming shared threat from a third power. That is what enabled President Franklin Roosevelt to ally with the Soviet Union against Nazi Germany and President Richard Nixon to align with Red China against the Soviet Union. But there was no such threat in existence or on the horizon – in part because the collapse of the Soviet Union and American preeminence put an end to great-power competition for a generation. President George W. Bush's attempt to portray terrorism as an existential threat collapsed after the shock of 9/11 wore off a year or two later.

And so, despite qualms about Russia's domestic trajectory, Clinton, George W. Bush, and Obama needed to preserve the public image of a democratizing Russia to continue their cooperation with it on their primary security concerns. And the futility of their approach was laid bare when a dramatic event – the 1998 financial collapse, the 2008 invasion of Georgia, or the 2014 annexation of Crimea – irrevocably stripped that image of any credibility.

The Hedge

While all three administrations staked the success of their policy on Russia's making progress toward free-market democracy on their watch, they nevertheless all prudently hedged against its radical destabilization (a major worry in the first post-Soviet years) or its reversion to its authoritarian, imperialist past (a concern that grew as the threat of destabilization receded). Arms control, NATO expansion, and geopolitical pluralism in Eurasia were the cornerstones of this hedging strategy. Administrations did not conceal that they were pursuing these objectives out of concern about Russia's trajectory. But that was not the only reason.

The greater vision was to bolster security in Europe after the Cold War trauma of a divided Europe, to make Europe "whole and free" and at peace, as George H.W. Bush advocated as the Cold War drew to an end.[37] That Europe would include Russia, should it make progress in its democratic transition. American leaders could thus argue that, while they took certain steps because of doubts about Russia's trajectory, they were not directed against it. Indeed, they were in Russia's interests, properly construed, and an added incentive for it to continue down the path to free-market democracy.

That Russia would object, and at times vehemently, did nothing to dissuade three administrations from their course. Each thought that Russia was too weak, and the power differential in America's favor too great, for Russia to be able to effectively counter their policies. The asymmetry was starkest during the Clinton administration. While Russia suffered a political and socio-economic collapse unprecedented for a major power not defeated in a great war – its economy contracted by roughly 45 percent between 1990 and 1998[38] – the United States enjoyed its longest period of uninterrupted expansion in history up to that point, as its economy grew by some 40 percent in the 1990s.[39] But, even after Russia's remarkable recovery in Putin's first two presidential terms, the United States remained vastly superior across all dimensions of power, except for nuclear weapons. In 2008, the Russian economy was just one-twelfth the size of American economy in nominal terms (or just over one-fifth in purchasing power parity terms).[40] Then the global financial crisis of 2008/2009 hit Russia hard, hardest of all among the G-20,[41] a shock from which Russia never fully recovered.

Arms Control

A top priority for the United States was to ensure the safety and security of the vast former Soviet arsenal of nuclear, biological, and chemical weapons and the infrastructure used to produce them, which were spread across Russia and three other former Soviet states. No one wanted to see the weapons or the material to produce them end up in the hands of terrorists or rogue states, which posed perhaps the gravest threat to the United States now that the Cold War was over and no great-power competitor lurked on the horizon. In 1992, the United States launched the Nunn–Lugar Cooperative Threat Reduction program with Russia to secure weapons of mass destruction and provide employment for the scientists and engineers with expert knowledge of the weapons and their delivery systems. This was a genuinely cooperative program. While there was some concern about American access to the jewels of their defense-industrial complex, Russian leaders shared concerns about proliferation and also welcomed the funding that would enable them to keep their arsenal safe and secure at a time of tremendous financial shortfalls. The program only ended in 2013, as relations deteriorated under Putin and Russia decided it had the financial means to ensure the security of its forces on its own.[42]

Moscow also welcomed the Clinton administration's decision in 1993 to intervene in its bilateral negotiations with Kyiv on the disposition of the nuclear forces in Ukraine. American pressure and blandishments were critical in convincing Kyiv to honor the commitment it had given in 1992 to send its nuclear weapons to Russia for dismantlement and join the Non-Proliferation Treaty as a non-nuclear weapons state, a critical step in ensuring that Russia would be the sole successor to the Soviet Union as a nuclear-weapons state.[43]

Ensuring the security and the safety of the former Soviet arsenal of weapons of mass destruction was only one part of the hedge, however. The other part was reducing the size of the Russian nuclear arsenal in exchange for reciprocal cuts in the US arsenal. The 2002 Strategic Offense Reductions Treaty and the 2010 New START treaty both served that purpose. Moscow was eager to engage because negotiations validated Russia as the equal of the United States at least in one realm critical to global security.

By and large, Moscow was therefore not troubled by America's hedge in arms control because it served its own needs as well. What it could not abide were American decisions to abandon agreements, notably the 1972 Anti-Ballistic Missile (ABM) Treaty. The United States may not have exited that treaty as part of a hedge against Russia – it rather wanted to develop the means to deal with what it saw as mounting threats from North Korea and Iran – but Moscow was not convinced. It feared the United States intended to develop a missile defense system that could neutralize its strategic deterrent. Even if that were not the case, the US exit from a treaty that Moscow considered fundamental to the preservation of strategic stability undercut Russia's standing as the other great nuclear power. Not taking Russia seriously was infinitely more disturbing than hedging against the resurrection of its power. Dealing with Russia's prickly pride was a constant challenge for American administrations, but not an insurmountable obstacle to the conclusion of mutually beneficial arms control agreements.

NATO Expansion

If US measures on arms control did little to unsettle relations, NATO was quite another matter. Moscow was adamantly opposed to the eastward expansion of an alliance that it considered fundamentally anti-Russian in character. Expansion would narrow the buffer zone in Eastern Europe that Russia had for centuries believed critical to its security and deny it a central role in deliberations about European security. If the United States proceeded with expansion, in Moscow's eyes, it could only be because it wanted to extend its geopolitical reach in Europe at Russia's expense at a time of extreme Russian vulnerability.

Moscow was not entirely wrong. NATO anchored the American presence in Europe. It provided the United States with a powerful tool to shape the security environment so as to prevent the continent's domination by a hostile power and reduce the risk of a major conflict that would inevitably draw in the United States, as the First and Second World Wars had. The challenge for the United States was to recast NATO's mission now that Cold War containment had achieved its goal in order to mollify Russia – even if East European states sought to join precisely for protection against Russia and the United States wanted to hedge against the resurrection of Russian power.

The solution was found in rediscovering another reason for creating NATO, namely, to reconcile former foes, especially France and Germany, and prevent the reemergence of interstate rivalries that would threaten the continent's stability, as they had throughout history. NATO would now be called upon to replicate that task in the East, where rivalries were resurfacing in the absence of Soviet domination.

And so, while NATO at core remained a military alliance, it would be fashioned into a tool to promote Europe's integration and, since all members were democracies at the Cold War's end, it would be integration on the basis of a common commitment to democracy. Membership was made contingent on an aspirant's progress in institutionalizing democratic practices and resolving territorial disputes. Expansion would not be a single act but a process that extended over years, since countries would meet the membership requirements at different speeds.[44]

The Clinton administration did not exclude membership for Russia, at least in the long term – as Talbott admitted in 1995 in an essay that made the case for NATO expansion, a Russia that joined NATO "would be a very different Russia from the current one."[45] But any attentive observer would have understood that was not serious. If the United States adamantly opposed the consolidation of a European pillar inside NATO that could challenge its leadership, why would it agree to membership for Russia, a country that by reason of its size, resources, military power, nuclear arsenal, and self-image as a great power could, and most assuredly would, challenge US leadership on its own?

With membership for Russia off the table and expansion inevitable, the question was how to manage Russian discontent. Arguments that Russia itself should have an interest in NATO's promotion of peace and stability in Eastern Europe predictably fell on deaf ears in Moscow. Declarations that the alliance's mission had changed, that it was no longer directed against Russia but against "out-of-area" threats, seemed disingenuous when the aspiring members made no secret of their desire for protection against Russia. Nor was Moscow impressed by the sharp drawdown in the US military in Europe – from over 300,000 troops in 1989 to a little under 110,000 in 1995 – that should have diminished its sense of threat.[46] In these circumstances, strengthening ties between Russia and NATO seemed to offer a more promising path. To this end, the Clinton administration advocated a NATO–Russia Founding Act,[47] which was signed in 1997 as the first invitations to join NATO were extended to the Czech Republic, Hungary, and Poland.

To ease Russian concerns about the military implications of expansion, NATO declared in the Act that it had "no intention, no plan and no reason" to deploy nuclear weapons in new member states or change its nuclear policies, nor would it station additional permanent "substantial" combat forces in the region "in the current and foreseeable security environment." This of course conceded little because the environment could change with time, and NATO alone would decide if it had. The Act also established the Permanent Joint Council, where Russia would meet with the NATO as an organization for consultations. It was a way of giving a voice in, but not a veto over, NATO decisions. Such steps were hardly major concessions to Russian sensitivities – they were longer on symbolism than substance. But Clinton thought he had to do little more because Russia was too weak to resist.[48]

Clinton thus set the stage for his successors to continue with NATO expansion. His immediate successor, George W. Bush, was all too eager to proceed. A "fierce believer in NATO," according to Secretary of State Condoleezza Rice,[49] he quickly decided that the second round of expansion would be a "big bang," bringing in seven countries, including the three Baltic (and former Soviet) states. Bush would not stop with this second wave, however. After the color revolutions in Georgia (2003) and Ukraine (2004), he pushed to put those two post-Soviet states on the membership track despite Russia's long-standing, vehement opposition.[50] Bush ran into resistance not only from Russia, however. Two key allies, France and Germany, were also opposed.[51]

At its 2008 Bucharest summit, NATO thrashed out a compromise that denied Ukraine and Georgia membership action plans but said the that two would eventually become members. Putin arrived the next day to warn that if Ukraine were to join NATO it would do so without Crimea and its eastern provinces.[52] Four months later, he sent his troops into Georgia. That cooled the ardor for further expansion into the former Soviet space, although NATO continued to add new members in the Balkans in subsequent years.

Geopolitical Pluralism

Like NATO expansion, the pursuit of geopolitical pluralism in Eurasia would poison relations. But not initially. Clinton was decidedly focused on Russia as his top priority, in the belief that a successful transition there would have a huge positive impact elsewhere in the region, while Russia, beset by ever-deepening domestic problems, had little time for managing the former Soviet space, even if it sought to maintain its presence through the Commonwealth of Independent States, the Collective Security Treaty, and other instruments. To be sure, the United States continued to provide assistance to foster economic and political reform to all the former Soviet space. And it encouraged the development of the energy resources of the Caspian Basin, but unsettled politics and economic woes hindered progress. At the same time, Clinton had helped resolve Russia's dispute with Ukraine over nuclear weapons in Moscow's favor. He may have built a framework for relations with Ukraine that paralleled that for Russia – senior officials paired trips to Moscow with stopovers in Kyiv, and both NATO and the United States set up bilateral commissions with Ukraine. But relations with Kyiv were never particularly warm.

The situation changed dramatically with the George W. Bush administration, especially after 9/11. Paradoxically, just as it was trying to forge close counterterrorism cooperation with Russia, Bush moved ever more aggressively to diminish the Russian presence in Eurasia. His administration stepped up efforts to promote the development of the energy resources of the Caspian region and the construction of pipelines that would circumvent Russia to deliver oil and gas to European markets. That would not only decrease Europe's dependence on Russian energy, but also reinforce the independence of the former Soviet states that no longer had to rely on Russia to bring their oil and gas to market. In a slap at Russia, the administration celebrated the launch of such an oil pipeline, from Baku through the Caucasus to Ceyhan in Turkey, in 2005 and a gas one, from the Shah Deniz gas field in the Azerbaijani sector of the Caspian Sea through the Caucasus to Turkey, the following year.

The United States also built military bases in Central Asia, albeit initially with Moscow's blessing, to prosecute the war in Afghanistan, but categorically refused to give Moscow a *droit de regard* as it forged closer security ties, especially with Uzbekistan and Kyrgyzstan. It upended a Russian-crafted resolution of the Transnistria frozen conflict in Moldova, in 2003, as it pressed Moscow to withdraw its troops from the country as it had earlier promised to do. And it backed the GUAM (Georgia, Ukraine, Azerbaijan, Moldova) regional organization, which sought to reduce Russian influence in the Black Sea and the Caspian regions.

All those steps sowed ill will with Moscow, but none compared with Bush's dealings with Ukraine in poisoning relations. Putin saw a US hand in the Orange Revolution in Ukraine that overturned the election of a candidate he had personally backed for the presidency in favor of a pro-Western politician. That event was in his view both a US rehearsal for regime change in Russia and a flagrant attempt to rip Ukraine out of Moscow's orbit. That was unacceptable. Ukraine, with its large population, abundant resources, industrial potential, and well-educated work force, was critical to Putin's plan to revive Russia as a great power.

The various economic and political structures he was forging with other former Soviet states made little strategic sense without Ukraine's participation. But that was exactly why Bush was keen on drawing Ukraine westward. He accepted Zbigniew Brzezinski's assertion that "without Ukraine, Russia ceases to be an empire, but with Ukraine suborned and then subordinated, Russia automatically becomes an empire [and a challenge to the United States]."[53]

After the Orange Revolution, Russia reassessed its relations with the United States and concluded that, without concerted resistance, the United States would drive Russia out of the former Soviet space, and doom it to the ranks of second-rate powers. The change manifested itself quickly. In 2005, Moscow engineered a call by the Shanghai Cooperation Organization that all non-regional powers (read, the United States) withdraw their military bases from Central Asia. And, as we have seen, when NATO declared that Georgia and Ukraine would become members, Moscow struck out against Georgia.

The new Obama administration got the message and put relations with the states of the former Soviet space besides Russia on the back burner as it launched the reset. That smoothed relations with Russia, as long as Medvedev was president. Putin's return to the Kremlin in 2012, however, reignited the competition.[54] When the Ukrainian president, under intense Kremlin pressure, reversed his decision to sign an association agreement with the European Union in November 2013, a massive protest movement erupted in Kyiv. Washington backed the protesters. And it cheered when the protesters ousted the president and installed a pro-Western, anti-Russian government in February 2014. Putin reacted quickly, seizing Crimea and fomenting rebellion in eastern Ukraine.

From Integration to Containment and Beyond

Those audacious actions brought an abrupt end to the United States' grand strategy of integrating Russia into the Western world. Why? Similar episodes in the past, notably Russia's invasion of Georgia in 2008, had been quickly followed by efforts to restore relations. But this time was different. Those earlier episodes had occurred toward the end of the Clinton and George W. Bush presidencies. A new president then took over, eager to outdo his predecessor in managing Russia. That a new leader – Putin in 2000 and Medvedev in 2008 – had emerged on the Russian scene as well with the expressed desire to rebuild relations proved a tremendous help in creating an atmosphere in which the ugly incidents could be pushed into the background in favor of a renewed focus on the benefits of cooperation.

By contrast, the Ukraine crisis erupted early in Obama's second term – he still had three years to serve. And the Russian president was once again the unsavory Putin, who, moreover, had underscored in his 2007 Munich speech Russia's waning interest in joining the West and his determination to take a more traditional Russian approach to world affairs that prided itself on strategic autonomy. Indeed, as we have seen, from the moment he declared his intention to reclaim the presidency in 2011, relations fell into a downward spiral.

Putin's illegal annexation of Crimea had also qualitatively changed the nature of the challenge Russia posed. This was the first seizure of territory by a great power in Europe since the end of the Second World War.[55] As such, it was a frontal assault on the norms that had governed European security for the past several decades. It could not simply be brushed aside to open up a path to US–Russian cooperation; nor was that ever considered because the agenda for cooperation was rapidly narrowing. Russia's intervention in Syria in 2015 to help the brutal dictator, Bashar al-Assad, crush Islamic State terrorists and the Western-backed moderate opposition, terrorists in Moscow's view, only further enflamed tensions. Russia's subsequent flagrant interference in the 2016 US presidential elections then congealed a solid bipartisan anti-Russian consensus in the United States that continues to this day.

The rapidity with which attitudes shifted is evidence of the pent-up frustration with Russia's resistance to integration on American terms that had grown since the end of the Cold War. In a few short months, Russia changed from a difficult but potential partner into a nettlesome rival – not, it should be noted, geopolitical foe number one, as Obama's Republican opponent in the 2012 presidential election had claimed. Obama had mocked that claim then, insisting that al-Qaida posed a greater threat. He would not change his view now.

Shortly after Russia's annexation of Crimea, Obama derided it as "a regional power that is threatening some of its immediate neighbors, not out of strength but out of weakness." Its use of military force in violation

34

of international law, he continued, indicated that it has "less influence, not more" over its neighbors. Granted, its actions created a problem, but, Obama insisted, Russia did not "pose the number one security threat to the United States." He remained "much more concerned about the prospect of a nuclear weapon going off in Manhattan."[56] He rejected the view that a new Cold War was in the making, as many commentators argued; he denied that he was seeking to contain Russia. Russia was simply not that important.

Nevertheless, Obama had to make Russia pay some price for its aggression. He turned to the tools the United States had historically used against emerging foes – diplomatic isolation, sanctions, and deterrence.[57] He ended "business as usual," severing most government-to-government channels of communication, including the Bilateral Presidential Commission. Russia was expelled from the G-8, which became once again the G-7 of major industrial democracies. The United States, along with its allies and partners, levied sanctions against a handful of individuals who had been directly involved in the seizure of Crimea, as well as some of Putin's "cronies," in the hope that they would urge him to reconsider his course. More damaging sanctions against the financial and key industrial sectors ensued after the Russian-backed separatists or the Russians themselves outraged the West by shooting down a civilian airliner over Ukraine in July 2014, killing all of the nearly 300 people on board. As relations with Russia tanked, Obama launched the European Reassurance Initiative to enhance the alliance's readiness to deter and defend against Russian aggression. This was containment, albeit limited in scope and intensity, no matter what Obama said.

But the effort never came close to the scale of the policy launched after Russia invaded Ukraine in 2022 for several reasons. To start, the Minsk Agreements on regulating the conflict in eastern Ukraine, first signed by Kyiv and separatist leaders in September 2014 and then augmented in February 2015, ended the acute phase of the fighting and opened up a negotiating track. That eased pressure to ratchet up sanctions against Russia. Russia's flagrant interference in the 2016 presidential elections did surprisingly little to raise the pressure. Obama hesitated to take strong actions that he feared might be seen as attempting to influence the elections, levying the first sanctions only shortly before he was to leave office in January. Meanwhile, Iran was making worrisome, rapid progress in developing a nuclear weapon, and the Islamic State, a vicious terrorist organization, was seizing large swaths of land in Iraq and Syria to add to its burgeoning caliphate. On both those matters, which were greater threats in Obama's mind than Russia's aggression, the Obama administration sought its erstwhile partner's cooperation.

The cooperation paid off with regard to Iran. In July 2015, the two countries, along with China, France, Germany, and Great Britain (the so-called P5+1)[58] reached agreement with Iran on the Joint Comprehensive Plan of Action designed to ensure that Iran's nuclear programs were exclusively for peaceful purposes. Cooperation on Syria was more fitful, and Russia eventually abandoned active talks with the United States in favor of an effort with Iran and Turkey to find a negotiated solution to the civil war. After Russia's military intervention in September 2015, however, the US and Russian militaries remained in close contact to deconflict their respective military operations in Syria.

Obama thus left office with relations in a curious state. On the one hand, they were the worst they had been since before the end of the Cold War; the alienation was near total; ties between the two governments were minimal. On the other, that did not matter that much to Washington. Russia's conduct abroad was problematic, to be sure, but few policymakers or members of Congress had much respect for it – it was a declining power, a nuisance, but hardly a grave threat to American interests abroad. Indeed, if Russia mattered, it was largely because of domestic political circumstances. Donald Trump's opponents consistently exaggerated Russia's influence in the just-concluded presidential elections – as if it could determine electoral outcomes in a mature democracy – as well as his ties to the Kremlin, to raise doubts about the legitimacy of his electoral victory and his fitness for office. From a significant foreign-policy concern, Russia had been reduced to a cudgel in a domestic political struggle.

Trump dramatically changed the atmospherics around Russia policy. He had little but praise for Putin; at the 2018 Helsinki summit, he famously sided with the Russian leader against his own intelligence community on the issue of Russian interference in the 2016 elections.[59] He stressed the virtues of "getting along with Russia." And he denigrated NATO as little more than a protection racket and played down the Russian threat. But he had little room to act on his views.[60] The Mueller

investigation and congressional probes on Russia's interference in elections and possible collusion between Trump and the Kremlin stymied
his efforts. Deeply concerned about his intentions, Congress passed
veto-proof legislation, the Countering America's Adversaries Through
Sanctions Act (CAATSA), that compelled Trump to maintain or levy
sanctions against Russia that could not be removed without its prior
consent.

But Congress was not the only obstacle. Surprisingly few of the
senior officials whom he had appointed, not to speak of the permanent
national-security apparatus, shared his assessment of Putin or Russia. To
the contrary, they saw an increasingly aggressive and malevolent Russia
and, often over the president's resistance, expanded and toughened the
measures Obama had taken to punish and contain Russia. High-level
contacts were intermittent and unproductive. The administration did
nothing to restore normal diplomatic relations. Rather, they expelled
Russian diplomats, at times in coordination with NATO allies, and
shuttered diplomatic missions, while levying additional sanctions to
punish Russia for malign acts, such as major cyber attacks against US
infrastructure or the poisoning of a former Russian intelligence officer in
Great Britain with a banned chemical weapon. They expanded funding
for the European Reassurance Initiative, now renamed the European
Deterrence Initiative, and they decided to provide Ukraine with lethal
defensive equipment, something Obama had refused to do so as to avoid
further antagonizing Russia.

Like the Obama administration, Trump's senior officials had little
respect for Russian power. Even if the *National Security Strategy* her-
alded a new era of great-power competition and identified Russia, along
with China, as a near-peer competitor and revisionist power bent on
undermining the US-led world order, China far outpaced Russia as a
strategic concern.[61] And the growing strategic alignment between Russia
and China raised few worries because it was assumed that that alignment
added little to the challenge China alone posed.

Where Trump had sown discord and disarray, Biden came to office
determined to provide clarity and consistency. He made two things
clear at the very beginning. First, he was not interested in a reset. The
United States and Russia were rivals and would remain so for at least
as long as Putin led Russia. The goals were minimal. As a senior official

put it, the administration was seeking "stability and predictability and areas of constructive work with Russia, where it is in our interest to do that."[62] Second, Russia would not be a priority. China was the much greater concern, a true strategic competitor around the globe and across all dimensions of power. By contrast, Russia was a destabilizing, and passing, threat on the global stage, a nuisance. Biden wanted to stabilize relations with it so that he could concentrate on China.[63]

Russia's military buildup along Ukraine's border in the Spring of 2021, however, compelled the new president to devote much more time to Russia than he had anticipated or wanted to.[64] He held an early summit with Putin – in Geneva in June. The two agreed to launch talks on strategic stability and cyber security. Biden hoped that would be sufficient to stabilize relations, and for a brief period it appeared to do just that. By the Fall, however, Russia had resumed its military buildup near Ukraine and demanded security guarantees totally unacceptable to the West – an end to NATO expansion and the withdrawal of NATO infrastructure back to the lines that existed in 1997 before the first post-Cold War wave of expansion. Faltering negotiations ended, when Putin launched a large-scale invasion of Ukraine on February 24.

That event marked a dramatic turn in US–Russian relations, exponentially more radical than the pivot after Russia seized Crimea eight years earlier. Biden decided to cast the conflict in world-historical, Cold War terms: "We have emerged anew in a great battle for freedom: a battle between democracy and autocracy, between liberty and repression; between a rules-based order and one governed by brute force," he told an audience in Warsaw in March 2022.[65]

The policy he chose was a hard-edged containment – his goal was not simply to constrain Russian behavior, but to punish and isolate Russia, to turn it into an international pariah, while also crippling its economy with sanctions that severed its access to global financial markets and cutting-edge technology. To defeat Russian aggression, the United States and its partners would provide Ukraine with advanced weaponry in greater numbers. At the same time, his ambition was to use Russia's aggression to revive the unity of purpose in the West, restoring NATO to its original purpose of defense against the Russian threat.[66]

It is much too early to judge whether Biden can succeed in his large ambitions. He himself has said that the battle will last for years.[67] But, more than thirty years after the end of the Cold War and the breakup of the Soviet Union, US–Russian relations are scraping the depths of Cold War hostility. This is not a Cold War redux, no matter what Biden's rhetoric might suggest. As I argued in the Introduction, the world has changed dramatically during the past thirty-plus years; US–Russian relations no longer define the international system, as they once did. But the conflict is extraordinarily dangerous, and will remain so as long as the two countries retain the nuclear weapons capable of destroying the other as a functioning society in thirty minutes.

Unanswered Questions

To be sure, no one wanted to wind up in this place. The end of the Cold War had offered broad vistas of a safer and more prosperous world. We have seen what the United States did to seize the moment and why. And we have seen how the United States reacted when the ambitious project of integrating Russia into the Euro-Atlantic community finally collapsed under the weight of Russian aggression against Ukraine in 2014. What we need to understand now is why the grand strategy of integration failed. Was there a fatal flaw in the original design? Did the United States hedge against failure in a way that increased the chances of failure? Did the United States overlook, or willfully ignore, something essential in the character of Russia that doomed its project from the beginning? Was the United States simply the victim of circumstances, undone by events that it could not have reasonably foreseen? Or, as is widely believed in the West today, was Russia, or more exactly Putin, from the very beginning driven by a profoundly anti-American animus, determined to avenge the defeat in the Cold War and restore Russia's grandeur at its rival's expense?

The answers to these questions are hardly academic. They will have implications for how we assess the likely outcomes of the course of hard-edged containment on which United States has embarked and, most important, how the United States should structure relations to best advance its interests both now and over the long term.

2

The Clash of Worldviews

The US effort to forge a democratic partnership with Russia in support of the US-led world order was a huge gamble in historical terms. Success would have broken with the pattern of competition, if not outright confrontation, that had marked relations since the United States emerged as a great power on the global stage at the end of the nineteenth century. Granted, the two countries had been "distant friends," in the words of historian Norman Saul,[1] for the first century after the American War of Independence. But ties were hardly close; they did not amount to what we would now call partnership. Each country was of marginal concern to the other. Geopolitical tension was absent because the two countries largely operated in separate spheres – the United States in the Western Hemisphere and Russia in Europe and the Far East. And, when tension did emerge over Alaska, Russia generally yielded in the face of American activism because it did not consider that region of vital interest. The gulf in values between the republican United States and the autocratic Russia may have been profound and unbridgeable, but the two powers insulated relations from ideological disputes. As John Gaddis, a prominent scholar of the Cold War, simply puts it, if relations were friendly, it was because there was no compelling reason to be rivals.[2] That experience surely provided no model for constructing relations in the post-Cold War world.

Shallow friendship turned to incipient rivalry as the nineteenth century drew to a close. The shift arose as a consequence of American dynamism, confidence, and self-regard, which propelled the country's geopolitical and ideological ambitions from the confines of the Western Hemisphere overseas into the Far East and Europe and nourished aspirations to propagate its way of life and institutions abroad as a foundation for American prosperity, security, and continued success. Russia, by contrast, remained much as it had been in domestic structure and geopolitical endeavor, despite internal stresses and shifting coalitions with

European great powers. Its foreign policy was driven by a sense of vulnerability and the need to keep up with its rivals, not by a grand mission. As Gaddis notes, it would have preferred to retain cordial relations with the United States. It certainly had no need to seek a new rival. But it had no choice but to resist as the United States pushed into regions it considered of vital interest and stepped up criticism of its domestic affairs. American ideological activism and geopolitical ambition ultimately shattered the fragile framework of comity that had existed since 1776.[3]

To understand the enduring nature of US–Russian rivalry, we need to look to the differing requirements each saw for the advance of its security and prosperity and to the competing forms of national purpose. As the historian William Appleman Williams once wrote, the history of US–Russian relations is the story of "the conflict of two destinies – both expanding and both avowedly manifest."[4]

Geography, Climate, and Geopolitics

Geography, climate, and geopolitical setting are not destiny, but they provide opportunities and raise challenges that shape the character of any nation. In this regard, the starting conditions for Russia and the United States could not have been more divergent. No great power has ever emerged from a more unpromising geographic, climatic, and geopolitical setting than Russia. And no great power has been more blessed in starting conditions than the United States. The harsh necessities of survival informed the Russian worldview, while Americans reveled in the possibilities of progress.

Muscovy, which rather than Kievan Rus is the true forerunner of the modern Russian state, lay at the same latitude as Hudson Bay. It was located on the heavily forested northern section of the great Russian plain. The winters were brutal, the growing season short, the soil poor in nutrients, clearing the forests for agriculture an arduous task. The land, as a result, could only sustain a small population and, even then, only at extraordinary cost and effort. The main source of revenue came from the abundance of the forests, in the form of furs and timber, which were also the main items Muscovy traded with the outside world.[5] But trade was limited. Muscovy lay far off the main trading routes. It did not control the rivers that would bring it to open seas and facilitate trade. It was thus isolated, remote from the main centers of civilization in Europe, the Middle East, and Asia.

Muscovy's security problem lay to the south, where the forests gave way to the steppe, a vast grassland stretching from Central Asia into Europe easily traversed by the nomadic tribes that inhabited it – and their highly mobile, skilled, and lethal horsemen. The warriors of Genghis Khan's heirs swept across the steppe from the east in the mid-thirteenth century to subjugate Kievan Rus, which included the lands that would later emerge as Muscovy. Moscow itself escaped from Mongol overlordship only in late in the fifteenth century. After that, it was still long subject to the wrath of nomadic warriors – it was sacked by Tatar tribes as late as 1571. The threat was eliminated only when Catherine the Great seized the northern littoral of the Black Sea and annexed Crimea in the late eighteenth century.

Geography, climate, and geopolitics thus conspired to embed a profound sense of vulnerability and insecurity in the Russian psyche. Disaster was never more than a poor harvest and merciless nomadic raid away. Risk needed to be carefully managed. But, given the lack of formidable physical barriers that would have provided protection, and the interlocking river system and vast steppe that facilitated movement across the Russian plain, expansion – pushing borders as far away as possible from the heartland – seemingly provided the surest path to security. Strategically, expansion was fundamentally a defensive operation but, more often than not, it was pursued through acts of aggression against rivals or emerging threats. Russia's neighbors, unsurprisingly, saw a preternaturally threatening power.

The United States, by contrast, emerged on the edge of a vast territory of unlimited possibilities. The middle third of the North American continent lies in the temperate zone. The greater Mississippi River basin, between the Rocky Mountains to the west and the Appalachians to the east, drains the largest contiguous tract of rich, arable land in the world. Its intricate network of rivers flowing into open seas at New Orleans facilitates the delivery of food products to population centers along the Gulf and Atlantic coasts. The heavily indented coastlines provide for numerous natural harbors on all three coasts, ideally positioning the continent for maritime trade. The land also bears one of the richest natural endowments in the world with most resources of easy access.[6]

Geopolitically, the middle third of the continent was well protected from external threats. Geographic and climatic conditions precluded the rise of a major power to the north or south. What became Canada was too cold; the future Mexico was too dry to sustain an agricultural system that could rival the productivity of the Mississippi Basin. Neither country had a system of easily navigable rivers or the same wealth of natural harbors. In the east and west, two vast oceans provided protection from non-continental great powers. The European great powers, in any event, were preoccupied with the balance of power in Europe; the American continent was never more than a secondary theater. Meanwhile, the land itself was initially inhabited by a number of less-developed Indian tribes, who could not mount a serious defense against a determined population of Anglo-American settlers.[7]

None of this meant that the settlers of the original thirteen colonies along the Atlantic coast were destined to be the forebears of a great power. To start with, they had to maintain unity among themselves to preclude the possibility of the emergence of a system of competitive states vying for the continent's bounty. That was hardly a given. Regional disputes and rivalries were a constant from the colonies' foundings. If they could remain unified, the colonies then needed to dominate the Mississippi Basin and eliminate any land-based threats to their control. If those three tasks could be accomplished, America's rise as a great power was next to inevitable. Spared the costs of defending itself against neighboring great powers, the country could focus its resources on creating wealth and economic power.[8]

Expansion was thus the road to greatness for the United States, and America's Founding Fathers aspired to occupy the continent from the very beginning. In this light, American expansion has borne a radically different character from Russian expansion, a character that is evident even today: If Russia expanded out of geopolitical necessity in an unending search for security, America did so out of ideological ambition to fulfill its destiny.

Russian Messianism v. Realpolitik

Many, perhaps most, Western commentators would take exception to that characterization of Russian expansionism. They would point to Russia's long messianic tradition with varying visions of Russia's destiny, if not to rule the world, then to ultimately shape its future. This tradition, it has been argued, has driven Russia's unprecedented historical expansion and lay behind its aggressive foreign policy. Russia, in short, is inherently – and exceptionally – aggressive, expansionist, and imperialistic.[9]

That messianism was a constant feature of Russian thought is not surprising. Such thinking is widespread in countries around the world, as elites seek to articulate their nation's character and historical role. So too is the tendency to identify attributes that elevate their countries above their neighbors and to find special missions that unfolded over long historical periods. In this, educated Russians, at least from the late fifteenth century onward, were no exception.

Orthodox, Slavophiles, Communists

Out of the profoundly religious milieu of late fifteenth to early sixteenth-century Muscovy there emerged two messianic ideas with expansionist overtones: Moscow as the Third Rome and Holy Russia. The first exalted the Muscovite state, intertwining its fate with the religious truth of Orthodoxy and making its rulers universal Christian sovereigns and defenders of the faith. According to one Russian Orthodox narrative, the ancient Rome of Christendom had fallen with the Great (Church) Schism of 1054. Constantinople assumed Rome's mantle as the defender of the true Orthodox faith, only to betray its divine calling by accepting reunion with apostate Rome at the Council of Florence in 1437–1439. The Turkish conquest of Constantinople ensued in 1453 as God's punishment. That left Muscovy as the preeminent Orthodox Empire. As Philotheus, a Russian monk from Pskov, wrote to Grand Prince Vasily III in 1511, "Two Romes have fallen, a third stands, a fourth shall not be." The Muscovite state marked the final stage in historical development.[10]

"Holy Russia," by contrast, elevated the land and its people, not the state, as the true bearers of the faith and the source of salvation. The earliest written references date back to the sixteenth-century reign of Ivan the Terrible, and they become more frequent in the seventeenth, after the Russian people drove the Polish invaders out of Moscow during the Time of Troubles. But the epithet attained its most profound messianic connotations in the 1840s, when the Slavophiles embraced it in their search for an authentic Russia to resist what they considered the corrupting influences of the state-supported Europeanization launched by Peter the Great at the beginning of the eighteenth century.[11]

The Slavophiles became the fount of messianic thinking in the nineteenth century, as they sought to counter the West's corrosive individualism, materialism, and abstract rationalism. They found solace in "Holy Russia," a Russia that was still illuminated by the Christian faith, and considered the peasant commune to be the most vivid manifestation of that Russia. Their idealized vision of the commune, a voluntary association of Orthodox peasants in which the individual expressed himself through the community, was far removed from reality, and their historical narrative lacked rigor – they opposed serfdom but ignored the fact that it had been instituted in Russia well before Peter's reign. They nevertheless urged a return to the pre-Petrine "authentic" Russia, not the further assimilation of debilitating foreign ideas and practices, as the solution to Russia's many ills. What's more, they argued that this Russia offered the model for the salvation of the entire civilized world. In this advocacy, according to the eminent historian of Russia Martin Malia, "Slavophilism culminated in a grandiose religious nationalistic messianism, in which the last of civilized nations [that is, Russia] became the first, and the most humiliated of peoples [that is, the Russians] the most exalted."[12]

Slavophilism was fundamentally conservative in its embrace of the pre-Petrine past and a purer form of Russian autocracy. But it nourished a revolutionary offspring, Russian populism, which was given its original form in the thinking of Alexander Herzen, who maintained a dialogue with the leading Slavophiles, despite his radical tendencies. He came to value the Russian peasant commune as the embodiment of the socialist ideal of equality through free association, at least in embryonic form. It also represented a total denial of the despotic centralized Russian autocracy that Herzen despised. In this, the commune was not only Russia's future, in Herzen's view, but also the ideal to which Europe itself was striving. And so, like the Slavophiles, Herzen and other early Russian populists discovered the salvation not only of Russia but of Europe as well in the Russian countryside. It was a revolutionary form of nationalistic messianism.[13]

After the Crimean War (1853–1856), the original Slavophilism gave way to the idea of pan-Slavism, a reactionary and imperialist form of Russian messianism, which gripped a substantial part of educated Russians amid the general rise of nationalist sentiment throughout Europe. Looking for a way to restore Russian power in Europe after a humiliating defeat, pan-Slavists turned toward the Slavic and Orthodox populations in the Balkans living under Ottoman rule. There, Russia could replicate the feat of Prussia in uniting German states into a powerful empire by forging a formidable Slavic–Orthodox entity, which would eventually attract other Slavs in Europe, including the Poles and Czechs. Never mind that the latter two were not Orthodox, nor were they particularly eager to be part of a union dominated by Russia. The point was to reassert Russia's prerogatives abroad. Russian action, in the pan-Slavic view, would eventually lead to a Slavic Orthodox empire that would dominate Europe, replacing the waning Romano-Germanic form of domination, banishing the heathen Turks, and marking a first step toward eternal peace in Europe.[14]

The twentieth century finally brought forth a potent secular form of Russian messianism: Bolshevism. The Bolshevik leaders, to be sure, had little affection for Russia per se. They loathed the autocracy; they considered the peasant commune to be reactionary. They exalted the proletariat, but it formed only a sliver of the Russian population. For them, Russia was the base from which to launch a worldwide socialist revolution; it would wane in importance as the revolution progressed. The failure to spark revolution in the more-developed West, where socialism should have triumphed first in the Marxist telling, eventually sapped Bolshevism of its messianism, in deed if not in word, and the country under Stalin applied itself to the task of building socialism in one country. But Soviet Russia could not abandon its revolutionary ideology, which was the source of its legitimacy. From a country that was to spark revolution and then fade into a worldwide socialist community, it became the center of international movement that communists across the globe were called to defend as their first duty.

Realpolitik at the Fore

There have thus been statist and populist, religious and secular strains of Russian messianism of greater or lesser appeal for more than 600 years. But have they driven Russian foreign policy? The historical record provides little evidence that they did before the middle of the nineteenth century. After that, messianic visions began to penetrate into state counsels, usually with pernicious effect: Russia has generally failed poorly when it succumbed to the siren calls of messianism and slighted the sober calculations of realpolitik.

In the sixteenth century, for example, Moscow might have been the Third Rome for Philotheus and his fellow monks. And that vision might have had a certain appeal among ordinary believers, comforting a hard-pressed people with assurances that their land had a special mission in the world. But grand princes and their secular servants had little use for a theory that in practice would have curtailed their authority by empowering the Church as a partner in ruling their lands. They did not evoke it to justify their aggressive expansionist policies, which they pursued largely for dynastic reasons, "to gather the Russian lands" of the Kievan inheritance.[15] That was the justification for expansion even when the claim was patently false, as when Ivan the Terrible launched the Livonian war in 1558 on the grounds that the Baltic territories of the Teutonic Knights were once ruled by Kievan princes.[16]

Spreading the Orthodox faith, similarly, played little role in Ivan's, and Muscovy's, first imperial conquests of the sovereign Muslim Khanates of Kazan and Astrakhan in the 1550s. He quickly abandoned an attempt to forcibly convert the Tatars to Orthodoxy, which had sparked widespread rebellion, allowing them to assimilate into the Muscovite state as Muslims. Much more important was eliminating the security threat from the southeast that had long plagued his realm and seizing the commercial opportunities that arose from control of the full length of the Volga.[17]

The story was the same for the first half of the Imperial period, from the reign of Peter the Great down through the Crimean War. While educated strata might have imagined ways Russia could save the world, Russian rulers were operating strictly on the basis of what came to be known as realpolitik within the European balance-of-power system. The great tsars of the eighteenth century, Peter and Catherine II, expanded

Russian sway westward in contests with the waning powers of Sweden, Poland, and the Ottoman Empire, to maintain their position vis-à-vis a rising Prussia and a still formidable Austria. As they did, Russian officials, many of whom like Catherine herself were not ethnic Russians, debated the benefits of various options for the power and security of the Russian state, not the implications for some fuzzy messianic idea.[18] In the event, their exploits produced the longest streak of military victories in Russian history, expanded the Empire's writ to the farthest point westward in Europe before Stalin's conquests in the mid twentieth century, and made Russia the preeminent continental power in the early decades of the nineteenth.

After the herculean efforts in the Napoleonic Wars, Russia became a status quo power, determined to preserve the balance of power and contain the scourge of revolution. At the Congress of Vienna in 1814–1815, rather than seizing as much land as possible, Alexander I helped to rehabilitate France as an essential element of the balance and divide up the territory of Poland and Saxony to ensure a stable equilibrium among the great powers.[19] He advocated for a Holy Alliance of major powers, but it had nothing to do with expanding the writ of Orthodoxy or creating an exceptional role for Russia in Europe. Indeed, it was ecumenical in inspiration, uniting Orthodox, Catholic, and Protestant powers on a common Christian, ethical foundation in the defense of monarchical legitimacy.[20] His successor, Nicholas I, followed with an even stronger defense, even as he eschewed territorial gain in Europe.[21]

The Crimean War marked an historic turning point in Russia's fortunes. It was the last major conflict in which realpolitik shaped policy largely unaffected by messianic yearnings, even if its origins lay in the long-standing dispute over who – the Orthodox or Catholic clergy – should have custody over the holy places in Palestine, which was then under Ottoman rule. Nicholas risked war in an effort to preserve Russia's paramount influence in Constantinople, the Ottoman capital. He considered that essential to maintaining the Ottoman Empire as a buffer zone to protect Russia's southern reaches on the Black Sea, and he feared it was threatened by the sultan's bending under French pressure to grant the Catholic clergy custody of the holy places.[22] The war was also the first time realpolitik had yielded a humiliating defeat, from which the

Russian Empire was never to fully recover in the decades leading to the catastrophe of 1917.

Messianic Delusions Intrude

The humiliation persuaded Nicholas' successor, Alexander II, of the urgency of modernizing the Empire to regain its position as the dominant continental power. To that end, he initiated what became known as the Great Reforms – the emancipation of the serfs, creation of an independent judiciary, grant of autonomy to universities, easing of censorship, and formation of zemstvos, institutions of local self-government. Those reforms empowered society and gave birth to public opinion as a potent political force, which only grew stronger as industrialization in the decades ahead gave rise to capitalists and professional classes that began to operate independently of the state.[23] By the turn of the century, political parties were taking shape, and their role was enhanced when revolutionary upheaval in 1905 compelled the autocrat to agree to the establishment of the Duma, the country's first true parliament.

As elsewhere in Europe, nationalist and socialist ideas found fertile soil among Russia's educated classes. As a result, public opinion would not be satisfied with a foreign policy grounded in the naked pursuit of state security – Russia needed to have a special mission in the world. And for a significant segment of the educated classes during the late imperial period that mission was pan-Slavic in inspiration. The ambitions of public opinion infected the Court and, at times, the tsars themselves. The practitioners of realpolitik, who had long dominated state counsels in the formation and execution of foreign policy, now had to contend with it.

Public opinion first demonstrated its sway in the run-up to the war with Turkey in 1877–1878. A massive pan-Slavist public campaign, tolerated if not encouraged by the Court, persuaded Alexander II that he had to come to the defense of Slavs in the Balkans, even though Russian diplomats were opposed to risking a European war for any purpose. Nationalist fervor swelled as Russian forces reached the outskirts of Constantinople, whose conquest pan-Slavists urged, to the alarm of the other European powers. Concerned by this mounting displeasure, Alexander halted the advance but then imposed a settlement that would have made Russia the dominant power in the Balkans. That was more than the other powers, especially Germany, could accept. Bismarck took the lead in rolling back the Russian gains at the Congress of Berlin in 1878 to restore the European balance of power. Pan-Slavists were outraged, but Alexander acquiesced in the stinging reversal, as the logic of realpolitik reasserted itself: Russia was in no condition to wage war against Europe's other great powers to hold onto to its gains.[24]

This setback paled in comparison to the tragedy of the First World War. The causes of that conflict are myriad, as are the considerations that shaped Russian diplomacy in the run-up. Pan-Slavic sentiment was among them. During the Bosnian crisis of 1908, pan-Slavists had reacted with fury when Vienna annexed Bosnia, while reneging on its promise to help Russia gain an adjustment in the Straits convention that would enable Russian naval forces alone of all European powers to enter them during peacetime. That was not only a blow to Russia's prestige but also to the interests of its Balkan client, Serbia. The pan-Slavists insisted that Russia could not sit by idly and watch Austria and Germany destroy Serbia without forfeiting its standing as a great power. That turned out to be a crucial factor in Russia's decision to back its client in July 1914, in resisting the Austrian ultimatum delivered after the assassination of Archduke Franz Ferdinand.[25] The rest is history.

The situation with the other great military debacle of the late Imperial period, the Russo-Japanese War of 1904–1905, is more complex, but is not without an element of messianic delusion. The main cause lay in the sharpening competition with Japan for control over Manchuria, which lay at the center of Russia's ambitious plan of rapid industrialization to enable it to keep pace with Europe's other great powers. But visions of national grandeur, especially on the part of Nicholas II, and racist denigration of Japan's capabilities played a major role in overriding realpolitik calculations that called for avoiding war in the Far East, as challenges in Europe mounted.[26] Japan's victory – the first time in the modern era that an Asian state had defeated a European great power – precipitated a revolution that put Russia squarely on the road to 1917.

Realpolitik Returns

The communist period seemingly reinforced the power of messianic thinking, only replacing nationalist ambition with Marxist–Leninist ideology as the framework for Moscow's foreign policy. But it was not that straightforward. Policy unfolded along two separate tracks. Moscow created the Comintern in 1919 to guide the global revolution, while it set up the People's Commissariat of Foreign Affairs (the *Narkomindel*) to pursue the interests of the state along traditional realpolitik lines. As hope for worldwide revolution faded, and the menace of war grew, state interests took precedence over revolutionary dreams.[27] The Comintern fell into disuse in the mid 1930s and was finally abandoned in 1943; realpolitik flourished, fashioning Soviet policy as it sought to avoid war and then to wage it.

Soviet policies toward two conflicts in the 1930s – the Spanish Civil War and the Sino-Japanese War – illustrate how realpolitik took precedence over ideological considerations. In both cases, Moscow confronted fascist powers, sworn enemies of Bolshevism and parties to the Anti-Comintern Pact. In Spain, in a contest that was framed in world opinion as pitting the political right against the political left, the Soviets could not possibly deny public support to the anti-fascist forces of the Republic battling the German- and Italian-backed fascist insurgents under Franco. But they had no interest in the complete identification of communism with the Spanish Republic, as long as they still hoped to ally with Great Britain and France against Germany. And so, in December 1936, Stalin urged the Spanish government to avoid social radicalism and ordered the Spanish Communists to rein in their anarchist and left socialist allies' extremism.[28]

At the same time, in the Far East, Moscow urged the Chinese Communists to collaborate with the nationalists under Chiang Kai-shek, even though the latter had paused his struggle against the Japanese invaders to focus on consolidating the Chinese forces, in part by eliminating the communists. After a bizarre incident that led to Chiang's imprisonment by a warlord in late 1936, the communists won his release, but only after he had pledged to end his struggle against them and take a strong anti-Japanese line. The renewal of Chinese–Japanese hostilities followed in 1937, and the Soviets provided massive aid to the Chinese. That development sharply reduced the risk of a Japanese attack on the Soviet Union and a two-front war in Europe and Asia that Moscow feared. Once again, realpolitik prevailed.[29]

And so it continued through the rest of the Soviet period. The ideology became little more than a framework for describing the world to the

Soviet people, an instrument of control in the socialist camp, and a ritual justification for actions driven mainly by considerations of hard power. When ideological concerns did prevail, as they did in Soviet interventions in the Third World in the 1970s, they led to ruin, most tragically in Afghanistan.

As this brief survey suggests, no matter what the fashions of educated society, statists usually dominated the counsels of the Russian state. To paraphrase the historian Geoffrey Hosking, throughout history the survival of the state and the maintenance of its territorial integrity were the paramount priorities for Russia's rulers, before which national, religious, economic and other priorities invariably yielded. The myth of the state as the core of Russian identity was powerful: it rested on pride in its size and diversity, as well as on military victories.[30] Realpolitik served Russia well in this regard. On those rare occasions when messianism infected Russian rulers, it led to humiliating setbacks, if not outright catastrophe.

American Exceptionalism and Ambition

There are multiple reasons why Russian messianism has carried so little sway in the conduct of Russian foreign policy. Many of the ideas were fuzzy, some were subversive. But surely one major reason has been that in a highly centralized authoritarian system rulers have, as a rule, little need to consult public opinion. Officials act on the basis of assessments of an action's implications for the state's power and security; the population lives with the results. This pattern could not hold for a democracy like the United States, where leaders are accountable to the people. American expansionism, therefore, reflected the aspirations of leaders and the people alike, which were informed by a shared myth of American exceptionalism.[31]

Puritanism and the Enlightenment Combine

Two strains of exceptionalism combined to define the new American nation in 1776. The first, religious, one arrived with the Puritan settlers in the seventeenth century. Persecuted in the Old World, the Puritans had come to North America to found a "new Jerusalem" and, in the words of John Winthrop, a leader who arrived in 1630, to create "a city on the hill" that would serve as a beacon of a new beginning for European civilization. Contrary to the conventional interpretation, this mission was not grounded in an isolationist impulse. Although geographically distant, the Puritans hoped that their home country of England would imitate New England, thereby reviving itself as the vanguard of humanity.[32] The Puritan ideology was reworked continuously in the seventeenth and eighteenth centuries and channeled into the mainstream of American Protestantism. Overall, as a leading historian of American political thought, Bernard Bailyn, argued, it "stimulated confidence in the idea that America had a special place, as yet not fully revealed, in the architecture of God's intent."[33]

The second strain was secular Enlightenment rationalism. The generation that won independence from Great Britain was steeped in the theories of natural law and social compact propounded by John Locke.[34] Those ideas inspired the Declaration of Independence, which is in essence a legal brief for separation of a free people from an increasingly tyrannical government. Two points are significant for our purposes. First, the ideas, grounded in reason, were universal in their application. The Founding Fathers were not only laying the foundation for their own country but also consciously creating a model for others who aspired to liberty. Second, they were also deliberately cutting the bonds of kinship that linked them to Great Britain. On the day the Declaration was signed, they ceased to be the Englishmen they had been and began to develop a distinctive American identity. Cut off from their British past, they could no longer use their British heritage to define themselves. Rather, they had to look to the future, to the unfolding of the ideas that lay at the foundation, for their national project.[35]

Both the Puritan and Enlightenment components of exceptionalism implicitly bore an expansionary impulse. The United States was either the vanguard or the magnet of humanity, the country that would lead the world into the future, or the one that would attract the allegiance of others, since it was based on a set of universal, rational ideas, not kinship or territory. Those views laid the groundwork for dynamic population growth, not so much by natural increase, but by the mounting influx of (mainly European) immigrants during the course of the nineteenth century.[36] The ideas also set the framework (and provided the justification) for rapid territorial expansion across what American leaders considered a largely vacant continent (the Indians didn't count, nor did the infrequent French or Spanish settler). Indeed, the Founding Fathers from the very beginning entertained a vision of a continental country. Jefferson spoke forcefully for the creation of an "Empire of Liberty," confident that the American republican system provided a model for accumulating territory without descending into despotism, as other empires had.[37] In time, Americans would seek to expand that empire overseas to the far corners of the earth. Grand ambition thus inspired America's expansion from the very beginning; it was never a matter of mere security.

One driving ambition has been to reform the world in its image. But how? According to Henry Kissinger, exceptionalism produced two approaches: One assumes that "America serves its values best by perfecting democracy at home, thereby acting as a beacon for the rest of mankind," while the other declares that "America's values impose on it an obligation to crusade for them around the world."[38] Both approaches – the exemplary and missionary – have coexisted throughout US history, although one or the other enjoyed precedence at specific times. Together they have imparted a unique character to American foreign policy.

Exceptionalism at Home

For the first 140 years of its existence, the United States focused on perfecting its democracy at home, creating the exemplar for the world to emulate, and eschewed democratic crusades. John Quincy Adams made that point empathetically in 1821: The United States "does not go abroad in search of monsters to destroy. She is the wellwisher to freedom and independence for all. She is the champion and vindicator only of her own."[39] In that light, the conventional wisdom has argued that the United States pursued an isolationist foreign policy, that it sought to insulate itself from European power politics.

There is much truth to that, but the term "isolationist" is misleading, for the United States was engaged in the world; Americans paid close attention to international affairs, especially to the European balance of power; a commercial nation, they were active traders in Europe and East Asia. But they were determined non-interventionists. They did not seek to manipulate the European balance – that would require the entangling alliances Washington and Jefferson had warned against. Rather they stoutly defended American neutrality in any great-power conflict so that they could continue to trade with all the belligerents. As the War of 1812 showed, they were prepared to go to war to defend their right to neutrality and unhindered trade. At the same time, the United States repeatedly exploited the shifting balance in Europe to advance its own interests, particularly the westward expansion across North America. This was a policy of prudence, especially during the early years of the republic, when the fledgling nation had little capacity for power politics and needed to devote its attention to building democratic institutions in the face of considerable domestic challenges, including the issue that was eventually to rip the country apart, slavery.

While non-interventionism might have described America's approach to Europe, it hardly applied to America's conduct in North America. For Americans, westward expansion was not a matter of foreign policy, but rather a fulfillment of what came to be known in the 1840s as their "Manifest Destiny" to spread across the continent. As an aspect of American exceptionalism, it did indeed lead to the greater sway of the American democratic, republican system, as territory was acquired and readied for statehood. The United States nearly doubled in size with Jefferson's purchase of the Louisiana Territory in 1803, and it added between 1845 and 1848 territories of greater dimension, with James Polk's annexation of Texas, conquest of what is now the US Southwest during the war against Mexico, and the settlement of the dispute with the British over the Oregon Territory. It rounded out its territorial expansion on the continent with the Gadsden Purchase from Mexico in 1854 and the purchase of Alaska in 1867.

Yet in this process, the United States was hardly acting as a democratic exemplar or crusader. Its action rather resembled those of other great powers in its lack of regard for the indigenous Indians, Creoles, and Catholic Spaniards and French who shared the continent; they were not deemed suitable for democratic rule or assimilation into the Anglo-American democratic experiment. The Indian tribes were driven from their lands, the others became at best second-class citizens. None of this, however, dimmed popular faith in American exceptionalism or manifest destiny.

Nor did the scourge of slavery. Indeed, for Southerners, slavery acted as a stimulus to extend the empire of liberty Jefferson spoke of, even as it led Northerners to hesitate, lest expansion upset the delicate balance of slave and free states in the Senate. The issue was joined in earnest when Missouri applied for statehood as a slave state. The Missouri Compromise of 1820, which admitted Maine as a free state along with Missouri, thus maintaining the delicate free state–slave state balance, and banned slavery above the 36°30' parallel except in Missouri, temporarily papered over the sectional rift.[40] The issue reemerged when Texas asked to join the country as a slave state, but this time it set in motion currents that would ultimately lead to the Civil War and the overcoming of this concern with the end of slavery.

Exceptionalism Goes Abroad

The extraordinary accumulation of wealth and power, the concomitant burgeoning faith in the American system, and the closing of the frontier in the late nineteenth century pushed the United States overseas toward more active engagement in global affairs. For advocates of global activism, the challenge was to reconcile their dreams with American exceptionalism to secure the popular support any foreign policy needs to succeed in a democracy. Two efforts failed in rapid succession.

The first attempt was by Theodore Roosevelt, an unabashed imperialist and realist in foreign policy. He believed that the United States should flex its muscles abroad and join the world's imperial powers in acquiring territories abroad. He and his allies were ardent supporters of the Spanish–American War that led to the US acquisition of new territories in the Caribbean and Pacific, most notably the Philippines.[41] But they understood that they could not sell imperial expansion to Americans as a matter of the power politics they believed in. In homage to American exceptionalism, they described the expansion as a mission to extend the sway of American virtues. American officials avoided any mention of empire and colonies, as they pursued a more interventionist approach abroad. They distinguished the United States from other imperialist powers, asserting that it was not acting out of selfish interests but rather to benefit the peoples of the lands seized from Spain.[42] Roosevelt himself was adamant that the main American goal was to bring civilization to backward lands.[43]

Despite this subterfuge, Roosevelt's imperial policies, especially the vicious counterinsurgency campaign against Filipino rebels, sparked a determined backlash. Many Americans saw them as running counter to the country's founding principles; others feared that compromising freedom abroad would undermine democracy at home.[44] Roosevelt was forced to pare back his ambitions. Annexation of further territory was out of the question. The most he could manage was to conduct "international police actions" in the Western Hemisphere to promote order and good government. He ultimately took steps to prepare the Philippines for independence as he left the presidency, although he had once foreseen a long occupation of the archipelago.[45]

Less than a decade later, Woodrow Wilson made a new attempt to break America's commitment to non-intervention and neutrality, but in a way that linked active engagement more closely to American exceptionalism. He himself believed deeply in exceptionalism and that the United States had a moral obligation to spread the benefits of the American experiment abroad. He was also certain that the United States had to play a more active role abroad to safeguard its interests. But, unlike Roosevelt, he did not propose to do that by manipulating the balance of power but rather by transcending that system with a new one based on justice, democracy, and international cooperation. In this, what Wilson was proclaiming, according to Henry Kissinger, "was not America's withdrawal from the world but the universal applicability of its values, and, in time, America's commitment to spreading them."[46]

In line with this thinking, Wilson brought a reluctant country into the First World War to make the world "safe for democracy." After the defeat of Germany, he became the leading advocate of the League of Nations, which was to replace the balance-of-power system. The country may have been prepared to follow the president into war. But it balked at his effort to redefine the international order and put the United States at its center. Despite a relentless effort on his part, which undermined his health, Wilson failed to persuade his countrymen to join the League. The country reverted to its non-interventionist tradition.[47]

Wilson's ideas triumphed a generation later. During the Second World War and ensuing Cold War, the United States turned its back fully on its foreign-policy tradition of neutrality, non-intervention, and unilateralism. It played the central role in the creation of the United Nations and affiliated bodies that grew up around it. It put in place a system of alliances that spanned the globe, and established military bases along the periphery of the communist bloc, to contain Soviet communism, few of which it abandoned in the post-Soviet era. And it renounced strict unilateralism in favor of multilateralism, even as it proclaimed its right to lead the multilateral coalitions it joined.

But the United States remained true to its sense of exceptionalism. It prided itself as acting on the global stage in a way no other great power had, not in pursuit of its narrow national interests but for the benefit of all peoples. That benefit consisted largely in spreading American values and principles of democratic self-government to the rest of the world, and the economic prosperity that Americans believed naturally flowed from democracy. The claims to leadership were present at the beginning and grew louder over time: The leader of the Free World during the Cold War became the "indispensable nation" that stood taller and saw further into the future in the post-Cold War period.[48] American exceptionalism and active global engagement were reconciled in a grand ambition to lead the world to a democratic future.

Russia's Ambitions Limited

Russia had no ambitions to lead the world, certainly not before the Bolshevik Revolution and after that event the matter is not as self-evident as many Western commentators have argued. Rather, rulers from Muscovite times to the present have considered their primary charge to be ensuring the survival of the state. That in itself has been a formidable task. State collapse has not been a rarity in Russian history. Genghis Khan's heirs dismantled the Kievan state in the thirteenth century. The end of the Rurik dynasty led the state to collapse in the early seventeenth century during the Time of Troubles. And the state collapsed twice in the twentieth, during the revolutions of 1917 and with the demise of the Soviet Union in 1991.

The Imperative of State Survival

The Russian state is a unique construct, at least in the European context, where Russia's most bitter and enduring contests have played out. Despite superficial similarities, it is radically different in essence and conception from its Western counterparts. It has never been conceptualized as an emanation of society, instituted to protect the rights of citizens, temper the consequences of conflicts among them, and advance the public weal. Rather, it emerged as an alien force invited to impose order and rule over an unruly people. "Our land is great and rich, but there is no order in it. Come reign as princes, rule over us," as the *Primary Chronicle*, written in the thirteenth century, describes the creation of the Russian state.[49]

For the elites, the state *was* Russia. It alone was capable of holding together a vast territory with a multiethnic population, which grew only more heterogeneous as the state expanded. It was not an exaggeration to argue that, without the state, there would be no Russia. Thus, the first task of the elite was to preserve the state, and preserve it in its unique characteristics, so that it could continue to hold together a disorderly empire. And, since the state and society, or the *narod*, the people, were two distinct entities, the elites without compunction exploited society for the state's purpose with little regard for the welfare of the people in most eras.

Russian rulers, admittedly, often spoke in different terms, positioning themselves as protectors of their people. Before the imperial period, the tsar was presented as just, merciful, and Orthodox (a sign of goodness in an Orthodox land). In the eighteenth century, emperors began to talk about the general weal, especially Catherine the Great, who was much influenced by Enlightenment thinkers. And the Bolsheviks were building socialism for the general welfare of their population. This was not all cynical posturing. Most were sincere in their belief that existing socio-political structures formed the basis of a just world order and guaranteed the general good. Their task was to maintain that order. But the order in fact was grounded in a darker reality.

The Muscovite order, the first incarnation of the Russian state, was in fact a highly centralized military and political system, built around the tsar (grand prince) and boyar clans, that ruled over a vast, sparsely settled territory in harsh, unforgiving climatic conditions. (And so were its successors: Although the titles changed over time, the Russian state has preserved that basic oligarchic structure with the same sharp divide between it and the country's population to the present.) The Muscovite state reached its exalted status among all Russian principalities in the sixteenth century by containing internal strife and growing its power, in a sense by surviving better than its rivals. Looking forward, survival for the Muscovite state and its successors entailed, first of all, continuing to avoid the political chaos that could arise from persistent conflict among the leading boyar clans (oligarchs) at the center of the system.[50]

Strategic Depth and Internal Control

If Russia's rulers managed the clans' competition effectively, they then faced two additional tasks: protecting the state from the masses and defending it against external enemies. The staggering dimensions of those tasks become clear with Ivan the Terrible's conquest of the Muslim Khanates of Kazan and Astrakhan, and the first steps across the Urals into Siberia, in the mid sixteenth century. The task was to defend that immense, sparsely populated, diverse country located on a territory without formidable physical barriers abutting unsettled regions or powerful states. Unfortunately for Russia's rulers, the external imperatives exacerbated the internal challenges.[51]

Externally, Russia sought safety in buffer zones, regional hegemony, defensible borders, and disruption of coalitions of hostile states, but most importantly in expansion, in the creation of strategic depth. As Catherine the Great explained, "I have no way to defend my borders but to extend them." There were three vectors of advance: western, southern, and eastern (with control of the Arctic littoral, there was little room or need for further expansion northward). Each bore its own particular challenges. To the west lay Russia's principal rivals, the great powers of Europe – initially Sweden, Poland, and the Ottoman Empire and, in time, Prussia (ultimately in the guise of a united Germany) and Austria. The southern vector was dominated initially by the nomadic-warrior tribes of the steppe, but by the nineteenth century the shadow of Great Britain loomed large. The east, by contrast, presented a vast opportunity in the largely unsettled, but incredibly resource-rich Siberian expanse and the tempting markets of China, which only turned dangerous in the late nineteenth century as Russia's European rivals and Japan scrambled to partition the Qing dynasty.

The pace of expansion varied along the three vectors, depending on the geopolitical resistance and physical obstacles Russia encountered, but

Russia pursued all three simultaneously. It did not, as many have argued, shift from one vector to the other, compensating for reversals in one place by advancing elsewhere. Rather it was the dynamic core of Eurasia, releasing its energy all along a periphery thousands of miles long.[52] The advance was extraordinary: From the small confines of Muscovy in the mid fifteenth century, Russia embarked on one of the grandest episodes of geopolitical progress in history, expanding more than 550 times in size in 450 years, to form the largest overland empire in the modern period.[53]

There were setbacks to be sure, and Russia abandoned territory that brought little benefit or that it could not reliably defend, Alaska being the prime example. And there were times when Russia claimed to be a satisfied power, notably during the reign of Nicholas I in the first half of the nineteenth century.[54] But the pause was never more than temporary – and even Nicholas, while not seizing territory, sought to project power further into Europe to defend monarchical legitimacy and suppress the spread of revolutionary ideas and actions. Even when Russia was vulnerable and arguably should have reined in its ambitions, it did not: witness its effort to expand into Manchuria in the late nineteenth and early twentieth centuries.[55] And so the expansion continued, until it led to disaster with the humiliating defeat at Japan's hand in 1905.

Nevertheless, the expansion resumed in the Soviet period. After the collapse of the Russian Empire and the Revolution, the Bolsheviks reasserted Russia's authority during the civil war over most of the once-imperial territory, minus the Baltic states, Bessarabia, Finland, and Poland. Less than two decades later, Stalin regained those lost territories, save Finland, as a result of the Molotov-Ribbentrop Pact with Nazi Germany. He then extended Moscow's sway over much of Eastern Europe as the Second World War drew to a close, creating the largest buffer zone Russia has ever controlled in Europe.

The creation of strategic depth paid off dramatically in the conflicts against Napoleon and Hitler in the nineteenth and twentieth centuries, enabling the country to absorb deep incursions, granted at great human and material cost, before turning the tide. But it came with a heavy long-term price, the exacerbation of the challenge of internal security. To begin with, it brought in large numbers of non-Russian and non-Orthodox peoples, heterogeneous elements that had to be assimilated. Until the middle of the nineteenth century, that was not an insurmountable task.

Local elites were absorbed into the country's socio-political structure on the same conditions that the ethnic Russian elites encountered.[56] But the rise of nationalism undid this happy situation, particularly in the western parts of the empire among the more advanced peoples attuned to the prevailing trends in Europe. The non-ethnic Russian communities were located primarily in the borderlands, and co-nationals as a rule inhabited land on the other side of the border. As a result, nationalist movements among Poles, Finns, Balts, Romanians, Ukrainians, and various Caucasian nations along the periphery were constant threats to the Empire's domestic stability and external security.

The second problem emerged from the empire's vast territory and long borders. Peasant unrest was a perennial problem. Massive rebellions, led by Stepan Razin and Yemelyan Pugachev, rocked the Volga region in the seventeenth and eighteenth centuries. As a consequence, a large army was needed both to defend (and advance) the extended borders and to garrison the interior against peasant and later nationalist unrest. The state was perpetually exercised by the need to divide its limited resources between external defense and domestic garrisoning. Moving troops to the borders always raised the specter of greater domestic unrest. Not accidentally, the great Pugachev rebellion erupted during a war against Turkey.

The internal and external imperatives thus combined to feed a persistent sense of vulnerability that never lay far beneath the surface in the consciousness of Russia's rulers. As Robert Kaplan has aptly put it, "Insecurity is the quintessential Russian national emotion."[57] Russian rulers struggled to mobilize the resources to ensure domestic order and defend against external foes, constantly shifting forces and attention between domestic and external threats as the need arose in a never-ending quest for absolute security.

One Among a Few

But that was hardly the same as a drive for global domination, even during the Soviet period. And, while there was persistent pressure to move the borders outward, the expansionist ambitions were not unlimited. Indeed, over centuries, the dialectic of expansion and resistance, and the imperative to balance the requirements of external and internal security, came to define Russia's geopolitical space, and the limits of its territorial ambitions, as north central Eurasia, that is, all of the former Soviet space. It is this zone, Russian rulers believe, where Russia must remain preeminent to guarantee its own security and territorial integrity. The borders of this zone, it must be noted, are not defined by imposing physical barriers, but rather by the contours of power between Russia and its neighbors and Russia's political calculation of when the benefits of expansion cease to outweigh the risks of internal instability.

This struggle for security, this unending effort to defend the unique character of the Russian state, came to define Russia's role in global affairs as a jealous defender of its own sovereignty, and by extension of the sovereignty of other great powers, if not all countries. In a world of sovereign great powers, balance-of-power politics came to be Russia's preferred approach to international relations, and a concert of great powers the desired structure for managing global affairs, on the understanding that Russia would be among the great powers and that it would have a veto, as would other great powers, on the workings of the concert. The Russian goal was not domination in the name of a Russian brand of universalism and exceptionalism, but rather a seat at the high table of global geopolitics among the few other great powers.

The Continuing Clash of Expansionary Missions

Physical and political circumstances and historical experience have thus combined to create two great powers with radically different views of their missions in the world. Both were inherently expansionist, but for different reasons. Russia expanded to vanquish its fears, America to fulfill its dreams. Russian expansion exacerbated internal contradictions as it strained the state's resources; American expansion muffled its contradictions by growing domestic prosperity. Except during rare moments of messianic delusion, Russia was forever seeking an elusive balance, against its external foes and between external and internal security and stability; America was forever seeking progress by transcending balances in the propagation of "universal" principles and the formation of an enduring rules-based order. For Russia, history was a tragic set of cycles of growth, collapse, and renewal; for America, it traced a triumphal arc of progress toward American ideals.

It was thus inevitable that American expansion to fulfill its destiny would eventually collide with Russia's expanding security perimeter in Eurasia. The conflict started in Northeast Asia in the late nineteenth century and slowly extended along Russia's entire periphery in Europe and Asia, with the peak of confrontation being reached during the Cold War.

But does this clash of expansionary missions continue today? As we saw in Chapter 1, the end of the Cold War and the demise of the Soviet Union only whetted America's expansionist appetite. There opened up the grand vista of extending and then consolidating free-market democracy in Eastern Europe and the former Soviet space, ultimately in Russia itself, America's great antagonist of the previous half century. That ambition has animated American foreign policy for the past thirty years, except for the four-year interlude of the Trump administration. Biden, however, quickly reasserted the centrality of this mission for American foreign policy. "America is back" was the message Biden wanted the world to hear, as he told his diplomats shortly after his inauguration.[58]

What about the new Russia? Surely, it would understand that borders were vanishing in a rapidly globalizing world. That strategic depth and buffer zones brought little security in a world where cyberspace was becoming an increasingly central element of political action and socioeconomic wealth. That the task was not to cordon the country off from the outside world but to learn how to manipulate interdependence to advance its own interests and to make itself secure. Alliances and partnerships, not *cordons sanitaires*, guaranteed security.

A truly democratic Russia may have recognized those realities and been prepared to jettison Russia's expansionary past, satisfied that other democratic states along its borders provided security at least as robust as strategic depth, although that is far from certain. Even a democratic Russia would have wanted to guard against the rise of a hostile power along its borders, and alliances with other democratic powers might not have proved possible or durable enough.

But Russia has never been democratic at any time since the breakup of the Soviet Union. At best, it was democratizing. And even an ostensibly democratizing Russia under Yeltsin saw strategic depth as essential to its security. Yeltsin is lauded in the West as the leader who played the largest role in bringing about the demise of the Soviet Union. But that did not mean he was interested in the waning of Russian influence in the former Soviet space. Quite the contrary. He broke up the Soviet Union so that Russia could undertake the reforms necessary to revive the economy and rebuild its power. That would provide the basis for reconstructing a Russian-dominated entity across the former Soviet landscape.

At the time, Yeltsin justified the dissolution of the Soviet Union and the creation of the Commonwealth of Independent States (CIS) as the sole alternative to "further uncontrolled decay of the Union."[59] Three years later, he argued that creating the CIS had been necessary "to quickly reinforce centripetal tendencies in the decaying Union, to stimulate a treaty process. The CIS offered at the time the only chance of preserving a unified geopolitical space," particularly after Ukrainians had voted overwhelmingly for independence.[60] His foreign minister, Andrey Kozyrev, made similar points to the Congress of People's Deputies in April 1992: "In line with the logic of attempts to recreate a renewed union in one shape or another, our priority is of course centered on multilateral institutions, not bilateral relations [with the other former Soviet republics]."[61]

One key multilateral agreement, the Collective Security Treaty, was signed in May 1992 by a subset of the CIS. That set up Russia as the security guarantor of the former Soviet space. Although Ukraine refused to join, Russia insisted on maintaining the headquarters of the Black Sea Fleet in Sevastopol in the now independent Ukraine – something that made the fleet a constant source of tension in relations between those two former Soviet republics. Similarly, Russia maintained troops in Georgia and Moldova, ostensibly for peacekeeping purposes but also as sources of influence, if not control.

Ukraine proved to be the greatest obstacle to Yeltsin's ambitions, because it insisted on its independence. As we have seen, Ukraine balked at sending the former Soviet nuclear arsenal to Russia for dismantlement and yielded only under American pressure. Russian leaders, other than Yeltsin, actively objected to the inclusion of Crimea in the newly independent Ukraine. They considered the peninsula sacred Russian territory, which Soviet leader Nikita Khrushchev, a former Ukrainian Communist Party boss, gratuitously transferred to Ukraine in 1954 to celebrate the 300th anniversary of Ukraine's union with Russia. Russia may have signed a Friendship Treaty with Ukraine in 1997 that recognized the inviolability of existing borders, but the issue was never fully settled in the minds of Russian elites.

Russian relations with Ukraine have only further deteriorated under Putin, especially after the Orange Revolution and the mounting US effort to bring that country into NATO. Strategic depth remains a concern – that was the point of Russia's demands made in draft bilateral treaties with the United States and NATO released in December 2021 that NATO cease to expand eastward into the former Soviet space and that offensive weapons capable of striking Russia not be deployed in Ukraine, or elsewhere in Eastern Europe. But Putin has added another element – his Ukraine policy is also a matter of reuniting Russian lands based on his own idiosyncratic reading of history. He denies that Ukraine has a right to exist as an independent state and insists that Ukrainians are ultimately Russians.[62] In invading Ukraine, he claims to be following in the footsteps of the Russian Empire's founder, Peter the Great, who, according to Putin, fought wars to recapture historic Russian lands from European powers.[63] But, we should remember, Peter took those lands in part to extend Russia's strategic depth.

And so, both Russia and the United States remain true to their traditions of expansion. That means there will always be an inherent tension in relations, as their expansionary impulses and great-power ambitions collide on the great Eurasian landmass. That reality does not preclude constructive relations. But, to endure, such relations require both Russian and American leaders to recognize the inevitable tension and understand the reasons for it. Only then can they craft ways to mitigate the stress in pursuit of greater mutual benefit.

They failed in that effort in the first Cold War decades, and that put them on the path to estrangement in 2014. Whether Russian and American leaders can reconcile these clashing worldviews in the years to come remains to be seen. But the ongoing conflict in Ukraine underscores the obstacles, for at one level it is a consequence of Russia's search for security as a great power crashing against America's ambition to spread democracy.

3

The Paradox of Russian Power

Since the breakup of the Soviet Union, the United States has had little respect for Russian power. "Upper Volta with nukes" was a phrase coined during the Cold War to underscore the vast discrepancy between Soviet military might and the population's low living standards, especially compared to the West's. The phrase, or variations on it, has been endlessly repeated in the post-Soviet period but with a different intent, to highlight not the co existence of military prowess and debilitating societal ills but rather the one-dimensional nature of Russia's power (based on nuclear weapons or energy resources) in a world where states compete across multiple dimensions of power. That is to say, Russia is not all that powerful, and certainly not the great power it claims to be.

That sentiment has infused US Russia policy for the past three decades. It gave confidence to the Clinton, George W. Bush, and Obama administrations that Russia would ultimately yield to its policy preferences, and to the Trump and now Biden administrations that they could impose crippling sanctions on Russia without fear of damaging retaliation. The issue for us is not so much whether that sentiment is accurate as whether a more nuanced view would produce better policy.

The Complex Challenge of Assessment

Russia is neither as strong as it seems nor as weak as we think. Some variant on that aphorism has been attributed to a number of leading statesmen, including Talleyrand, Metternich, and Churchill. A wise leader would heed it. History is littered with rulers and warriors who lacked respect for Russia's power and paid a heavy price, notably Napoleon and Hitler.

The exaggeration of Russia's strength has played out in less spectacular ways, but with no less consequence for global affairs. The widespread concern about Russia's growing might in the years before the First World War – the Prussian General Staff in particular was alarmed at the expansion of Russian power – fueled the volatile alliance diplomacy and accelerated the drift toward war. Yet a closer look revealed glaring weaknesses in the quality of Russia's industrial growth and the capabilities of the autocratic regime.[1] In the late 1940s, US President Harry Truman was advised to "scare the hell out of the country" to win backing for steps to block Soviet domination of Greece and Turkey, although the region was not high on Stalin's list of geopolitical priorities and his country was still reeling from the devastation of the Second World War. Thus was born the Truman Doctrine, which put the policy of containment into practice and laid the basis for US global leadership throughout the Cold War.[2]

The assessment of any country's power is admittedly a complex, uncertain task, but particularly so with Russia, which shrouds in secrecy pertinent information and goes to great lengths to hide its vulnerabilities, while boasting of its prowess. Some elements of power are theoretically subject to concrete measurement – total population, territorial expanse, natural resource endowment, size of economy and growth rates, defense spending, investment in research and development, educational standards, public health, and so on – although experts debate how best to measure those elements, especially for the purposes of determining power relationships. The measurement of GDP illustrates the problem, which is important for our purposes, since GDP is regularly used as an indicator of a country's overall standing on the global stage. Measured in current dollars at current exchange rates, Russia's GDP is less than one-twelfth the size of the US economy; measured in purchasing power parity terms, it is roughly one-fifth as large. That is not a small difference. Despite these pitfalls, it is possible to deduce a more or less accurate estimate of the material resources that any country, including Russia, can bring to the conduct of foreign policy.

Other elements of power are intangible: political will, leadership skills, societal cohesion and resilience. They determine how effectively material resources can be mobilized and deployed to advance national objectives. Judgments about such matters are of necessity highly subjective. Leaders constantly take the measure of their counterparts, particularly during interactions at multilateral and bilateral fora. They study their reactions to foreign policy and security challenges and assess their mastery of domestic politics. The character of a people is discerned through the way they have endured armed conflict and economic adversity in the past. The natural tendency is to shade assessments – to see a more or less able rival – to support one's preferred course of action.

An added layer of complexity and uncertainty arises from the fact that the situation is dynamic. A leader doesn't need a snapshot of another country's power but a motion picture that traces its trajectory from the past to the future, which more often than not will include fluctuations in both absolute and relative power as a consequence of domestic developments and geopolitical shifts. In Russia's case, the fluctuations have been dramatic. Just take a look at the last century, which is bookended by the collapse of seemingly mighty Russian states in 1917 and 1991. Yet, in between, the Soviet Union won a spectacular victory with a rare display of sacrifice and tenacity that saved Europe from domination by Hitler's Germany. Similarly, in the nineteenth century, Russia saved Europe from conquest by Napoleon's France and played a central role in shaping the peace at the Congress of Vienna in 1814–1815. Yet less than a half century later it suffered a humiliating defeat at the hands of Great Britain, France, and the Ottoman Empire in the Crimean War, from which it never fully recovered.

Even in shorter periods, consequential fluctuations have caught observers by surprise. Rare was the analyst in the mid 1980s who imagined the collapse of the Soviet Union in 1991. In the mid 1990s, few foresaw Russia's remarkable recovery in the 2000s under President Vladimir Putin. More recently, the prevailing view in January 2022 was that Russia's military machine – widely considered to be the second most potent force in the world after the US armed forces – would easily roll over Ukraine. The West was prepared for a Russian blitzkrieg and occupation of Ukraine, not the prolonged war of attrition that has developed and could possibly end in Russia's defeat.[3]

The final factor in the assessment of another country's power is the state of the beholder. In foreign policy, it is not absolute power but relative power that is decisive. Leaders confident in the power of their own country will tend to see Russia as less of a threat, no matter what rhetoric they might use to garner public support, although hubris can cause them to perilously dismiss Russia, as was true of Napoleon and Hitler. Contrariwise, leaders of countries in crisis will tend to exaggerate the Russia challenge no matter what the objective state of its power.

As the eminent historian of Russia Martin Malia notes, Europe was little concerned about the supposedly enlightened Empress Catherine the Great, although she posed a clear challenge with her rapid expansion westward, partitioning Poland, driving the Turks from the northern shore of the Black Sea, and adding 200,000 square miles of territory to the Empire. The European Enlightenment was an age of growing confidence in humanity's ability to master the environment around it that was not fixated on Russia's ambitions. But European elites in the throes of domestic upheaval as rising democratic forces challenged monarchical rule in the post-Napoleonic age demonized Nicholas I as the gendarme of Europe, a looming threat, although he was a status quo leader who advanced Russian territory not one inch into Europe.[4] In short, as a rule, a West in turmoil fears Russia, whereas an optimistic West sees little reason for concern, no matter what the objective reality of Russian power and ambition. As we shall see, the United States might be the exception that proves the rule in the post-Cold War period.

Upper Volta with Nukes?

American officials have rarely compared Russia to Upper Volta in public pronouncements, but all post-Cold War presidents have shared the sentiment. They were not always wrong to do that. During the Clinton years, Russia was mired in a prolonged systemic crisis that led to a dramatic plunge in economic output, the gutting of the military, and the crumbling of the central state apparatus, while the United States, unchallenged on the global stage, was enjoying one of its longest periods of economic expansion in history. The gaping asymmetry in power enabled Washington to dictate policy with little fear of any consequential Russian resistance.

Even though both the George W. Bush and Obama administrations were caught off guard by Russia's use of force in Georgia and Ukraine, respectively, neither saw reason to change their low assessment of Russia's power. To be sure, Bush was not in office for that long after the war in Georgia, and the global financial crisis soon absorbed all his administration's attention, but Obama did not enter office a short while later with a heightened concern about Russian power. Nor did he change his opinion after its seizure of Crimea in 2014. Rather, he derided Russia as a "regional power" that was acting out of weakness, not strength.[5] Despite Russia's recovery during the 2000s, the power asymmetry had hardly narrowed enough to shift Washington's low opinion of it.

That assessment seemed to change abruptly with revelations of Russia's flagrant interference in the 2016 presidential election. Russia's impressive cyber capabilities by all accounts posed a significant threat. Leading Democrats, including their presidential candidate, Hillary Clinton, spoke as if the Kremlin had determined the election's outcome, putting in the presidency its preferred candidate, Donald Trump. Democrats launched a series of investigations not only to uncover the details of Russia's interference but also to expose Trump's alleged subservience to the Kremlin. Nevertheless, even as the Russian threat served as a convenient cudgel to use against Trump, his critics' other actions suggested they in fact had little respect for Russia's power. Congress mandated wide-ranging sanctions, and pressed the administration to levy additional ones, with little evident fear that Russia might retaliate, even with cyber weapons, in a way that might do serious harm to American interests.

The Trump administration itself acted in a similar fashion, repeatedly levying sanctions and expelling Russian diplomats to punish "malign" behavior, even as it warned of the return of great-power competition, with Russia and China as the main rivals. It walked away from the Intermediate-Range Nuclear Forces (INF) Treaty, which had been a pillar of the bilateral arms control architecture. Granted, it did so because of Russian cheating but if it had been truly concerned about Russian power it would have exerted more effort to resolve differences with Moscow. Rather, focused on what it saw as the rising strategic challenge from China, the administration wanted to free itself of obligations that prevented it from deploying an entire class of nuclear weapons in East Asia. The Russia challenge paled in comparison; it was a fading nuisance not a genuine strategic competitor, even if the administration's *National Security Strategy* might suggest otherwise. That the Russian economy was stagnating only reinforced the administration's assessment.

No matter what its opinion of Trump, upon taking office the new Biden administration was clear that it shared that view. Its interim national security strategic guidance, released in March 2021, devoted little attention to Russia, dismissing it as a country determined to "play a disruptive role on the world stage."[6] That stood in stark contrast to the way it presented China: a strategic competitor that was "potentially capable of combining its economic, diplomatic, military, and technological power to mount a sustained challenge to a stable and open international system."[7] In these circumstances, Biden's team had no intention of making Russia a foreign-policy priority.

Nevertheless, Russia's buildup of forces along Ukraine's border compelled Biden to pay attention, leading to an early summit meeting he would otherwise not have sought. The two presidents launched working groups on strategic stability and cybersecurity, which the administration hoped would placate Russia and not be too demanding of its own time and energy, so that it could focus on China. That was not to be, as Russia escalated the tensions with Ukraine once again in the Fall and ultimately launched a large-scale invasion in February 2022.

For a moment, the Russian threat loomed large, and then its disastrous military performance reinforced the view that Russia was a declining power. To be sure, Washington had to focus intently on the imminent risk of a weakening Russia's lashing out, including with nuclear weapons, with catastrophic results. But that is quite different from preparing for a long-term contest with a strategic competitor. As the Biden administration's *National Security Strategy*, written in the wake of the Russian invasion, makes clear, China remains the sole strategic challenger, and Russia only an "immediate threat" to the international order, lacking the capacity to remake it.[8]

But a Burgeoning Threat?

Paradoxically, from the mid 2000s onward, American policymakers' dismissal of Russian power at first glance sits uneasily with the intelligence community's description of a burgeoning Russia challenge. In their annual survey of worldwide threats in 2007, the analysts noted that high energy prices were fueling greater Russian confidence and assertiveness, which they predicted would "continue to inject elements of rivalry and antagonism into US dealings with Moscow, particularly our interactions in the former Soviet Union, and [would] dampen our ability to cooperate with Russia on issues ranging from counterterrorism and nonproliferation to energy and democracy promotion in the Middle East."[9] Two years later, the analysts acknowledged that "Russian challenges to US interests now spring more from Moscow's perceived strengths than from the state weaknesses characteristic of the 1990s."[10]

Early in the next decade, as terrorism finally faded away as the central organizing threat to the United States, attention turned to other dangers that had seemingly proliferated in the meantime. Risks in cyber space were accumulating; the United States was profoundly vulnerable to cyber attacks on critical infrastructure; it was unprepared to deal quickly and effectively with information warfare, disinformation, and social disruption propagated with cyber tools. Adversaries were also rapidly advancing their capabilities in space, developing anti-satellite weapons that could disrupt the communication networks on which the US military relied and which had become essential to socio-economic processes. Organized crime, drug trafficking, and corruption were eroding the foundations of prosperity in many of the United States' allies and partners around the world. To make matters worse, the decades of great-power amity were rapidly giving way to renewed competition. In all these areas, the intelligence community judged, Russia was a major actor and mounting challenge to American interests.

Moreover, beginning in 2009, a recurrent theme in intelligence assessments was Russia's modernization and expansion of its military capabilities, both conventional and nuclear. That lay the foundation for a much more assertive foreign policy, increasingly at odds with American interests. Russia was acting ever more aggressively to reassert its hegemony in the former Soviet space, especially in Ukraine and Belarus, and extending its reach further into the Middle East, Africa, and Latin America. It was building ever closer links to China, cooperating with Iran, and backing North Korea, all countries of continuing concern for Washington. More troubling, in partnership with China, Russia was ever more brazenly challenging international norms and institutions, the very foundations of the US-led international order. Curiously, and disturbingly, Russia was acting more assertively abroad, even as its economy was at best stagnating.[11]

In 2019, the intelligence community highlighted the growing challenge of Russia–China strategic alignment. "China and Russia are more aligned than at any point since the mid 1950s, and the relationship is likely to strengthen in the coming year, as some of their interests and threat perceptions converge, particularly regarding perceived US unilateralism and interventionism and Western promotion of democratic values and human rights." Their competition with the United States, it noted, "cuts across all domains, involves a race for technological and military superiority, and is increasingly about values."[12]

Just before Russia invaded Ukraine, American intelligence issued perhaps its most alarming assessment since the end of the Cold War. It foresaw Russia remaining "an influential power and a formidable challenge to the United States amid the changing geopolitical landscape during the next decade," a country that was "pushing back against Washington where it can – locally and globally – employing techniques up to and including the use of force." It had a wide and expanding array of tools to advance its own interests and undermine the United States. It remained the largest and most capable nuclear rival. It was a top player in the cyber realm. It was a major foreign influence threat and a key competitor in space. Its considerable military capabilities were augmented by private military companies, which it was using to extend its influence in the developing world at low cost and risk.[13] Russia was back as a power to be reckoned with.

Not Compared to China

The intelligence community, like the military, is not paid to minimize challenges and threats, or, perhaps more cynically, it does not get paid if it does that. But there is no gainsaying that Russia is considerably stronger and a much greater presence on the global stage now than it was when Putin rose to power nearly a quarter century ago. The gap in power with the United States is narrower, although still large, and by most accounts Russia is the third most active geopolitical actor, after the United States and China.[14] Not surprisingly, American administrations, starting with Obama's, have spent considerable effort to deal with the challenges emanating from Russia.

And yet, for American leaders Russia has remained a declining power, a nuisance or disruptor, in world affairs, unworthy of the respect accorded to China. Tellingly, despite warnings about Russia's strategic alignment with China, administrations have pursued policies – crippling sanctions, diplomatic isolation – that only drive it more tightly into China's embrace. While splitting Russia from China might be an impossible task – both have good strategic reasons for seeking better relations – Washington could take steps to attenuate ties, but never has. The unspoken reason is quite simple: Washington does not believe that Russia adds much to the challenge that it faces from China alone in terms of economic capability, technological prowess, military might (save for nuclear weapons), and global ambition. The cost of distancing Russia from China through, for instance, sanctions relief despite Russia's continuing hostilities in Europe, far outweighs any potential gain.

In American eyes, the contrast between China's and Russia's power and ambition is stark. China's power is multidimensional; Russia's, one- or at best two-dimensional (nuclear weapons plus gas). China's economy is growing robustly; it has become the world's leading workshop; it has grand plans for technological innovation. Russia's economy, by contrast, is stagnating; it manufactures little that the rest of the world wants; its investment in high-tech innovation is meager. China uses its vast resources to build infrastructure abroad to extend its reach and to win allies and partners – that is the essence of the Belt and Road Initiative. Russia builds little infrastructure abroad, beyond nuclear reactors in a few select countries, and its signature economic initiative, the Eurasian Economic Union, is designed to protect Russia from foreign competition in countries it considers vital to its security and prosperity. China is modernizing and expanding its military capabilities to defend its far-flung assets. Russia uses its military assets largely to bolster its presence in its immediate neighborhood.

Most strikingly, China is focused on building the future in competition with the United States. It envisions a world order that it can dominate – not a genuinely multipolar order. Talk of one is little more than a useful rhetorical tool for eroding support for the American-led order. By contrast, Russia is focused on recreating the past, on regaining its lost grandeur. It seeks a genuinely multipolar world order because that would guarantee its power and prestige in a world it has no hope of dominating. China aspires to reshape to its advantage the current world order from which it has benefited so greatly; Russia's only hope is to disrupt that order to create more space for itself.[15]

Like China today, the United States is a forward-looking power. It has always thought of itself as a country that is building the future in its own image. Contrasting visions of the future drive their competition.

Because China is a near peer, that contest will absorb America's energy for decades to come, as the Cold War with the Soviet Union once did. Meanwhile, Washington will devote the resources its needs to thwart what it sees as Russia's largely destructive policies, confident that future developments will steadily erode its capabilities. What it will not do is give Russia the respect it craves until it demonstrates that it is a creative, future-oriented force in world affairs.

. . . Or the Soviet Union

The Russia challenge then is not one that continues deep into the future, from Washington's perspective. It also falls far short of the threat that the Soviet Union once posed during the Cold War. The Soviets' nuclear arsenal, economic capabilities (the CIA estimated the Soviet economy at its peak to be about half the size of the United States'),[16] technological prowess, ideological appeal, and geographical reach into Latin America, Africa, and Southeast Asia gave rise to a global existential struggle, in which America's triumph was hardly assured.

With the collapse of the Soviet Union, Moscow almost overnight lost one quarter of the territory, one half the population, and two-fifths of the productive capacity it once controlled.[17] And the United States strove to ensure that Russia would never again approach the Soviet Union in power potential. That was the essence of its hedging strategy against Russian recidivism, which drove Russia out of Eastern Europe and encroached upon its positions across the former Soviet space. What Washington saw as Russia's faltering effort to build a modern, competitive economy – it was dragged down by excessive bureaucracy, pervasive corruption, over-reliance on hydrocarbon exports, insufficient protections for private property, subservient courts, and predatory state practices – only further diminished Russia's standing,

Russian displays of power – Georgia in 2008 and Ukraine in 2014 – may have caught the United States flat-footed and upended policy toward those two countries. But in the end both events were at most of secondary importance to the United States, and Russia's military performance was hardly overwhelming; in the five-day Georgian war, for example, Russia lost six planes, two to Georgian air defenses and the others to friendly fire; the seizure of Crimea proceeded flawlessly but without any serious combat that would have tested the military's fighting skills.

From the moment the Soviet Union broke up, the view that Russia was a weak and declining power slowly took hold in Washington and gained a momentum of its own. Caught between a future China challenge to the United States that it could not match, and a past Soviet threat to American interests that it could not replicate, Russia cannot shake Washington's conviction that it need not pay much attention to its power in the long run, even if it must counter its disruptions in the present.

The Future of Russian Power

Is that conviction well grounded? Is Russia simply a disruptive force that will eventually fade away as it fails to keep pace with other world powers? Or will that capacity to disrupt persist decades into the future, requiring the United States to devise a long-term strategy for managing relations with Russia, as opposed to short-term palliatives to deal with immediate challenges? The answer depends on an assessment of Russia's ability to generate power in the future and the skill of its leaders in mobilizing it for state purposes.

Russia begins with major advantages: a large nuclear arsenal, a rich natural endowment, and a critical geopolitical location in the heart of the Eurasian landmass. They are not however sufficient to guarantee Russia's future power. Nuclear weapons have to be maintained and modernized. Russia must hedge against a technological breakthrough that might abruptly diminish the power potential of these weapons. Natural resources need to be transformed into instruments of power and influence. Geopolitical location matters little if Russia cannot generate power to project abroad.

The future of Russian power thus depends in the first instance on Russia's economic possibilities, technological capacity, and demographic vitality. How does Russia measure up?

Economic Possibilities Constrained

After the steady recovery during Putin's first two presidential terms, the Russian economy took a serious hit during the 2008–2009 global financial crisis, from which it has yet to fully recover. Growth stalled in the 2010s – the economy was less than 15 percent larger at the end of the decade than at the beginning (by comparison, the Chinese economy nearly doubled, and the US economy grew by just under 18 percent).[18] The outlook for the next fifteen years was troubled, even before the West unleashed a concerted effort to hobble the Russian economy in response to the invasion of Ukraine.

In 2013, the Russian Ministry of Economic Development presented three scenarios for the economy out to 2030: The conservative one, which posited active modernization of the energy and natural resources sectors and a continuing lag in civilian technologies, projected an average annual growth rate of 3.0–3.2 percent, with Russia's share of global GDP declining from 3.8 percent in 2012 to 3.6 percent in 2030. A second more promising scenario saw Russia investing heavily in a modern transportation system, a competitive high-tech sector, and a knowledge economy, as it continued to modernize the energy sector. Growth would average 4.0–4.2 percent per annum, and Russia's share of global GDP would rise to 4.3 percent by 2030. The third scenario built on the second, adding into the mix a much more active private sector, the creation of a large non-resource exporting sector, and significant foreign investment. The annual growth rate might then reach 5.0–5.4 percent and, by 2030, Russia's share of global GDP could be 5.3 percent.[19]

Even before the invasion, Russia lagged far behind the conservative scenario, let alone the two more promising ones. That was not due simply to circumstances beyond the Kremlin's control. To the contrary, it was reluctant to undertake the critical reforms needed to move the country toward an innovation and knowledge economy, such as reining in the predatory state sector, introducing reliable protections for private property, and advancing the rule of law. The reason was clear: Such steps would have entailed taking on the vested economic interests that undergird Putin's authority. In the place of reform, the Kremlin focused on the professionalization of the economy, bringing into government and state-owned enterprises younger and better educated cadres, to make the current system run more efficiently. That in fact improved economic performance, in part by minimizing the negative impact of Western sanctions, but it was and remains insufficient to spark the rapid growth Russia needs.

The coming decade only promises to be more challenging, especially if, as seems likely, relations with the West do not improve. Western investment, technology transfers, and management skills played a central role in Russia's economic development during the past twenty years. Moscow's aggression against Ukraine put an abrupt end to productive engagement. Harsh sanctions have crippled Russian access to credit markets and high-technology goods of Western origin. Hundreds of Western companies have abandoned Russia or plan to do so in the near future. The situation will not dramatically improve even if the war in Ukraine ends. Russia is no longer the attractive market it once was; its deep hostility toward the West raises unacceptable risks to anyone considering a long-term investment. Moreover, no Western government is likely to encourage investment in Russia as most once did – the war in Ukraine shattered the once prevailing illusion that closer commercial ties would help stabilize bilateral relations.

In these circumstances, Russia will have to develop a new economic model. Since the West levied its first major sanctions in 2014, the Kremlin has pursued two options: import substitution and a pivot to the East. So far, the benefits have proved meager. Import substitution has lifted a few sectors, notably agriculture, but overall it has failed to provide substitutes for Western industrial, and especially high-technology, goods that can match their quality and price. More to the point, Russia's economy is too small to manage on its own across the range of sectors it needs to back up its great-power aspirations.[20]

The Kremlin hoped it could find the needed partners in the East. That remains a distant hope. Trade has grown to a significant degree only with China; elsewhere, it has in fact mostly decreased. Outside of a few mega projects focused on China, foreign investment in Siberia, the Russian Far East, and the Arctic has been minuscule. Asian investors, including the Chinese, find Russia's investment climate as inhospitable as most Western investors do.[21]

In these circumstances, Russia at best faces a decade or more of slow growth, barring major reforms and normalization of relations with the West that could still unlock its tremendous potential. Its share of global GDP will almost certainly decline, unless major disruptions elsewhere shift into reverse the steady growth the world has seen in recent decades. That is not impossible, given the current global turmoil, but Russia is hardly likely to emerge unscathed from a broader global disruption.

Further out, the situation appears only more dire for Russia. The growing appreciation of the existential threat of climate change is accelerating the move away from fossil fuels, which have been the backbone of Russia's economy in recent decades. Anywhere from a quarter to two-fifths of federal government revenue comes from the export of oil. Gas exports are essential to the income of the state gas monopoly, Gazprom, which the Kremlin can use for political and socio-economic purposes. What can replace this revenue over the long run is an open question. Even if Russia develops a new economic model to deal short term with the loss of Western investment, technology, and management skills, it will soon need to find yet another model to compensate for the diminishing role of oil and gas in economic performance.[22]

Technological Capacity Lagging

Russia faces considerable hurdles in keeping up with the rapid technological advance that defines the current era. Today, it ranks 47th (just ahead of Vietnam and Romania) and far behind the leading Western countries in the World Intellectual Property Organization's Global Innovation Index.[23] Russia's share of global trade in high-tech products is a fraction of one percent.[24]

This is not a novel situation for Russia. Historically, it has trailed behind the West technologically, at times with dire consequences: the failure to keep up played a large role in the defeat in the Crimean War; the inability to master the information revolution as it began to unfold in the 1970s was a major factor behind the Soviet Union's demise in 1991. Thus, the repeated efforts by the Kremlin to spark technological innovation.

The most prominent attempt was launched not by Putin, but by Dmitry Medvedev during his brief presidential term. A year in, he issued an appeal for the creation of an innovation economy. Russia, he wrote, needed to free itself from an excessive reliance on commodities, especially oil and gas. He proposed that it seek to be a global leader in five areas: energy efficiency, nuclear technology, information technology, space, and medicine. And he promised to undertake the political reforms necessary to promote innovation, including creation of an independent and reliable judicial system.[25]

His showcase was a technological hub and incubation center located just outside Moscow. The Skolkovo Innovation Center, as it was called, was launched with great fanfare in 2010, with the goal of becoming Russia's answer to Silicon Valley. It included a technopark, which attracted some of the world's leading corporations, including Boeing, Cisco Systems, Intel, Johnson & Johnson, Microsoft, and Nokia, among others, and an Institute of Technology, which was set up in collaboration with the Massachusetts Institute of Technology.[26] Once Medvedev left office, however, Skolkovo fell out of favor, a victim to elite strife and corruption scandals. Western companies drifted away as relations between Russia and the West deteriorated. Other incubation centers across the country suffered similar fates.

Their plights reflect a broader problem. For all the talk about the need for innovation and technological advance, the government does little in fact to create a suitable environment. It spends relatively little on research and development. Under Putin's leadership, Russia has never invested more than 1.3 percent of its GDP in such activities (by contrast, the US level in 2000 was 2.63 percent, rising to 3.45 percent in 2020).[27] Poor facilities and working conditions, plus increasing impediments to working with foreign colleagues, do little to attract world-class scientists, while they drive home-grown talent abroad in search of opportunities and inclusion in the global scientific community, thus nourishing innovation and scientific advance elsewhere in the world. The results are ironic: Russia's investment in educating scientific talent in practice increases not Russia's competitiveness but that of other countries to which Russian scientists emigrate. Similarly, Russia's poor record in commercializing new technologies means that they are often bought by foreigners who commercialize them, once again for the benefit of other countries.[28]

Even the military might no longer be an exception to this rule, as it was during the Soviet period. Granted, Russia can still mobilize the talent it needs to develop the military applications of new technologies; witness its formidable capabilities in cyberspace. But the question is whether it can develop those new technologies on its own and turn them to productive uses. Similarly, Russia can produce some sophisticated weapon systems, such as the strategic armaments Putin touted in an address to the

Federal Assembly in 2018, including a nuclear-powered cruise missile, a nuclear-capable underwater drone, a new heavy intercontinental ballistic missile, and hypersonic weapons.[29] But the question is whether Russia can produce the sophisticated components for such systems on its own or whether it is reliant on foreign sources. The latter appears to be the case. In any event, the technical inspection of Russian weapons captured in or fired at Ukraine reveals that Russia's military modernization program has made extensive use of microelectronics manufactured in the West.[30]

Demographic Vitality Uncertain

Russia's demographic challenge has its origins in the Soviet period. In the mid 1960s the total fertility rate fell below replacement levels and stayed there, with rare exception, until the collapse of the Soviet Union. In the post-Soviet period deaths began to outnumber births in most years, leading to a sharp decline in natural growth, offset to some extent by immigration, primarily from former Soviet states. The population will continue to decline for the next fifteen years, according to most forecasts, from the current total of almost 147 million (which includes Crimea, or just over 144 without Crimea) to less than 135 million, if the worst projections come true.[31]

This shrinking population will also be aging. Most forecasts see the number of people over 65 years of age rising sharply until 2030, and then more slowly, and the working-age population continuing the decline it began in 2011.[32] Those developments will only slow the pace of economic growth and create manpower issues for the armed forces, as the number of young men available for service wanes. Such problems are far from unique to Russia. Most Western countries face similar circumstances. But they are more serious for a country that insists that it must be a great power.

A falling population, however, is hardly evidence of waning power, and a small population in the twenty-first century does not in and of itself connote weakness, as it might have in the nineteenth or early twentieth century.[33] Much more important is the health and education of the population, that is, the quality of human capital. Those matters have figured centrally in Kremlin deliberations since at least Putin's second presidential term, as it sought to increase natality, promote a healthy lifestyle, and raise educational standards.[34] In 2018, demography, health, and education were among the fourteen national priority projects the Kremlin announced to jumpstart economic growth and set Russia on an upward trajectory this decade.

Results so far have been mixed. The population may continue to shrink, but its health is rapidly improving. Spending on health care has been rising slowly during the past decade, although the amount – under 6 percent of GDP – is roughly half the Organization for Economic Cooperation and Development (OECD) average.[35] One widely cited statistic can stand as an indicator of the general trend: male life expectancy. Although it still lags substantially behind Western levels, it rose from a dismal 59 years in 2000 to 68 years in 2019, before falling back to 66 years as a consequence of the coronavirus pandemic.[36]

Education presents a similarly contradictory picture. Russia retains a well-educated population by OECD standards. It is among the leaders with regard to adults with at least upper secondary education, with over 95 percent (the OECD average is 80 percent), and those with tertiary education at 57 percent (the OECD average is 40 percent).[37] But there are questions about the quality. Only one university – Lomonosov Moscow State University – ranks in the top 100 worldwide,[38] and a respected ranking of higher education systems ranked Russia 35th out of 50 in 2019.[39] Moreover, the future is uncertain, as Russia underfunds secondary and tertiary education by OECD standards; in 2020, it devoted 3.4 percent of its GDP to education, compared to the OECD average of 4.8 percent, which translates into about half the dollar amount per student.[40]

Mobilization Capacity in Doubt

In the years ahead, Russia thus faces formidable impediments (economic, technological, and demographic) to generating the resources it will need to pursue its great-power ambitions. Wise policy can help overcome them, but only so much in the next ten to fifteen years. The economy, technological conditions, and demographic situation are complex systems that evolve incrementally over time, even if the slow accumulation of gains or losses can produce abrupt changes at certain points. In these circumstances, Russia's ability to project power beyond the limits of what its physical resources would suggest, to be more than a secondary power, will depend on the quality of Russia's leaders, the state's capacity to mobilize resources, and the population's willingness to bear hardship.

Since he assumed power, Putin has shown extraordinary will to restore Russia's grandeur. By all accounts, Russia has under his leadership punched far above its weight on the global stage, projecting power into the former Soviet space and extending its reach into Latin America, Africa, and the Middle East. Putin has repeatedly forced Russia onto America's agenda, even when administrations have had other priorities, most recently in the Fall and Winter of 2021/2022, as he raised tensions around Ukraine.

Whether Putin can continue to raise Russia's international profile is an open question. His actions in Ukraine increasingly appear to be a debacle that will raise questions about his judgment, sap Russia's power, and tarnish its reputation. In the Fall of 2022, the first serious cracks in his elite support became visible, as hardliners publicly questioned how the war was being prosecuted.[41] Meanwhile, former Soviet states saw opportunities to settle scores with their neighbors, as Moscow, bogged down in Ukraine, proved unable to spare forces to police the region; for example, frontier skirmishes erupted between Azerbaijan and Armenia and Kyrgyzstan and Tajikistan in September 2022.

A tremendous advantage in most circumstances, Putin's vaunted political will becomes a great liability if it is too far out of sync with reality, as is the case with Ukraine. His predilection to double down rather than acknowledge setbacks and readjust goals is stretching Russian resources to the breaking point. This problem will likely only grow as Putin, now in his seventies, advances in age and his circle of trusted advisers narrows, with allies falling out of favor or departing the political scene by reason of death or ill health. That is, of course, assuming that those advisers have a better grasp of reality than he does, which may not be the case. If they don't, they will only reinforce his illusions, to the country's ruin.

This situation will only end with Putin's departure. How and when that occurs will shape the challenge his successor will face in consolidating power and putting his own stamp on Russian foreign policy. But there will almost certainly be a period of at least a few years when Russia will act more cautiously abroad as domestic affairs absorb elite energies. Thereafter, the details of Russian foreign policy, if not its general contours, will depend on the character of the new leader. If he is determined to assert Russia's prerogatives abroad as a great power, he will have to turn to the state apparatus to mobilize the country's shrinking resources and put them to effective use.

The central state apparatus is undoubtedly in better shape than it was in the 1990s. Among other things, it can now effectively collect taxes to fill the state coffers in order to pursue national goals. But its performance since Putin assumed power has been uneven. On the one hand, the professionalization of the macroeconomic bloc and the Central Bank has enabled Russia to weather Western sanctions since 2014 in much better shape than anticipated. In particular, Western capitals have been surprised by Russia's resilience in the face of what they thought were crippling sanctions levied after Russia's invasion of Ukraine. On the other hand, the government's implementation of the fourteen national priority projects launched with such fanfare in 2018 has, for the most part, lagged behind their targets. To be sure, worsening economic conditions have been part of the reason, but government inefficiency and corruption have also played a large role.

Most spectacular, because of Putin's attention and the vast sums devoted to it, has been the failure of the military modernization program. Since it was launched in 2009, Russia has spent over $750 billion (in constant 2020 dollars) on defense.[42] The effort appeared to pay off handsomely in Russia's military operation in Crimea in 2014 and in Syria in 2015.[43] And it led the West to grossly overestimate Russia's military capabilities on the eve of the war in Ukraine. That war has, however, turned out to be a disaster. Uninspired leadership, inept operational plans, faulty equipment, and demoralized troops led to humiliating setbacks and staggering losses of men and material in the first months. Pervasive corruption throughout the government and military ranks drastically undercut the efficacy of the whole modernization effort. In the wake of the ill-fated Ukraine campaign, it will take years to rebuild the military's morale and to replace the lost equipment.[44]

In January 2020, Putin appointed a new prime minister, Mikhail Mishustin, who had earned the reputation of being a superb manager as the head of the tax services; he had used modern digital technology to ensure prompt payment of taxes and narrow the scope for evasion. Putin's evident hope was that he would transfer his skills to the government as a whole. Mishustin is, in fact, introducing more modern management practices to increase efficiency and reduce waste. But progress will be slow and uncertain, as he encounters stiff resistance from a deeply conservative state apparatus.[45]

Mishustin is, however, only responsible for a part of the central government. The power ministries are the president's bailiwick, and they will likely be shielded from the prime minister's policies. For Putin, loyalty takes precedence over competence when it comes to the heads of agencies that are essential to his staying in power. The key figures have long worked with Putin, tend to be around his age, and have been in office since 2016 at the latest – two of Putin's closest advisers, Security Council Secretary Nikolay Patrushev and FSB director Aleksandr Bortnikov, have held their positions since 2008, while a third, Defense Minister Sergey Shoigu, has been at his post since 2012.

Moreover, Putin has shown no desire to take on the corruption problem within the power ministries. To the contrary, it has grown in recent years as he became ever less inclined to devote the necessary attention and energy to managing elite competition and looked for easy ways to ensure the loyalty of his key allies. There is no reason for that to change, especially as Putin inevitably grows older and less vigorous.

Popular Support Limited

The Russians are among the world's great survivors. Disciplined by a harsh, unforgiving climate, the Russians have learned skills that have enabled them to survive crop failures and other natural disasters, as well as foreign invasion and arbitrary rule. Admittedly, Russian peasants rebelled with great frequency, as did workers in the last tsarist decades and even at times during the Soviet period; but their fury was directed at landlords and local authorities and not at the country's leaders or central state apparatus, with only rare but profoundly consequential exceptions, such as the revolutions of 1917 and the last years of the Soviet Union.

More often than not, however, across centuries, Russians have been prepared to endure tremendous sacrifice in the defense of the homeland. Swedish King Charles XII marveled at how Russian peasants burned their crops rather than let them fall into the hands of Swedish invaders. That deprived the king's armies of the ability to live off the land and ultimately played a role in his defeat at Poltava (in present-day Ukraine) in 1709. Napoleon suffered a similar fate in 1812, as Russians laid waste to the lands he traversed on his way to and from Moscow. And Hitler ran into the heroic sacrifice that enabled Russians to withstand the 900-day siege of Leningrad and prevail at Stalingrad in an epic battle that marked the turning point of the war on the Eastern front.

In exchange, in times of peace, Russians have demanded that that the state maintain order and security in the country and, as the country became more urbanized, provide a minimal standard of living. Otherwise, they preferred that the state stay out of their daily lives. That was a key element of the implicit social contract Putin offered the country when he assumed power; he would leave average people alone as long as they forsook active involvement in politics. In addition, Putin promoted a foundation for national unity based on what he called the traditional Russian values of patriotism, statism, belief in Russia as a great power, and social solidarity, which he thought would resonate with a basically conservative population and nourish the resilience the country would need to survive inevitable periods of hardship.

The people's resilience has its limits, however. Stubborn in the defense of the homeland, Russians are less eager to bear sacrifices for foreign adventures. That is one lesson learned from the war in Ukraine, and the response to the partial mobilization Putin ordered in September 2022, when tens of thousands of young Russian men fled the country. In other words, the population as a whole only enhances Russia's power when its leaders can credibly make the case that they are defending genuine Russian national interests and not pursuing narrow personal ambitions dressed up as national concerns.

Implications for the United States

Washington is not wrong in its assessment that Russia is a relatively weak and largely disruptive power that poses a challenge nowhere near as consequential as the one China does, even if it remains imperative to maintain an effective strategic deterrent against Russia's nuclear arsenal. What is less certain is the widespread opinion in the foreign-policy establishment that Russia's ability to thwart American initiatives will fade with time, as domestic constraints prevent it from keeping pace with the world's leading powers, notably China and the United States itself, or that at some point Washington can push Russia aside (except in the nuclear realm) to focus the overwhelming share of its resources on out-competing China. Nor is it self-evident, as Washington seems to believe, that it does not need to make an effort to attenuate Russia's strategic alignment with China because Russia adds little to the challenge China alone poses.

Contrary to the widespread expectations, in the first decade or so of this century, Putin did a remarkable job in rebuilding Russia's power. But he ran out of steam shortly after he reclaimed the presidency in 2012. His further time at the helm may yield only stagnation for Russia. And his debacle in Ukraine may undo much of what he has achieved. Nevertheless, his successor will still inherit a resilient country that is potentially rich and powerful and primarily in need of economic and political reform to tap that promise.

In that regard, we should remember that Russian history is a story of repeated efforts to catch up with the world's leading powers, that is, the West, for the past 300 years or more. Russia has generally succeeded, at least to the extent that it has been able to hold its own among the world's great powers, by adopting the practices of the leading powers without sacrificing its fundamental characteristics, which are as a rule out of sync with Western values and American interests. One of Putin's successors will eventually launch this effort, for being a great power lies at the very core of Russian national identity. We just don't know when that will happen.

And we don't know the degree to which the new leader will succeed. But Russia is never as weak as we think it is because of the intangibles of political will and national resilience, which are often overlooked in the focus on quantitative data about its socio-economic conditions. If the past is any guide, those intangibles will eventually lead to a resurgence of Russian power.

The current period of strategic failure will not last forever, perhaps not even for a long time. While American policymakers can make short-term decisions based on the assumption of Russian weakness, that should not be the premise for long-term planning. And so, while Washington should be considering how it can constrain Russian power or limit its ability to disrupt American initiatives for the moment, it should also give serious consideration to how it might harness future Russian power to its own interests, especially in the face of what will remain the enduring strategic challenge of China. If continued weakness turns out to be Russia's future, Washington loses little now by working through the consequences of its resurgence. Quite the opposite would be the case, if it acted on the assumption of long-term weakness and Russia returned as a great power, as it has repeatedly in the past.

4

Russian National Interests and Grand Strategy

American exceptionalism posits that the United States is acting in the best interests of peoples around the world; in other words, American interests are theirs too, rightly construed. Resistance is then taken as a sign of misunderstanding or malevolence. In fact, however, other countries have interests that often do not align with America's. This is self-evidently true of adversaries, but it is true of allies and partners, as well. It has been true of Russia during the years when Washington considered it a partner and in recent years of adversarial relations.

Throughout, however, Washington has had difficulty coming to terms with Russia's national interests. Since the end of the Cold War, the question regularly asked in the halls of power has been whether the interests Russia espouses are "legitimate" or not. Does Russia, for example, have *legitimate* security interests in Europe or the former Soviet space that the United States needs to respect? Although they never say so in so many words, by "legitimate" American policymakers mean "congruent with American goals." If they are not, Washington is quick to reject those interests as illegitimate, with the understanding that it is free to ignore Russian concerns or actively undermine them. More often than not, that is the way Washington has assessed Russia's avowed interests in Europe and Eurasia.

Such a posture put US–Russian relations on shaky ground from the very end of the Cold War. It became problematic from the standpoint of America's own interests, as Russia slowly regained the means to defend its interests – in Georgia in 2008 or Ukraine in 2014 – and throw around its weight as a great power. The task now is not to judge the "legitimacy" of Russian interests, but rather to understand how Russia defines them, what considerations lie behind them, and how and why they have evolved over time. That assessment then provides the basis for determining not how the United States can persuade Russia to redefine its interests to its liking but rather how Washington can best manipulate them to advance its own goals.

The Importance of the State

As we argued in Chapter 2, the preservation of the state has throughout history been the paramount mission of Russia's rulers. In their eyes, the hyper-centralized military-political order has been indispensable to holding together a heterogenous population spread across a vast territory that grew only more diverse as the country expanded. Many observers have objected that the rulers' interest runs contrary to that of the broader population, and therefore cannot be properly considered to be the national interest of Russia. That view carries a certain appeal. After all, the rulers have maintained the state by ruthlessly extracting resources from the people with little regard for their well-being in most eras, no matter what their rhetoric about a just order and the common good. And surely there are other forms of governance that can hold a vast country together while raising the people's standard of living – an American-styled federation, for example. That has been a constant refrain of Russia's liberal and democratic thinkers, dating back at least to the reign of Catherine the Great.

But, curiously, each time this traditional Russian state collapsed – in the early seventeenth century during the Time of Troubles, in the revolutionary year of 1917, and in the Cold War's wake in 1991 – the vast majority of the people acquiesced in, and many actively supported, its reconstitution. The guise of the state may have changed from the tsarist to the communist and now to the post-Soviet, but its essence has remained unchanged for centuries. The words of the Primacy Chronicle have echoed at times of crises: "Our land is great and rich, but there is no order in it. Come reign as princes, rule over us." History confirms that the rulers' interest in the preservation of the traditional Russia state is indeed the nation's.

Even today, President Vladimir Putin's continuing effort to rebuild and preserve the state resonates with the elites and the broader population. To be sure, there is anecdotal evidence of elite displeasure with Putin's direction. Some spilled out into the open after Russia's humiliating setbacks around Kharkiv and Kherson in the Fall of 2022. Many in the business community would prefer less hostility toward the West, where they have forged lucrative partnerships and shelter their wealth,[1] while hardline ideologues, who have gained influence in the military and security services, want more aggressive anti-Western measures.[2] And polls show that, on occasion, the public would prefer Putin to devote more attention and resources to pressing domestic needs than to foreign adventures. Yet, whenever Putin acts decisively abroad, in seizing Crimea, or intervening dramatically in Syria, or launching a large-scale military assault on Ukraine, his popularity soars for an extended period. And those bold actions are all first of all intended to defend the interests of, and thereby preserve, the Russian state.

In recent years, observers have focused on the kleptocratic nature of Russia's current political regime to argue that the Kremlin does not care about national interests. By definition, kleptocrats cannot be invested in the well-being of the nation they are looting. But neither, it is argued, are they much interested in the state as such. Rather, Kremlin policies are designed to preserve the personalistic regime centered on Putin, along with the opportunities for personal enrichment that brings to his extended, yet still relatively small coterie of "cronies," once including perhaps the 110 billionaires who controlled 35 percent of the county's wealth, according to an oft-cited figure from 2013.[3] In this, Putin has been likened to a mafia don, not the leader of a proud nation.[4]

This view may help explain domestic politics, where ruthless, often extra-legal battles for control of lucrative property are a constant. But it is of little worth in illuminating Russia's foreign policy. The years-long conflict over Ukraine, for example, has provoked onerous Western sanctions that have destroyed value for Russian elites, but, at least until quite recently, it has certainly been in line with the costly efforts of previous Russian rulers to control that territory to create strategic depth, or a buffer against European rivals. Likewise, continuing efforts to drive wedges between European states and between Europe and the United States have boomeranged against Russian wealth in the West, but they are in line with Russia's traditional endeavors to disrupt hostile coalitions along its borders. In other words, these policies have been designed primarily not to ensure regime survival, narrowly construed, or to provide opportunities for self-enrichment, but to enhance state security. Realpolitik remains a better guide to Russian foreign policy than greed or self-preservation.

There are, of course, exceptions. Private military companies (the Wagner Group is the best known) engage in warfare – in Libya, Syria, and now most dramatically in Ukraine – as arms of the state, for all practical purposes. But they also conduct operations elsewhere that are arguably more for commercial profit than to advance state interests. Wagner's presence in the Central African Republic, Mali, and Sudan, for example, appears aimed mainly at gaining access to mineral resources, even if it serves the Kremlin's interest in countering Western influence in Africa, has Kremlin sanction, and some of the profits find its way into the pockets of senior officials.[5] Such operations, however, lie far from the core of Russian foreign policy and security interests, which are concentrated along the country's long periphery on the Eurasian supercontinent. They do not negate the central role of state interests in the conduct of Russian foreign policy.

Making Russia a Great Power Again

Mere state survival, however, is far from describing the whole of Russia's national interest. For at least the past three centuries, since Peter declared Russia an empire in 1721, its rulers have insisted that their country has to be a great power, that is, one of the few countries that determine the structure, substance, and direction of global affairs. As Putin himself declared on the eve of his ascension to the presidency, one of Russia's traditional values is "belief in the greatness of Russia." "Russia," he wrote, "was and will remain a great country. That is due to the inherent characteristics of its geopolitical, economic, and cultural existence. They determined the mentality of Russians and the policy of the state throughout the history of Russia. They cannot but do so now."[6] Or, as Dmitry Medvedev starkly put it during his short stint as president, "Russia can exist as a strong state, as a global player, or it will not exist at all."[7]

Focused on Russia's survival as a great power, its rulers, with rare exception, have been unreconstructed realists when it comes to world affairs. In their view, only great powers matter. Lesser states are at their mercy, locked in spheres of influence, used as buffer zones, or fought over. Transnational corporations, religious communities, civil society associations, and even terrorist groups and other non-state entities are not autonomous agents but instruments of state power wielded to advance state interests. To survive, great powers are predestined to engage in a never-ending struggle for power and influence and a seat at the head table of global geopolitics. Consequently, relentless competition is the essence of international affairs, and hard power, military might, and the will to use it are decisive, in the minds of Russia's rulers. It is an unforgiving, harsh view of the world.

As realists, Russia's rulers believe that Russia labors under a constant imperative to augment its power to stay abreast of its rivals; if it doesn't, it will eventually fall from their ranks. It was just that threat that haunted Putin when he assumed power nearly a quarter century ago. "Russia," he warned his countrymen at that time, "is going through one of the most difficult periods in its long history. For the first time in the last 200 to 300 years, it faces, let us say, a real danger of falling into the second, and even the third, rank of the world's states. To prevent this from happening, we will have to expend all our nation's intellectual, physical, and moral vigor. We need coordinated creative work. Nobody will do this for us. Everything now depends only on our ability to realize the degree of danger, to unite, to commit ourselves to long, arduous work."[8]

Certainly, back then Russia was far from meeting the criteria for being a great power. It was not a truly sovereign state, which governs itself free of outside interference, pursues an independent foreign policy, and can hold its own among the other great powers on the global stage. The two foundations of true sovereignty, a capable military and a reliable currency, had been eroded during the 1990s. Starved of state funding and deeply corrupt, the heirs of the once formidable Soviet Red Army were defeated by Chechen rebels in the mid 1990s. The ruble was displaced as a means of exchange by the dollar, and nearly half of all economic activity took place in the black market, beyond the reach of the state's tax collectors. More broadly, the Kremlin's authority had crumbled, as regional barons seized control of state assets within their provinces and brazen oligarchs privatized parts of the central state apparatus for their own parochial purposes. Even more humiliating, the Kremlin had to rely on repeated infusions of Western cash to sustain itself in the absence of a reliable tax-collection system. In these circumstances, Russians feared that their country would collapse, much as the Soviet Union had a short decade before.

Not surprisingly, such a weakened Russia commanded little respect on the global stage. Western, especially American, officials shamelessly interfered in its domestic affairs, claiming that they were only assisting the country in its transition to free-market democracy. They trampled on Russian interests in the former Soviet space, as they sought to advance their own geopolitical and commercial agendas. Despite Moscow's vehement objections, the United States set in motion the process of NATO's post-Cold War expansion, which, in the first wave, admitted the Czech Republic, Hungary, and Poland, all former Soviet satellites. Shortly thereafter, NATO launched a military operation against Serbia, Russia's traditional ally in the Balkans, without authorization from the UN Security Council, where Russia with its veto could have blocked or at least shaped that mission. That NATO was acting to end Serbia's brutal campaign of ethnic cleansing against Kosovar Albanians was of little import to Russia – the humiliating fact was that Western leaders were acting aggressively in a region of traditional Russian strategic endeavor, and elsewhere, as if they lived in a "world without Russia."[9]

Rebuilding the State

Putin thus faced extraordinary internal and external challenges as he assumed power on the eve of the new millennium. He set, as his principal task, the restoration of the authority of the Russian state, first at home and then abroad. In his initial weeks in power, he started to rein in the regional barons and oligarchs. He divided the country into seven federal districts, each headed by a personal presidential representative, to monitor the activities of regional leaders to ensure their compliance with Kremlin policies. He stripped the governors of their ex officio seats in the Federation Council, the upper house of Russia's legislature, thus depriving them of direct input on federal laws and legislation, as well as the immunity from criminal prosecution that all deputies enjoyed. He pushed through legislation that granted him the authority to dismiss governors and disband regional legislatures for actions that violated federal law.[10]

At the same time, Putin was taming the oligarchs. The deal he proposed was straightforward: If they ceased to meddle in Kremlin politics, they could hold on to the property, the vast commercial, financial, and industrial empires, they had amassed through corrupt means and at knockdown prices during the previous decade. Otherwise, he would launch criminal investigations against them. To show he meant business, he took aim at two of the most notorious, Boris Berezovsky and Vladimir Gusinsky, who cynically wielded their media assets to attack commercial and political rivals, including Putin himself. The new president quickly stripped them of those assets, putting them in the hands of loyalists, and hounded them into exile. Three years later, he turned against Russia's then richest man, Mikhail Khodorkovsky, owner of the Yukos oil empire, who was assiduously working to deprive Putin of a majority in the Duma to be elected in 2003. The oligarch eventually lost not only Yukos but also his freedom: he was convicted to eight years in a Siberian labor camp. Other oligarchs took notice.[11]

As he was taming domestic actors, Putin also worked diligently to limit the scope for foreign influence. He used the windfall profits from rapidly rising oil prices to pay off Russia's debt to the International Monetary Fund and to the Paris Club of sovereign creditors, in 2005 and 2006, respectively, thus freeing Russia of Western tutelage over its federal budget and financial policies. The color revolutions in Georgia, Ukraine, and Kyrgyzstan, convinced him that he needed to constrain the activities of foreign-funded non-governmental organizations in Russia, especially any that were even loosely engaged in what might be considered political issues (very broadly defined by the Kremlin).[12] In addition, Putin took steps to fortify the Kremlin against a Western-inspired color revolution, including the formation of youth movements that would provide the needed street muscle during political crises.

Putin's determination to rebuild an authoritative state took the country down an authoritarian path, well-trodden in Russian history. His actions slowly but steadily restricted the space for autonomous political activity and squeezed competition out of the system. In the 2007 Duma elections, the party of power, United Russia, gained a constitutional majority, which it has not since relinquished. That party also came to dominate regional politics across the country. By the end of Putin's second term, the mass media and courts were reliably in the hands of Kremlin loyalists. Political activism had withered, and the popular political passivity that Russian rulers have historically valued as essential to state security and stability was once again deeply entrenched. Putin had become the new tsar, ruling over a reconstituted state in its traditional, authoritarian mold.

Rethinking Relations with the United States

As Putin consolidated domestic power, and rising oil prices fueled an economic recovery, he began to push back more confidently against what he saw as American efforts to undermine Russian interests abroad. His hopes for a strategic partnership with the United States grounded in a common struggle against terrorism after the horrific attacks on New York and Washington in 2001 faded quickly.

The turning point came in the Fall of 2004, bookended by two events: The terrorist attack in Beslan, a small town in the North Caucasus, in September (the attack on the public school ended with the deaths of more than 300 people, including 186 children), and the Orange Revolution in Ukraine in November, December, and January (massive protests against a rigged election prevented Putin's choice from taking over as president in favor of a pro-Western candidate).

Beslan convinced Putin that the United States was using counterterrorism cooperation as a smokescreen for advancing its interests in the former Soviet space at Russia's expense. Days after the attack, he warned that some countries wanted to tear away a "juicy" piece of Russia, convinced that Russia, "one of the greatest nuclear powers in the world," posed a threat. Terrorism was simply a tool for achieving that goal.[13] No one doubted he had the United States in mind. And not without reason. While it spoke of cooperation against a common enemy, Washington had offered little support for Moscow's struggle against Chechen terrorists; indeed, Washington insisted that some of the rebels were moderates with legitimate grievances, with whom Moscow should be prepared to negotiate. It even allowed a representative of the anti-Russian Chechen government-in-exile to live undisturbed in the United States as he built support for the Chechen cause.

Likewise, the Orange Revolution persuaded Putin that Washington's democracy promotion in the former Soviet space was little more than a cynical ploy for ripping states out of Russia's orbit. The United States, he believed, had trained Ukrainian activists in the dark arts of protesting against allegedly rigged elections to overthrow governments it did not favor. Regime change and geopolitical advance, not democratic transition, was Washington's real goal. Speaking in New Delhi in December, he rejected efforts to reorder diverse civilizations according to the "barrack principles of a unipolar world." Dictatorship in international affairs, he asserted, would solve none of the world's problems even if it was packaged in "pseudo-democratic phraseology."[14]

To be sure, the role of indigenous factors in these two events overshadowed any US interference by a wide margin. Russia's relations with its North Caucasian provinces, especially Chechnya, had been troubled from the moment it conquered the region in the mid nineteenth century, and Ukrainian voters had ample reason to reject a presidential candidate enmeshed in the deeply corrupt practices of the current government. That made no difference to Putin. He saw a geopolitical struggle first of all. His reaction was an early manifestation of an inclination that would grow more pronounced with time, that of seeing malevolent external actors as the drivers of developments in the former Soviet space he found threatening.

Reflecting this mindset, the Kremlin undertook a thorough reassessment of its relations with the United States, concluding that it had to counter American encroachments on its interests much more aggressively. This new approach received its full-throated public articulation in Putin's denunciation of America's allegedly hegemonic designs at the Munich Security Conference in February 2007. Putin ended his remarks with a thinly veiled warning: "Russia is a country with a history that spans more than a thousand years and has practically always used the privilege to carry out an independent foreign policy. We are not going to change this tradition today."[15] It was his declaration that Russia had returned to the world stage as a great power.

The Kremlin's World in 2012

Five years later, Putin returned to the Kremlin as president, pushing aside his loyal lieutenant, Dmitry Medvedev, who in retrospect had only served as a caretaker, while Putin sat out a presidential term in deference to the constitutional ban on serving as president for three *consecutive* terms. He could look back at his dozen years in power with tremendous pride. He had inherited a shambolic country of little consequence on the global stage and step by step restored some of its earlier grandeur. A military modernization program he had promoted as prime minister had produced a seemingly capable force for use in contingencies along

Russia's borders and perhaps farther afield.[16] Russia was now a force to be reckoned with, among the world's three most active geopolitical players, along with China and the United States.

Putin's ambitions had grown dramatically. Being a fledgling great power no longer sufficed. The pillars of Russia's global position had to be consolidated to secure its long-term future. To that end, he was now set on using Russia's new-found power to erode the standing of the United States as the dominant world power and harden the foundation of a multipolar world, in which Russia would manage the world's affairs along with a very few other great powers: China and the United States, to be sure; India, likely; perhaps Japan and a few major European states.

Putin had no illusions that this would be an easy task. The world was in a state of enormous flux, presenting myriad challenges and opportunities. The global financial crisis of 2008–2009 had accelerated radical changes in the geopolitical landscape. China was on the rise, having just overtaken Japan to become the world's second largest economy. More generally, economic and political dynamism was rapidly flowing to the Asia–Pacific region away from Europe. The West was losing the dominant position it had enjoyed in world affairs for half a millennium, and it would hardly accept without a fight its reduced status. The Arab Spring was upending the geopolitical order in the Middle East.[17] New technologies were revolutionizing the way countries communicated, manufactured goods, and, perhaps most ominously, conducted conflicts. Potent cyber tools encouraged hybrid warfare – the combining of efforts to erode from within a rival's societal cohesion, decision-making capacity, and will to resist with traditional military means of coercion. The line between war and peace was fading away.

It was in this fluid environment that the Kremlin had to craft approaches to a set of interrelated problems. At the strategic level, the critical question was how to position Russia between the United States, the preeminent world power, and China, the rising challenger, to maximize its strategic autonomy. Below that level, Russia's immediate neighborhood, the so-called "near abroad," as well as the regional dynamics in Europe, the Middle East, South/East Asia, and the Arctic, called for wedding traditional Russian concerns and current circumstances into coherent, mutually reinforcing policies to advance Russia's interests. Success would require fashioning an overall balance of interests built on hedges and counter-hedges at the strategic and regional levels.

The Strategic Puzzle

For all the achievements Putin touted, Russia remained a weak great power. It lagged far behind the United States and China along most dimensions of national might. Raw statistics from 2012 underscore the predicament. With a population of just under 145 million people, Russia was in demographic decline. By contrast, the United States' population of over 310 million was continuing to grow, and China's, while nearing stagnation, still numbered 1.35 billion.[18] Russia's share of global GDP was a mere 2.0 percent, the United States', 24.7 percent, and China's, 13.0 percent.[19] Russia spent on defense roughly one-fifth and one-half of what the United States and China did, respectively.[20] Russia devoted a mere 1.0 percent of its GDP to research and development, while the United States allocated 2.7 percent, and China 1.9 percent, of much larger economies.[21] Russia operated five of the world's top 500 supercomputers, whereas the United States had 252 and China, 68.[22] No Russian university ranked in the world's top 100 universities; 28 American and two Chinese universities did.[23]

Only in two areas was Russia in the same league as the United States and far superior to China: nuclear weapons and energy resources. Russia and the United States had roughly equivalent stockpiles of deployed nuclear weapons (1800 and 2150 warheads, respectively), as they were reducing arsenals to the levels agreed in the New START treaty. They were far ahead of China with about 240 warheads (with an uncertain number deployed).[24] As for oil and natural gas, Russia and the United States were among the top three producers of both fuels,[25] although the United States remained a net importer of both to the order of about 40 percent of its oil and some six percent of its natural gas consumption.[26] Although China had significantly increased production of oil and natural gas, it was a net importer of both and on a path to becoming the world's largest importer of hydrocarbons, as production fell rapidly behind soaring demand.[27]

Raw statistics, of course, capture only a small part of the picture. Actual power depends on the political will of leaders and their ability to mobilize the country's resources for their purposes. In this regard, Putin excelled, enabling Russia to punch far above its weight in global affairs as it recovered from the profound crisis of the 1990s. But China, too, was in an upbeat mood, having easily weathered the recent global financial crisis and now certain that its economic model was superior to that of the United States, and that it would surpass its rival as the world's largest economy in the not-too-distant future. And, while the United States seemed mired in a crisis of confidence, weighed down by intractable conflicts in Afghanistan and Iraq, a global financial collapse sparked by American excess, a maddeningly slow recovery, and acute political polarization, Silicon Valley was still driving the digital revolution and the American energy sector was unleashing one in shale.

Moreover, even if the United States was in decline, as the Kremlin fervently wanted to believe, it still posed the gravest threat to Russia's status as a great power. A unipolar world after all had no place in it for other great powers. And the United States was taking concrete steps to undermine Russia. Deployment of missile defense systems in Europe, the Kremlin feared, would upset the strategic balance by defanging Russia's strategic deterrent. The United States continued to encroach on Russian interests in the former Soviet space, especially in Central Asia and the Caucasus, as it prosecuted the war in Afghanistan. US-led NATO was building up infrastructure along its frontier with Russia.

Moscow was increasingly looking to China as a strategic counter-weight, buoyed by the conviction that Beijing shared its interest in a multipolar world order. But problems remained: Moscow was worried by China's rapid commercial penetration of Central Asia, possible massive Chinese migration into East Siberia and the Russian Far East, and China's growing regional and global ambitions. It must have also sensed that China had as little respect for Russian power as the United States did, and certainly was not prepared to sacrifice geopolitical and commercial gain in the interest of building closer relations with Russia.

The Neighborhood

For at least the four centuries up to the collapse of the Soviet Union, Russia was the dynamic core of Eurasia, extending its sway in all directions to form the largest contiguous empire in the modern era.

Its erstwhile control of what was now the former Soviet (and former Imperial Russian) space had once given it geopolitical heft and provided the foundation for its security and prosperity.

The Soviet collapse reversed the arrows of influence. Even if Russia remained the dominant outside power in most former Soviet states (the Baltic states were the exception, having escaped Russia's grip for the safety of NATO and the European Union), Western ideas, radical Islamic ideologies, and Chinese money were penetrating its historical sphere of influence at an alarming pace. In a sign of Russia's weakening influence, not one former Soviet state – not even Belarus which was nominally part of a union state with Russia – had recognized the statelets of Abkhazia and South Ossetia, which Moscow declared independent after the 2008 war with Georgia. More worrisome, fragile institutions, pervasive poverty, and simmering interethnic and interstate tensions made the outbreak of radically destabilizing conflict an ever-present risk.

Europe

Russia remained, Putin wrote in 2012, "an inseparable, organic part of Greater Europe, of the wider European civilization. Our citizens feel themselves to be Europeans. We can hardly be indifferent to how things develop in an integrated Europe."[28] Nevertheless, it had in fact been slowly driven out of Europe since the end of the Cold War, as Euro-Atlantic institutions expanded eastward. In 2012, Russia probably played a lesser role on the continent than it had at any other time since Peter brought Russia into the European balance-of-power system 300 years earlier. That was a huge psychological blow to a country that historically demonstrated its great-power prowess on the major battlefields and at the grand diplomatic conferences in Europe and prided itself on having twice saved Europe from domination by a single power in the past 200 years by defeating Napoleon and Hitler.

The psychological shock was the smaller part of the problem, however. In the previous two decades, the slow political and economic consolidation of the European Union, in 2012 a region of over 500 million people with a GDP of more than $13 trillion, or 19 percent of the world economy,[29] raised the possibility of the emergence of an entity on Russia's Western flank that would dwarf it in population, wealth, and power potential, much as the United States already did. Even if the Transatlantic tie were to break down – one of Moscow's abiding wishes – a truly united Europe would present Russia with an immense security challenge.

Yet this potentially threatening Europe remained a seemingly indispensable economic and commercial partner. In 2012, the European Union was Russia's main trading partner, accounting for over 40 percent of Russia's overall bilateral trade. Russia sent one-third of its oil and nearly all of its gas exports westward to the EU. The EU accounted for about 60 percent of foreign direct investment stock,[30] and served as a critical source of the high-technology goods and managerial skills that Russia needed to build a modern, competitive economy.

The Middle East

The broader Middle East, stretching from Morocco to Afghanistan, was perhaps the most volatile region in the world in 2012. Sectarian strife, bitter interstate rivalries, and myriad terrorist and extremist groups, coupled with fragile, often poor, states, a bulge of unemployed or underemployed young men, and a sea of weapons, made for a witch's brew of threats that Russia could not ignore. The war in Afghanistan was entering its eleventh year with no end in sight, as terrorist influences and narcotics spilled across its borders, including into Central Asia and Russia. The Arab Spring had led to the ousting of authoritarian leaders in Egypt and Libya, among others, and civil war had broken out in Syria, a long-standing Russian client in the region. Jihadist terrorists with ties to Middle Eastern extremists were still active in Russia: The attacks on the Moscow metro in March 2010 and the Domodedovo International Airport outside Moscow in January 2011 were the most recent reminders of the threat.

Iran posed a special challenge. It was a valuable commercial partner, particularly in the field of nuclear power. Despite Western objections, Moscow had helped Tehran bring a nuclear power reactor in Bushehr on line in 2011. But Moscow had no interest in Iran's developing a nuclear weapon. Albeit not without friction, Moscow had worked with the United States in passing UN Security Council resolutions to deter

Iran from seeking nuclear weapons and to ensure outside powers that its nuclear ambitions were entirely peaceful. It had done this also in no small part to reduce the risk that the United States, or more likely Israel, would attack Iran's nuclear facilities and spark a regional war that would almost certainly spill over into the former Soviet space.

Indo-Pacific Region

China of course dominated the picture in the East. To help manage its rise, Russia looked to India, Japan, South Korea, and Vietnam, all of which were themselves wary of China and saw Russia as a possible partner in constraining its room for maneuver. Russia had developed a strategic partnership, including close military-technical cooperation, with India, starting in the mid 1950s. It remained India's major arms supplier. Much the same was true of Vietnam – Moscow had been its major supporter during its war against the United States in the 1960s and early 1970s and remained a key arms supplier. Meanwhile, ties were warming with Japan and South Korea, American treaty allies, who hoped to keep the resource-rich regions of East Siberia and the Russian Far East from falling captive to Chinese markets.

The flip side of managing China's rise was sustaining Russia's presence in the sparsely populated, isolated Far Eastern regions. Shortly after he came to power, Putin had traveled there and warned that "the question of the perspectives for the development of the Far East and Transbaikal has been posed sharply, I would say even dramatically, for the country. In essence, we are talking about the existence of the region as an inseparable part of Russia." And, he added, if Russia did not urgently undertake a concerted effort to develop the region and integrate it fully into Russia, then "even the primal Russian population in a few decades would be speaking mainly Japanese, Chinese, and Korean."[31]

North Korea's nuclear ambitions added one final piece to the geopolitical puzzle in East Asia. Moscow had little influence in Pyongyang, but it wanted to ensure that efforts to contain North Korea did not destabilize Northeast Asia, a region critical to the economic viability of Russia's eastern provinces. Active Chinese and American engagement on North Korea, moreover, made it part of the global strategic competition that so engaged Russia.

The Arctic

The Arctic region was of immense economic and security importance to Russia. It accounted for roughly 80 percent of Russia's gas production and nearly a fifth of its oil production. The continental shelf held vast mineral resources, besides oil and gas. The Northern Sea Route through the region was a potentially lucrative maritime route that significantly cut the transit time between East Asia and Europe compared to the usual routes through the Suez Canal or around the Horn of Africa. The Arctic, moreover, was home to key elements of Russia's strategic nuclear deterrent, including the ballistic missile submarines of the Northern Fleet and early warning systems.[32] Global warming was opening up the region to greater commercial activity, but the melting ice meant that Russia would, for the first time in history, have to defend its long northern border, except for a small portion around the White Sea, from land and sea attack.

The geopolitical setting on the Eurasian landmass thus added further tasks to the strategic challenge of positioning Russia properly in the US–China rivalry. How could Moscow reassert its predominance in the former Soviet space? How could it retard, if not reverse, the consolidation of Europe without damaging vital economic and commercial ties? How could it contain the terrorist contagion and risk of nuclear proliferation in the Middle East without alienating its regional partners? How could it constrain China without losing it as a strategic counterweight to the United States? And how could it exploit the promise of the Arctic without provoking excessive geopolitical competition? Each of these regions posed a geopolitical conundrum on its own. Managing them effectively simultaneously called for a nuanced strategy – and a huge dose of luck.

The Shifting Contours of Grand Strategy

Grand strategy identifies only a strategic goal, a broad direction for policymaking. It does not dictate concrete policy or tradeoffs among priorities. Those depend on the geopolitical landscape and the predilections and imagination of policymakers. The United States, as we know, successfully pursued a grand strategy of containment against the Soviet Union during the Cold War. But, during more than forty years, the key features of US policy shifted. John Gaddis, the historian of containment, identifies six different geopolitical codes that framed US policy from the Truman through the Reagan administrations.[33] Likewise, the details of Russia's grand strategy – the concrete ways of containing the United States and consolidating the foundations of a multipolar world with Russia as a great power – have been worked out in a shifting geopolitical context, guided by the biases and vision of its leaders.

One will look in vain for a single document that fully articulates Russia's global strategy at any point since the end of the Cold War. Various foreign-policy and national security concept papers have laid out Russia's view of the global environment and the challenges it faces, as well as guiding principles for approaching global governance, key countries and regions, and international threats. But they do not explicitly link all these matters into a coherent whole with clear priorities and trade-offs, nor do they indicate how Russia will generate the means to achieve its goals.

Nevertheless, a strategic logic can be distilled from the analysis of these documents, the pronouncements of Putin and other senior officials and Russia's actual conduct. Russia's foreign policy, upon examination, turns out to be an intricate set of priorities with multiple hedges against failure, all aimed at fortifying it as a great power and enhancing its security through the traditional means of creating strategic depth and establishing regional hegemony, disrupting the formation of hostile coalitions along its borders, and carefully managing domestic politics.

The details of Russia's strategy have changed radically during the Putin era. In retrospect, 2012, Putin's return to the Kremlin as president, marks a transition between two diverging orientations – between a Western/European-centric policy and a pivot to the East, between restoring Russia as a great power and undermining the US-led global order, between constraining the United States through partnership to countering it through strategic alignment with American rivals.

Contrary to conventional thinking, the eruption of the Ukraine crisis in 2014 did not cause this shift. It served more as a catalyst, dramatically accelerating a transition Putin had already decided to make. But it did lay bare for all to see the depths of antagonism between Russia and the West, as the United States severed normal diplomatic relations, Russia was expelled from the G-8, and the West levied a series of diplomatic and economic sanctions against Russia. And it did underscore how the world had changed. In the West, Russia's seizure of Crimea was denounced as the first violent land-grab in Europe since the Second World War; in Russia, it was hailed as the end of Russia's geopolitical retreat and the start of a new advance. Either way, the post-Cold War world had run its course.

In Gorbachev's Footsteps

How did Russia come to this turning point in 2012? Ironically, by Putin's following in the footsteps of a Soviet leader he despised, Mikhail Gorbachev, who had figuratively abandoned him as a KGB officer confronting a hostile crowd in Dresden shortly after the Berlin Wall was breached in 1989. When Putin asked for help, the response he received was "Moscow is silent"; he was on his own. Gorbachev thus became in Putin's mind the gravedigger of a great Russian state, and the affront was personal. Putin nevertheless initially adopted his approaches to the United States, Europe, China, and the former Soviet space.

Gorbachev had futilely offered President George H.W. Bush a strategic partnership at the end of the Cold War in an effort to shore up the Soviet Union as the other superpower, as it undertook a jolting, but in Gorbachev's view necessary, set of far-reaching internal reforms. Likewise, Putin initially aspired to build a partnership with the United States, hoping to harness its extraordinary power to Russia's purposes. Close ties would ease Russia's return to its traditional regions of strategic endeavor in part by demonstrating that greater Russian influence in the former Soviet space, or Europe, or the Middle East, no longer posed a threat to American interests, as it had during the Cold War, but rather could help advance them. If all went well, Russia would eventually enjoy a "special relationship" with the United States, which would afford it the influence over American policy it believed London's relationship with Washington did.

To gain leverage over Washington, the last Soviet leader sought to improve relations with key European countries. He called for a "common European home," stretching from Lisbon to Vladivostok, built on shared democratic norms and a commitment to peaceful resolution of disputes. It would be a home with separate rooms for each nation, so as to preserve the Soviet Union's role as the major power *in* Europe and prevent the consolidation of a new Europe (minus the Soviets) as a strategic actor. For similar reasons, Putin promoted the formation of a Greater Europe. As he told the German Bundestag in September 2001, Russia was a "friendly European country" that wanted to overcome Cold War suspicions to foster European integration.[34] But the Greater Europe would be a Europe of states not a European state – Putin was determined to return Russia to its traditional and, in his view, rightful role as a major power *in* Europe, despite US efforts to push it to the continent's margins. Accordingly, Moscow gave preference to bilateral ties with leading European states over relations with the European Union's multilateral bodies. It also used what levers it could to sow tensions among states, setting, for example, different prices for its natural gas based on the state of a country's relations with Moscow.

Within Europe, Germany, America's key ally on the continent, became Gorbachev's chief interlocutor, particularly after that country's reunification. He wagered that he could parley good relations into a lever of influence over the United States. Similarly, Putin built robust relations with Germany, which was Russia's leading trade partner, until overtaken by China in 2010, and its largest foreign investor. To foster better relations, in 2001 the two countries launched the St. Petersburg dialogue, which brought officials, businesspeople, media representatives, cultural figures, and civil society activists together for regular meetings. As Putin hoped, the ties did provide some leverage over Washington: Russia and Germany, along with France, opposed the American decision to invade Iraq in 2003, and Germany, once again along with France, thwarted US plans to put Ukraine and Georgia on a fast track to NATO membership in 2008.

Beyond Europe, Gorbachev repaired relations with China so that the United States could no longer play the China card against the Soviet Union, as it had since the era of detente under President Richard Nixon. Putin went a step further – he hoped to use China as a strategic counterweight to the United States. Shortly after he assumed the presidency, Putin signed the Treaty of Good-Neighborliness and Friendly Cooperation with China. Four years later, he and his Chinese counterpart, Hu Jintao, issued a joint statement on the international order in the twenty-first century, which laid out their common vision of a multipolar world, deeply at odds with the US vision of a rules-based world order.[35] The two countries finally delimited their long border, over which they had violently skirmished in 1969, thus enabling Russia to devote more resources to what it saw as more pressing challenges on its Western flank.

Finally, Gorbachev desperately worked to hold the Soviet Union together as the source of Moscow's heft on the global state. His effort to negotiate a new Union treaty, however, crashed against the opposition of Russia, which aimed to take over the Soviet Union albeit in the form of a genuine federation, and Ukraine, which was set on achieving genuine independence. As for Putin, he continued Russian efforts to rebuild its presence in the former Soviet space as critical to the country's great-power ambitions. In 2003, the Collective Security Treaty was transformed into something akin to a post-Soviet NATO, making Russia for all practical purposes the security guarantor of much of the former Soviet space. That same year, Putin signed, along with the leaders of Belarus, Kazakhstan, and Ukraine, a declaration of intention to create the Single Economic Space, which would lead to progressively closer economic integration of the four post-Soviet states that accounted for the overwhelming share of the erstwhile Soviet Union's landmass, population, productive capacity, scientific and technological capability, and military might. Ukraine, however, quickly abandoned this initiative. As was true for Gorbachev and then Yeltsin, Ukraine's jealous defense of its independence was a serious blow to Putin's strategic plans.

Losing the West

Like Gorbachev, Putin lost his wager on the United States. The attempt to forge a counterterrorist alliance with the United States after the horrific attacks of September 11, 2001, fell far short of his goals. Washington may have appreciated Putin's decision to overrule his security chiefs and raise no objection to the United States establishing military bases in Central Asia to prosecute the war in Afghanistan, as well as the valuable intelligence Moscow supplied in the initial phases of the conflict. And Washington may have been pleased to receive Russia's support in what rapidly turned into a global war on terrorism.

But Washington was never prepared to repay Russia in kind. Support for Russia's war against its terrorists in Chechnya was lukewarm at best.

Washington spurned Russian efforts to get more directly involved in Afghanistan, whether by providing strategic airlift to Kabul or helping rebuild Soviet-era infrastructure, with the lame excuse that the Afghans would never accept a Russian presence after the brutal Soviet military campaign of the 1980s, never mind that Russia had been the primary backer of the Northern Alliance opposition to the Taliban after the United States largely abandoned the country in the wake of the Soviet military withdrawal in 1989.

More important, Washington categorically refused to concede to Moscow a sphere of influence in the former Soviet space, Putin's unspoken quid-pro-quo for supporting the American war on terrorism. And Bush would never expend the political capital to normalize trade relations with Russia and accelerate its path to the World Trade Organization by lifting the Jackson-Vanik amendment, a Cold War relic if there ever was one – the amendment originally linked normalization to free Jewish emigration from the Soviet Union, but post-Soviet Russia had long since lifted any restrictions on that. Washington, Putin concluded, was still mired in Cold War thinking; partnership would never be more than a one-way street.

Meanwhile, the European hedge also yielded less than hoped for. To be sure, commercial ties were growing robustly. But on the geopolitical front that mattered most to Moscow, Europe was in lockstep with the United States. It strongly supported NATO expansion into Eastern Europe, even if Germany, France, and some others later balked at considering membership for Georgia and Ukraine. The big European powers – Germany, France, and the United Kingdom – joined the United States in backing Kosovo's unilateral declaration of independence from Serbia, Russia's historical ally in the Balkans. Moscow took a relatively benign view of EU expansion, until it began to seek ways to impose its values and rules on former Soviet states along its expanded borders in the late 2000s – something that jeopardized those countries' trade ties with Russia and turned EU expansion into a geopolitical threat.

That left China. The strategic partnership continued to develop along with trade ties. But closer relations would entail at least in part Moscow's overcoming long-standing suspicions of China. Would Beijing's mounting regional and global ambitions, coupled with the increasing disparity in Russian and Chinese economic fortunes, eventually create a challenge on the Eastern flank equivalent to the one Moscow already faced in the West? Moscow was of two minds in 2012.

The Pivot

As Putin returned to the Kremlin in 2012, policy was in need of repair. He knew the direction in which he wanted to take the country, toward a more openly confrontational approach to the United States. This shift had been long in the making, at least since his verbal assault on the United States in Munich in 2007. The first signs in fact had surfaced in the year and half after that speech, in a more threatening approach to Georgia, which eventually erupted into a brief war in August 2008, shortly after Medvedev took over as president. The new approach did not take root at that time, however. Medvedev was granted some leeway to exercise his presidential powers, even as Putin lurked in the background, and the new leader was eager to reset relations with President Barack Obama.

The Turn Against the United States

By 2011, the reset had run its course, in Putin's view. It was time to return to the course he had adumbrated in 2007. Two developments on the eve of his new presidential term reinforced that conviction: the sadistic murder of Libyan strongman Muammar Gaddafi and the Russian protests against the rigged Duma elections in October and December 2011, respectively. Gaddafi's murder came after the United States had morphed a UN-endorsed humanitarian intervention in Libya into a regime change operation amid the euphoria over the democratic promise of the Arab Spring. For Putin, however, that was a clear case of the United States cynically twisting international law to eliminate a leader it did not favor, made all the more humiliating by the fact that Russia had abstained on the UN Security Council resolution authorizing the initial intervention. Putin suspected that Gaddafi's fate was not far from what some circles in Washington had in mind for him.[36]

Far more disturbing were the Moscow protests, which Putin was convinced were part of a deliberate American regime change operation directed at him. The Obama administration had not concealed its opposition to his reclaiming the Russian presidency – Vice President

Joe Biden had, after all, traveled to Moscow in the Spring to advise him against seeking a third term.[37] When the protests erupted, Putin immediately blamed US Secretary of State Hillary Clinton, who had voiced "serious concern about the conduct of the elections," and called for a "full investigation of all reports of fraud and intimidation" the day after the election.[38] That was the well-tested US playbook of proclaiming electoral fraud and instigating protests that had led to color revolutions in Ukraine, Georgia, and elsewhere. In his victory speech after being formally elected president in March, Putin declared, "We showed that no one can impose their will on us. Not anyone, and not in any form."[39] The color revolution had been averted; Putin's resentment of the United States swelled.

The December protests were a sign that the struggle with the United States would take place across a broad front. Geopolitics would no longer be the sole critical dimension, as it had been during Putin's first two presidential terms. Ideology would now claim a prominent place, as Putin sought to defend what he considered Russia's unique character against the onslaught of decadent Western ideas and promoted principles of world order that clashed with the American precepts of a unipolar world, dressed up, Putin would say, as a rules-based order. The confrontation would take on a hybrid form, waged not only in foreign lands but also inside both Russia and the United States. National resilience, the moral fiber of the nation, would be critical to success.

At home, Putin promoted a renewed patriotism to fortify the Russian people against Western attempts to undermine the country from within. Patriotic and religious instruction was reintroduced into school curricula at all levels. The teaching of Russian history was revamped to highlight the country's achievements and play down the more troubling episodes, such as Stalin's terror. The Kremlin allied with the Russian Orthodox Church to propagate traditional Russian values and conservative Christian morality in opposition to Western decadence, especially when it came to sexual mores. Putin put ever greater emphasis on the May 9 celebrations of the Soviets' triumph over Nazi Germany, and endorsed a civilian procession, the Immortal Regiment, in which people carried portraits of their ancestors who had fought in the war, to reinforce the emotional ties of today's population to that heroic feat. Eventually, patriotism – pride in the country and its achievements at home and abroad – became the source of the regime's legitimacy and Putin's popularity, replacing rising standards of living, which had played that role during Putin's first two terms but no longer could as the economy stagnated and real disposable income declined.

Accompanying the promotion of patriotism was a concerted effort to curtail dissent by individuals and groups supporting Western values. Shortly after Putin's inauguration, Russia adopted a Foreign Agent law, which essentially required any organization with non-Russian funding to register as a foreign agent and make note of that status on any public communication. "Foreign agent" was a loaded term in Russia, signifying spying, espionage, and subversion. That was exactly the association the Kremlin wanted Russians to make. Initially directed against foreign-funded non-governmental organizations, it was extended to foreign-funded media outlets and internet sites and eventually to individual journalists.

To justify these measures, Putin doubled down on the Western threat. Mounting tensions, Putin argued, were not simply the consequence of geopolitical rivalry, or even of ideological differences. They arose from a deep-seated Russophobia in the West, a refusal to abide a country that would not bend to its will or abandon its way of life to adopt Western practices. He traced this attitude back to the moment Russia first entered the European system in the early eighteenth century. "In short, we have every reason to assume that the infamous policy of containment of the eighteenth, nineteenth, and twentieth centuries continues today. They are constantly trying to drive us into a corner because we have an independent position, because we maintain it, and because we call things like they are and do not engage in hypocrisy," he told a gathering of the Russian elite as Russia prepared to annex Crimea in 2014.[40] That Russia had been an integral part of the European balance-of-power system in the eighteenth, nineteenth, and early twentieth centuries, and that a deliberate policy of containment only surfaced during the Cold War, were facts Putin preferred to ignore. He needed an enduring Western threat for his purposes.

The defense of traditional Christian values resonated not only at home; it also found a receptive audience in many conservative and populist circles in the West. The Kremlin had, knowingly or not, fashioned an instrument of soft power, which now became a central element of the hybrid war Russia was waging with increasing vigor against the West. Although Western commentators christened this style of warfare the "Gerasimov Doctrine," after the Russian chairman of the General Staff, who had described its parameters in a short article in a military journal, the Kremlin was in fact modeling its actions on the tactics it believed the United States deployed to foment regime change in the former Soviet space and during the Arab Spring and was now applying to Russia. The Kremlin was turning the table by conducting hybrid warfare against the West, although the goal was not so much regime change as promoting chaos to erode governments' ability to conduct coherent foreign policies. Russia's interference in the 2016 US presidential elections was evidence of how brazen it had become in confronting the West.

As Russia interfered in American domestic affairs, Putin mounted an ever more strident rhetorical attack on the US-led world order. American exceptionalism, the firm belief in the superiority of the American system, and the accompanying effort to impose American values on the rest of the world sowed chaos, stimulated the spread of weapons of mass destruction, and fueled terrorism: witness Iraq and Afghanistan.[41] He presented the so-called rules-based order as nothing more than a cynical system in which the United States unilaterally made, interpreted, and enforced self-serving rules that ran contrary to international law, which was established on the basis of consensus by the international community. The West's much vaunted liberalism, Putin declared, had outlived its purpose.[42] His strident remarks, to be sure, won Russia little favor in elite circles in the West, but they resonated with elites elsewhere.

As the ideological standoff heated up, the geopolitical competition continued apace, especially in the Middle East. Russia allied with Iran and Hezbollah to defend Syrian President Bashar al-Assad against American-backed rebels, starting with a dramatic military incursion in September 2015 that saved him from almost certain defeat. After an abortive coup attempt in Turkey in 2016, Putin rushed to support Turkish leader Recep Tayyip Erdogan, as Washington hesitated, forging a relationship that has bedeviled the United States and NATO ever since. When the UN-sponsored Geneva process to resolve the Syrian civil war bogged down, Russia turned to Iran and Turkey to fashion a solution, which did not lead to peace by any means but resulted in a military equilibrium once the United States finally withdrew in 2019. More broadly, as the

United States retrenched, Russia moved in to build relations with many traditional American partners, including Egypt and Saudi Arabia.

Despite this confrontational approach, Putin was not opposed to cooperating with the United States on concrete matters. But the cooperation was of a different character from what it had been in his first years as Russia's leader, when he was currying favor with Washington. Now cooperation had to show that Russia was the equal of the United States, at least with regard to the issue at hand. That was the case with the negotiations that eventually produced the nuclear deal with Iran in 2015, known as the Joint Comprehensive Plan of Action, in which Moscow played a critical role in obtaining Tehran's agreement.

Better yet was cooperation that could be portrayed as Russia helping the United States out of a predicament of its own making. Such was the case in 2013, when the United States backed away from a punishing attack on Syria for its use of chemical weapons, which Obama had loudly proclaimed was an American red line. Putin floated the idea of a joint US–Russian-led international effort to eliminate Syria's stockpile of chemical weapons, which Obama quickly seized.

But acts of cooperation were few and far between, and they did nothing to slow the growth of mutual antagonism. Putin's call for a grand coalition against terrorism at the United Nations in September 2015, which he likened to the coalition against Nazi Germany seventy years earlier, fell on deaf ears in Washington. American officials considered it a thinly veiled attempt to distract attention from Russia's aggression against Ukraine. In any event the United States much preferred to cooperate on its terms, not Putin's.

Disillusionment with Europe

Putin's new approach inevitably strained relations with Europe, which prided itself on being a normative power that shunned great-power politics for relations based on liberal–democratic norms. The gap in values had always been an irritant in relations. But, after he returned to the Kremlin, Putin gave them a sharper geopolitical edge, especially in Eastern Europe.

The European Union launched the Eastern Partnership in 2009 as a means of managing relations with the former Soviet states that became neighbors after the latest round of expansion in 2004. There was no desire to bring these countries into the EU itself, but Brussels wanted to develop commercial relations with them based on its own norms. What from Brussels' standpoint was primarily a socio-economic initiative was immediately perceived as a geopolitical challenge in Moscow.[43] The adoption of EU norms by former Soviet states could have only adverse effects on their commercial ties with Russia, which operated by a radically different set of rules. And that would slowly pull these countries out of Russia's orbit.

This contradiction came to a head in Ukraine in 2013, as Kyiv drew close to concluding an Association Agreement. It was this battle over economic ties that provoked the massive demonstrations in Kyiv in the Fall, after the Ukrainian president backed away from signing the agreement under immense pressure from Moscow. The struggle ultimately led to the ouster of the president in favor of pro-European forces in February 2014 and shortly thereafter to Moscow's seizure of Crimea. Tellingly, Putin justified that act in geopolitical terms; it was imperative to prevent a situation from arising in which Russians would find themselves being greeted by NATO officials should they visit the peninsula, the site of glorious Russian military exploits.

Relations spiraled downward, as the EU and Russia levied sanctions and countersanctions. Moscow ratcheted up interference in Europe's domestic affairs, using hybrid war tactics to influence, among other things, the 2016 Brexit referendum, the 2017 French presidential elections, and the 2017 German parliamentary elections. It continued to fund populist forces across the continent, notably Marine Le Pen's right-wing National Front in France, to exacerbate internal divisions. And it fostered closer ties to Hungary's own populist leader, Victor Orbán, to complicate internal EU politics.

Efforts to resolve the Ukraine conflict only exacerbated tensions. Germany and France played central roles in bringing about a ceasefire in eastern Ukraine and developing a program for resolving the conflict, known as the Minsk Agreements. The key provision, which quickly became the stumbling block to its implementation, provided for extensive autonomy for the regions under separatist control, which was to be codified in Ukraine's constitution. If enacted, those steps would have given Moscow an effective veto over Ukraine's foreign and security policy. Although party to the agreement, Kyiv balked – these provisions were politically toxic; parliamentary approval for the constitutional amendments was unachievable. Moscow expected Berlin and Paris to put sufficient pressure on Kyiv to compel compliance. They never did. That was just a further illustration of Western perfidy for Moscow.[44]

As relations deteriorated, Moscow grew more dismissive of Europe. It demeaned European states, even Germany and France, as little more than American vassals, incapable of independent action in their own national interest. That was admittedly a provocation to some degree – Moscow hoped that Germany and France, at least, would oppose American policies on some matters to demonstrate their independence. But, fundamentally, it reflected Moscow's conclusion that Europe could no longer provide the hedge against the United States that it sought.

The East Beckons

In these circumstances, Russia had little choice but to look to the East for a strategic counterbalance to the United States. Thus emerged the support for a Greater Eurasia (or Asia),[45] which with time became a central element of Russia's foreign policy. As Putin said in May 2022, "Greater Eurasia is without exaggeration a grand civilizational project, and the main idea is to create a common space of equal partnership for regional organizations. The Great Eurasian Partnership is called to change the political and economic architecture, to become the guarantor of stability and prosperity on the entire continent, taking into account of course the diversity of models of development, culture, and traditions of all peoples." This was the natural outcome, he noted, as more and more countries wanted to pursue independent policies, and no "world gendarme," read the United States, could stop this natural global process.[46] Quite naturally, relations with China lay at the center of this concept. Ties improved rapidly from the time of Putin's visit to Shanghai for a summit with Chinese President Xi Jinping in May 2014. In the face of the West's attempt to isolate Russia diplomatically over Ukraine, the Russian leader was determined to demonstrate that he had other options. The centerpieces of the talks were a $400 million gas deal and a joint naval exercise.

Troubled relations with the United States, complementary economies, authoritarian political systems, and personal rapport between Putin and

Xi provided the foundation for increasingly close strategic alignment. Relations reached new heights on the eve of Russia's invasion of Ukraine in February 2022. The two leaders issued a joint statement on February 4, in which they laid out their shared views on a wide range of global issues and a common vision of global politics. For the first time, a Russian–Chinese joint statement explicitly criticized NATO for its "ideologized cold war approaches" and opposed its further enlargement. In a statement that caught the West's attention, the two leaders declared that "friendship between the two States has no limits, there are no 'forbidden' areas of cooperation."[47] There remained frictions of course. But the key from Moscow's standpoint was that China vowed not to undermine it on the international stage. "Not always for but never against" is the way Russians described relations. That was sufficient for Moscow's purposes.

Strategic alignment manifested itself in multiple ways. At the diplomatic level, Russia and China coordinated their positions in international fora, notably the UN Security Council. The two countries agreed to harmonize the Russia-led Eurasian Union and Beijing's Belt and Road Initiative. Bilateral trade grew robustly, from $65 billion in 2015 to over $110 billion in 2019 and then, after a drop due to the pandemic in 2020, rebounded to $147 billion in 2021.[48] In 2022, Russia overtook Saudi Arabia as the top supplier of petroleum to China,[49] and after the Power of Siberia gas pipeline came on line in December 2019, it quickly became its third largest supplier of natural gas.[50] Moscow lifted earlier restrictions on Chinese investment in strategic sectors, although that did not produce a surge in investment. It talked of greater cooperation in the Arctic, reversing earlier policy aimed at limiting China's role.

Military-technical cooperation also blossomed. Joint military exercises became routine and grew in complexity and ambition. In Fall 2022, China for the first time sent all three components of its armed forces, land, air, and sea, to participate in a joint exercise, Russia's quadrennial Vostok drill. Russia began to sell China some of its most sophisticated military equipment, including the advanced Sukhoi SU-35 jet fighter and the S-400 air defense system. It is now helping China build a ballistic missile early warning system, which when complete will make China only one of three countries in the world with such a system, the other two being Russia and the United States.

While Russia touts this alignment, it is not without friction. Indeed, while both countries rhetorically support a multipolar world order, their views of the future are quite different. China wants to restore its preeminence in Asia and beyond. It is not necessarily opposed to a rules-based order; it just wants the rules to be written with Chinese characters. Russia, meanwhile, seeks a genuinely multipolar world, in which it would be one member of the concert of great powers that would manage global affairs.[51] How to reconcile those views is not readily apparent, but it is unnecessary for the moment in face of the challenge from the United States.

But that situation will not last forever and, when that time comes, Russia, as the junior partner, has to fear that diverging worldviews will erode relations, and problems that have plagued them in the past will reemerge. As was true earlier in its relations with the United States, Russia needs hedges against ties turning sour. The ideal hedge of course would be the United States or the West (including Japan and South Korea) more broadly, but that option is off the table, at least for an extended period. The hedge has to be found in Greater Eurasia or in the global South, and it has to be created in a way that does not cause undue tension with China.

The solution Moscow has wagered on is enveloping China in multilateral networks that can be billed as alternatives to Western-dominated security and economic structures: two in particular, the Shanghai Cooperation Organization (SCO) and the BRICS (Brazil, Russia, India, China, and South Africa).

The SCO, established in 2001, grew out of an earlier effort by China and the four former Soviet states it borders – Russia, Kazakhstan, Kyrgyzstan, and Tajikistan – to regulate border and defense-related issues. Since then, its mandate has broadened to include foreign-policy matters, broadly construed, transportation and energy issues, and economic and commercial matters. Its membership has also expanded: Uzbekistan joined at the time the SCO was formally founded; India and Pakistan in 2017 and Iran in 2022. Belarus, an observer state, is now seeking membership, while Afghanistan and Mongolia are observers. With this mandate and membership, the SCO is now a central institution in the organization of Greater Eurasia, with the clear intention of eroding Western influence. But it also provides a forum in which Russia can work with other countries, especially India, in shaping China's role.

The BRICS does in global economics and finance what the SCO does in Eurasia. Launched at the ministerial level at Russia's initiative in 2006, the four original members (South Africa joined in 2010) held its first summit in 2009 to discuss a range of financial and economic issues. The goal was not so much to provide an alternative to the International Monetary Fund and World Bank as to offer the leading developing countries a way to operate independently of those Western-dominated institutions. The BRICS have set up their own development bank, payments system, and reserve arrangement. Putin regularly boasts that the combined GDP of the BRICS exceeds that of the G-7, and that the five countries account for over 40 percent of the world's population. But the critical unspoken benefit it provides Moscow is a lever to influence China.

If these hedges prove less than adequate, Moscow is hoping that the strategic alignment, the special relationship it is building with Beijing, will still afford it some influence. Previously, a similar effort bought it little sway over American policy. It will likely have no more success with China.

Will Russia Succeed?

Russia has embarked on an ambitious and risky course. It has turned away from its centuries-long orientation toward the West, pivoting to the East and, to a lesser extent, to the South, hoping to ride the wave of a shift in global dynamism from the Euro-Atlantic region to the Asian-Pacific. It has aligned itself with China, a robust giant that is far outstripping it in economic and technological development with which it has had a long, troubled history. The bet is that Moscow can constrain it with multilateral arrangements among Eurasian states and other developing countries in the global South and thereby preserve its own strategic autonomy. Success would mean that Russia could then use alignment with China to upend the foundation of the US-led order and replace it with a truly multipolar one, in which Russia counted among the few great powers. Failure, however, would turn Russia into a Chinese vassal, at best.

While Putin has had some success – he has made Russia one of the world's top three geopolitical actors – formidable challenges remain, some of his own making. He has, for example, consolidated Russia on the basis of patriotism, which should fortify the country against the ups and downs in economic fortune that all countries inevitably confront. But the tools he has used to squeeze dissenters discourage the innovation and creativity Russia will need to build a competitive economy that can generate the resources to sustain great-power ambitions in the decades ahead.

The situation in the former Soviet space is likewise uncertain. Russia is playing an active role, but the region remains a drain on Russia's resources. Moscow exploited the troubles Belarusian President Aleksandr Lukashenko faced after a rigged election provoked a massive protest in 2020 to extend its control over its neighbor, but Moscow's actions have done nothing to alleviate the causes of widespread discontent. Moscow forced a settlement on Armenia and Azerbaijan after their brief war in 2020, and it deployed a small contingent of peacekeepers to the region, but the tension between the two South Caucasian states remains unabated, and Moscow had to concede a growing Turkish presence in the region.

Russian troops saved Kazakhstan President Kassym-Jomart Tokayev from an elite revolt in January 2022, but that did not prevent him from distancing his country from Russia's "special military operation" against Ukraine. The success of that operation hangs in the balance but, whether Russia wins or loses, it has produced a wasteland in eastern Ukraine that will only suck up resources, if it is to be rebuilt, or remain a wellspring of instability, if it is not. Moreover, it has drained resources that Moscow needs to maintain its position in Eurasia.

Meanwhile, Russia's invasion of Ukraine has breathed a new sense of purpose into NATO, which has rediscovered its original mission of containing Russia, but at a line that has move hundreds of miles eastward toward Russia's own borders since the end of the Cold War. A military operation that was ostensibly launched in part to prevent NATO's further expansion convinced Sweden and Finland to abandon their traditional neutrality in favor of NATO membership. And the European Union is taking urgent steps to wean itself off Russian energy, which hitherto had been a major lever of Russian influence on the continent. It will take a generation at least to restore anything that approaches constructive relations between Russia and Europe.

The same is probably true of US–Russian relations. By no means does Putin or Russia bear full responsibility for the break in relations. But that does not alter the reality that the United States remains the most powerful counterbalance to China, if only Russia could find a way to wield it. Nothing that Russia might be able to craft in Eurasia can compare. In the end, Russia's strategic autonomy will reach its greatest extent if it can maneuver deftly between the two superpowers. The challenge then is to repair relations with Washington, even in the face of the latter's resistance – and to do so without compromising its own core interests.

Putin is probably incapable of taking up that challenge – his anti-Americanism is too deeply embedded, and he has lashed his fate too tightly to that of Chinese leader Xi Jinping. But a future Russian leader will not be burdened with the same psychological and political constraints in confronting Russia's strategic conundrum. That is an eventuality Washington should never lose sight of.

5

The Putin Factor

"No Putin, no Russia," the president's deputy chief of staff, Vyacheslav Volodin, told a group of foreign-policy experts in October 2014. According to an organizer of the event, he was referring to the immediate situation surrounding Russia's seizure of Crimea and instigation of rebellion in Eastern Ukraine and the mounting Western campaign in response to punish and isolate Russia.[1] But few have heard that qualification. The quip may have been hyperbole, but for Western commentators, and not a few Russians, it was a true reflection of direction and aspiration.

The dominant narrative in the West is that Putin inherited a fitfully democratizing country and step by step walked it down a path to ever stricter authoritarianism. Putinism has emerged as a regime type of intense study in the West. Many now consider him a dictator, the evil genius behind Russia's aggressive conduct abroad and ever harsher domestic repression. His character and mindset are thus central to any assessment of Kremlin policy. Some would go so far as to argue that that they are the only things that matter.

That of course is an exaggeration. Like all leaders, no matter how seemingly powerful, Putin operates within a political context, an amalgam of tradition, structures, and contemporary political forces that frames the exercise of power, imposes obligations a ruler must fulfill to maintain legitimacy, and necessarily limits the range of options.[2] The extent to which a ruler can imprint his preferences on policy depends on his will, skill, imagination, and vision. The analytical task is to distill the personal factor from the broader contours of policy and, in our case, to determine Putin's unique contribution to the conduct of Russian foreign policy.

This is hardly an idle, academic question. To craft a successful Russia policy, both short-term and long-term, American policymakers need to assess how much of the challenge they face is due to the enduring characteristics of Russia as a major power on the global stage that will outlast any leader and how much is due primarily to the leader's preferences. In other words, does the United States today confront a Russia problem or a Putin problem? The answer is likely a bit of both. That said, getting the proportion right is critical to successful policymaking.

The Limits of Putin's Power

Who is Mr. Putin? That question has preoccupied Western observers ever since a journalist posed it to a panel of leading Russians at the Davos World Economic Forum in January 2000, shortly after Putin took over as acting president. Why the panelists hesitated to reply – because they had no good answer, or out of concern about crossing a new leader – is of little importance. Deliberately or not, they fed an aura of mystery that has hung about Putin since he rose to the pinnacle of power, from being a virtual unknown nearly a quarter century ago. The natural opacity of the Kremlin and the efforts of its myth-makers have only further obscured the answer.

In this vacuum, observers have latched onto one or another aspect of Putin's biography – former KGB officer is a favorite – or a trenchant phase – "The breakup of the Soviet Union was the greatest geopolitical tragedy of the twentieth century" is often cited [3] – as if it explains all that we need to know about Putin. Such superficiality abets the demonization of Putin; it does nothing to foster understanding. It is a sign of intellectual laziness. For Putin has, in fact, said and written much in the past 25 years that provides insight into his character and mindset, to his goals and motivations. More to the point, it demonstrates that he lay well within the traditional framework of Russia's political and strategic thinking, at least until he launched the invasion of Ukraine.

The Dictates of History

Like his predecessors, Putin is a *gosudarstvennik*, or statist, a fierce defender of the traditional Russian state; its restoration and future progress have lain at the center of his mission as the top leader. His service in the KGB, which prides itself on being the most faithful defender of the state, the most patriotic of all institutions, provided both the philosophical and the practical foundation for his statist beliefs.[4] He is convinced that Russia requires a strong state to survive and thrive. As he wrote in an essay, "Russia at the Turn of the Millennium," released in 1999 on the eve of his ascension to power, "[In Russia], the state, its institutions and structures have always played an exceptionally important role in the life of the country and the people. A strong state is not an anomaly for Russians, not something to struggle against, but rather the guarantor of order, the initiator and main driver of any changes."[5]

Putin also believes that a strong Russian state has to be a great power. He sees the requirements for the defense and preservation of that status much as previous Russian rulers did, that is, in strict control over the society; strategic depth, buffer zones, and spheres of influence; and disruption of coalitions of hostile powers along the country's long periphery in Eurasia. Like the great tsars before him – Peter, Catherine, and Alexander II – and Stalin, he considers himself called to extend Russia's sway. For him, as for his predecessors, it is not so much a matter of conquest of foreign lands as of gathering lands lost to Russia after the collapse of Kievan Rus in the thirteenth century, or later after other geopolitical catastrophes. As he told a group of young entrepreneurs in June 2022, even though Europeans believed Peter had seized Swedish lands during the Great Northern War, what he had done in fact was regain land that was historically Russian. That, he assured the group, was what he was now in the process of doing with the special military operation in Ukraine.[6]

This adherence to tradition is bound up in Putin's fascination with Russian history. He is reportedly an avid reader of works on his country's past.[7] He has authored two long treatises on controversial historical issues, the Molotov–Ribbentrop Pact concluded on the eve of the Second World War[8] and the unity of the Russian and Ukrainian peoples[9] – both, to be sure, written in support of current political goals. He absolved the Soviet Union of any responsibility for the outbreak of the horrific European war to preserve unsullied Russia's triumph over Nazi Germany as a core element of the regime's legitimacy, and he laid out the historical justification for his invasion of Ukraine to restore Russia's unity.

These works were part of a larger effort to inspire patriotism by restoring the bonds of the country's thousand-year existence, which had been severed during the Yeltsin period. His immediate predecessor had presented post-Soviet Russia, not only as a sharp break with 74 years of

Soviet totalitarianism, but also as a renunciation of a thousand years of Russian authoritarianism. That was a thin reed, in Putin's view, on which to build Russian pride and legitimate the new Russia. It ignored the great achievements of the tsarist and Soviet periods that elevated the country's global standing, and it denied the inheritance that made Russia great.[10] His determination to restore the bonds of Russian history, and bolster the new Russia's legitimacy, was revealed in his early choice of state symbols. He revived the Soviet national anthem, keeping the stirring melody but changing the lyrics to reflect current realities, while retaining the tricolor of revolutionary Russia as the state flag and the tsarist double-headed eagle in state heraldry.

Putin may appropriate Russia's past for his political purposes, but that does not erase the critical point that he places himself within the broad span of Russian history and tradition. He interrogates the Russian past, the leading statesmen and thinkers, as he seeks answers to his country's current challenges. He most certainly wants to go down in history as a great Russian ruler who continued and enriched a grand tradition.

The Ties that Bind

While history and tradition offer guidance for Russian rulers, the structure of the state imposes broad tasks they must carry out to maintain their power. In the oligarchic, political–military order that is the Russian state, the ruler is the ultimate source of political legitimacy, and proximity to him is the critical element of any oligarch's power and influence. But that hardly makes the ruler all-powerful. Rather, as Edward Keenan, a leading historian of Russia, argued in his seminal work, "Muscovite Political Folkways," the rulers serve as the anchor of the political system, "the focal point – and the *hostages* . . . of a ruling oligarchy of boyar clans."[11]

The ruler's task, in Keenan's view, was to manage the competition among the elite factions to ensure that it did not spin out of control and endanger the survival of the system as a whole. Deft management would also maximize the ruler's own power and authority. But he could not rule against the wishes of the oligarchs as a class. As no less a practitioner of autocratic power than Catherine the Great responded when complimented on her extraordinary power:

It is not as easy as you think. First, my orders would not be carried out precisely if it were not convenient to implement them. You yourself know how cautiously and carefully I move toward the issuance of my decrees. I analyze the circumstances, I let the enlightened part of the people know what I am thinking to see what kind of action my decree will likely elicit. When I am confident of general approval, I issue my order and have the satisfaction of seeing what you call blind obedience. That is the foundation of unlimited power.[12]

Coercion of course can ensure compliance in the short term, but it erodes the vitality of any polity over time – that was the great lesson of the Soviet period.

Elite support is thus the critical foundation of a ruler's power. But he cannot ignore the wishes of the population as a whole. He must also protect the system, the elites, from the people, who appear as an autonomous force in Russian history only as an enemy of order, a destructive force, the "the senseless and merciless" *bunt* (popular uprising) of Pushkin's imagination. Rulers would resort to brutal punitive operations to put down popular rebellion in centuries past. Today, when an educated, skilled population is needed to run a modern economy, the preference has been to mollify incipient discontent with temporary outpourings of cash or minor concessions to their demands. Doing that effectively requires identifying sources of friction in a timely fashion, which is one reason why the Kremlin does so much polling of popular opinion.

In post-Soviet Russia, one critical way in which the president demonstrates his mastery of the political system, and earns the confidence of the elites, is oddly enough through largely uncontested elections, especially presidential ones. Because the winner is known in advance, turnout, rather than share of the vote, is the key indicator of the president's strength. He has to demonstrate that he can mobilize the support of a population that he otherwise seeks to keep passive out of considerations of regime stability by bringing them out to vote in essentially meaningless contests. Successful mobilization depends to a great degree on the active efforts of officials at all levels of government, as well as the leaders of businesses and civic organizations. If the turnout is within an appropriate range, generally around 70 percent for a presidential election, the president will have demonstrated his sway with both the elites and the population as a whole.[13]

Elections thus send critical messages to the elites about the president's strength. They can provide confidence that he can protect them against the masses, while managing their own competition effectively to maintain the stability of the regime. Political polling serves a similar function. An appropriately high popularity rating for the president, and a sufficiently wide margin of superiority over other leaders, minimizes the risk that the elites will lose confidence in the president. Falsification of results, ironically, does not undermine confidence in the leader, as long as it is not flagrant and excessive. To the contrary, it is yet another indication of the president's mastery of the system.[14]

Not every Russian ruler has successfully navigated this dance with the elites and the people. Recent Russian history is replete with cautionary tales of rulers who alienated the elites or riled the people. Tsar Nicholas II was forced to abdicate after he lost the confidence of the elites with inept leadership during the First World War. Soviet leader Nikita Khrushchev was ousted in a palace coup for "hare-brained schemes" that undermined the power and authority of his colleagues at the peak of power. The last Soviet leader, Mikhail Gorbachev, lost his balance, and ultimately his position, between reactionary forces threatened by his reforms and progressive forces pressing for more rapid change. As for the people as a whole, the revolutions of 1917 and the mass protests of the late Soviet period underscore the dire consequences of alienating them to the point of open rebellion; not only did the rulers fall, the state collapsed around them.

Institutional Restraints

Contemporary Russian politics is the third element that shapes Putin's options. It is often said that Russia lacks institutions. This is certainly true as far as genuinely *political* institutions are concerned. The Federal Assembly is a rubber-stamp parliament; political parties are for show; and civic organizations, at least the ones that are not repressed, are arms of the state at various levels. Nevertheless, there are centers of power that Putin must control, usually through the appointment of loyalists to lead them, to undergird his authority, while the need to mediate between these competing centers necessarily limits the range of his options. In the first circle are the so-called power structures: the military and the special services, the men with the guns to protect or overthrow him. In recent years, Putin's trusted circle of advisers has reportedly narrowed down to a subset of the heads of these agencies, especially as far as foreign and security policy is concerned.

Also important are the key centers of socio-economic power, those entities, most state monopolies, that both generate the wealth to fund the state's ambitions and provide country-wide networks that can be used for political control. Among the most prominent are Gazprom and Rosneft, the natural gas and oil national champions, respectively; Russian Railroads; Sberbank, the largest bank; Rostec, a defense conglomerate; and Rosatom, which specializes in nuclear energy. The Central Bank manages the currency, and several large media companies oversee the broadcast industry. These entities may not be involved in key foreign-policy decisions, but Putin does rely on their technical skills to manage the socio-economic fallout of his choices. For them to do that, his decisions must not jeopardize their continued economic viability.

Besides these structures of power, Putin also has to deal with popular discontent. This comes, broadly speaking, in three guises: socio-economic dissatisfaction, liberal political opposition, and conservative nationalist forces. He has met these challenges, once again in broad terms, with money and minor concessions, repression, and co-optation, respectively.

In particular, Putin has worked to prevent the liberals from linking up with the socio-economic discontent to create a massive protest movement akin to the one that helped topple the Soviet regime. This is one reason for his harsh crackdown on Alexey Navalny, who, uniquely among the non-system liberal opposition leaders, had a knack for connecting with broader segments of the population. The approach Putin has used with noteworthy success is to paint these opposition leaders as tools of the West, while promoting patriotism among the population as a whole.

The conservative nationalist forces, in the Kremlin's view, pose less of a threat. They tend after all to be statists and supporters of a great Russia, who can be bought off with rhetoric and actions that underscore Russia's role as a great power. What Putin has to guard against is the rise of ethnic Russian nationalism as a major political force that would jeopardize the unity of a multiethnic country; thus his appeals to patriotism, not nationalism, as a traditional Russian value.

Putin or Russia?

So how powerful is Putin? How much of his foreign policy has been the outcome of potent historical currents that would have led any Russian leader to see a similar array of challenges and range of options? To what extent have his choices been constrained by domestic political forces that he had to co-opt or appease? How much has been due to his idiosyncrasies? And, perhaps most important, to what degree have his choices exceeded the traditional contours of Russian foreign policy to pose a new, unfamiliar threat to the United States?

Putin certainly brought a distinctive style to Russian foreign policy: blunt, aggressive, cynical, confrontational but also pragmatic, with a keen sense of Russia's limits. His anti-Americanism has taken on a sharper and more vicious edge the longer he has been in power. But, at least until the invasion of Ukraine in February 2022, he operated well within the parameters of Russia's foreign-policy tradition. His broad goals, his sense of how Russia should act as a great power, resembled those of his predecessors from the Soviet and tsarist eras. National-interest arguments, realpolitik, could easily account for his actions during the Orange Revolution in 2004, the short war against Georgia in 2008, the seizure of Crimea and the instigation of rebellions in Eastern Ukraine in 2014, and the incursion into Syria in 2015. The Putin factor was not needed to explain the broad outlines of his foreign policy, even if it could illuminate specific tactics.

Is the invasion of Ukraine of a different order? Would another ruler have assessed the challenge Russia faced and the range of possible responses much as Putin has? Would he have likely gone to war to defend Russia's interests? In short, is this Russia's war or Putin's?

The Importance of Ukraine

Ukraine is an existential issue for Russia, Putin would have us believe. Why, is not obvious. Certainly, Russia with its abundant resources and vast territory would continue to exist even if Ukraine were fully independent and outside a Russian sphere of influence. Allied to a hostile power, Ukraine might pose a security threat but it is hard to see how that would endanger the very survival of Russia, as, say, a nuclear conflict with the United States most assuredly would. An assertively independent Ukraine could of course strike a fatal blow against a certain *idea* of Russia as an East Slavic nation, composed of Great Russians, Little Russians (Ukrainians), and White Russians (Belarusians). A Western-oriented, democratic, and prosperous Ukraine could pose a powerful theoretical and practical challenge to an anti-Western, authoritarian Russian regime, given the close historical ties between Ukrainians and Russians. And a Russian defeat in the ongoing campaign to subjugate Ukraine could put an end to Putin's political career. But all those developments are quite different from the demise of Russia as an independent state or even as a great power.

That said, for centuries Ukraine has been of immense importance to Russia, and its separation would complicate the challenges Russia faces at home and abroad, in the eyes of the Russian elite. Russian identity, security, and status are inextricably intertwined with its fate. Russians consider it the cradle of their civilization, the progenitor of their state-hood, and the source of their religious identity. Historically, Ukraine has provided a buffer against hostile powers in Europe, and until the mid eighteenth century against Tatar raiders along the North shore of the Black Sea, while also serving as a gateway to markets in Europe and the Black Sea region. From the mid nineteenth century, Eastern Ukraine was a major industrial region that undergirded Russia's standing as a great power. Moreover, Ukrainians (Little Russians in the tsarist nomenclature) were essential to making the Empire Russian in the later quarter of the nineteenth century and the first decades of the twentieth, and were invaluable partners in running the Soviet Union. For all those reasons, any Russian leader would want to keep Ukraine close, if not necessarily as an integral part of Russia itself.

The Cradle of Kievan Rus

Russians, like Ukrainians (and Belarusians), trace the origins of their state back to a loose federation of East Slavic principalities, known as Kievan Rus, that was founded in the late ninth century and disappeared with the invasion of the Mongol Hordes in the mid thirteenth. During that period, the city of Kyiv was the hub of East Slavic trade with regions further south bordering on the Black, Azov, and Caspian Seas. It also served as the main line of defense against raids by nomadic steppe tribes and the defender of the river routes to markets in the South.

This strategic position enabled the princes of Kyiv to gather under their rule all the East Slavic principalities, including the one from which the Muscovite state would eventually emerge. In the view of the eminent late nineteenth to early twentieth-century Russian historian Vasily Klyuchevsky that made Kievan Rus the first Russian state, even though its population was ethnically diverse and there was no sense of Russian national identity at the time.[15]

Kievan Rus was important in more than just a political sense. Kievan Prince Vladimir I accepted Orthodoxy in 988, thus giving Russians their religious identity. His choice also led to a flowering of literature and the fine arts throughout his realm, something that would not have taken place, at least not as rapidly and extensively as it did in fact, had he chosen Catholicism instead. Unlike Roman Catholicism, Byzantium ensured that the key sacred texts, as well as other philosophical works, were translated into the local vernacular. Indeed, Greek missionaries, Cyril and Methodius, developed an alphabet for Slavonic, the language of the East Slavs, a century before Vladimir accepted the Orthodox faith. As a result, the educated elite did not have to learn Greek in order to gain access to Greek culture. Kievan Rus thus became the source of Russia's literary language and legal tradition, among other things.

One final element – dynastic – links modern Russia to Kievan Rus. The first rulers of Muscovy came from the same Rurikid dynasty as the grand princes of Kyiv and presented themselves as the heirs of the Kievan inheritance. Not surprisingly, when Muscovy began its period of rapid expansion in the late fifteenth century, it started by "gathering the Russian lands" of Kievan Rus.

The Indispensable Buffer and Fulcrum of Power

As the Muscovite state expanded, the lands of which are now Ukraine became essential to its security. Muscovy faced four major threats, from Poland and Lithuania in the West and from the nomadic steppe tribes and the Ottomans in the South. The Russian state acquired its first large piece of Ukraine in the middle of the seventeenth century as a consequence of the decision of the Cossacks under Hetman Bohdan Khmelnytsky to seek the tsar's protection against their Polish overlords. The Cossacks were granted substantial autonomy, which was slowly whittled away until their lands were fully absorbed into the Empire as three separate provinces under Catherine the Great.

The Empress added further Ukrainian land to the Empire through a series of wars with Turkey and the partitions of Poland, in collaboration with Prussia and Austria. With successive defeats of the Turks, Russia gained full control of the northern littoral of the Black Sea. Crimea was formally annexed in 1783, and shortly thereafter one of Catherine's favorites, Prince Grigory Potemkin, founded the Black Sea Fleet with its principal base at Sevastopol, the superb natural harbor on the peninsula. With the partitions of Poland, Russia acquired most of the land in that state that was inhabited by Orthodox believers, essentially Ukrainians and Belarusians. With those acquisitions, Catherine brought all the territory of today's Ukraine into her Empire, save Galicia and a few other minor territories.[16]

Catherine's policies substantially enhanced the security of the Russian Empire by creating strategic depth to the West and gaining a natural, defensible border to the South in the form of the Black Sea. But the territory was of more than geopolitical importance. It also provided the resources that helped generate the power Russia needed for defense and conquest, particularly in the later half of the nineteenth century and most of the twentieth. In 1897, Ukraine's population numbered more than twenty million, or 16 percent of the Empire's total. In 1914, Ukrainian land produced one-third of the empire's wheat, most of its exported grains (a critical source of state revenue), and 80 percent of its sugar. The Donbas in Eastern Ukraine, rich in coal and iron ore, became by the end of the nineteenth century the major zone of industrial development in the Empire. On the eve of the First World War, the region produced 70 percent of Russia's coal, 68 percent of its cast iron, and 58 percent of its steel. No other region of the Empire could compete with it, until Stalin created the Urals/Western Siberian industrial zone in the 1930s.[17] As the historian Dominic Lieven notes, "Without Ukraine's population, industry, and agriculture, early-twentieth-century Russia would have ceased to be a great power."[18] That is one reason why the Bolsheviks were so keen to reconquer Ukraine after the Revolution, no matter what their rhetorical support for national self-determination.

During the Soviet period, the agricultural and industrial potential of Ukraine remained a critical element of Soviet power, despite the horrors of forced collectivization and the man-made famine of the 1930s, known as the Holodomor, that killed millions. In particular, Ukraine was a central component of the Soviet military-industrial complex. The Soviet navy's largest ships were built in the port of Mykolaiv (Nikolayev) on the Black Sea. After the Second World War, Kyiv became the center for Soviet aircraft design and manufacturing, producing the famed Antonov strategic airlift planes. Motor Sich in Zaporizhzhia became the critical manufacturer of helicopter engines, and Yuzhmash in Dnipropetrovsk produced key components for ballistic missiles for the Soviet Strategic Rocket Forces.[19]

In addition, the Soviets built an extensive natural gas transportation system in Ukraine, including two trunk lines, Brotherhood and Soyuz, which carried the overwhelming volume of gas exports to Europe. In the post-Soviet period, upwards of 80 percent of Russian natural gas exports to Europe transited Ukraine until 2011, when the first Nord Stream pipeline on the Baltic seabed came on line, linking Russia and Germany directly. That pipeline was built expressly to reduce Russian dependence on Ukraine as a transit country. Nevertheless, until Russia's invasion of Ukraine in 2022 roughly one-third of Russian gas exports to Europe transited Ukraine.

Making the Empire Russian

Ukrainians played one last critical role for the Russian state beginning in the mid nineteenth century. They could decide whether it was Russian or not. Ethnic differences had not mattered much for the greater part of Russian history. As Muscovy expanded, the local elites, no matter what their ethnicity, were generally assimilated into the country's elite. During the Imperial period, many senior diplomats and military officers were not ethnic Russians and spoke Russian poorly. Indeed, one of the most consequential tsars, Catherine II, was by birth a minor German princess.

The age of nationalism, in the nineteenth century, changed the equation dramatically. Nations become the foundation of states, which was one reason for the unification of Germany and Italy in the middle of the century. Great empires, such as the British, the French, the German, had solid national cores; the multinational Austro-Hungarian and Ottoman empires struggled. Russia quite naturally wanted to be a great empire.

If Ukrainians and the far less numerous Belarusians counted as Russians, and, in the nomenclature of Imperial Russia, they did, as Little Russians and White Russians, then the Empire had a solid national core. According the 1897 census, over three-quarters of the population were Russian. But if the Little Russians and White Russians became distinct Ukrainian and Belarusian nationalities, Russians accounted for only 44 percent of the population. In what sense then was the Russian Empire Russian?[20] For that reason, the imperial government worked assiduously to suppress the first shoots of a Ukrainian national movement – as elsewhere, manifested in the promotion of the Ukrainian language among the educated classes – from the middle of the nineteenth century onward.[21]

The Soviets were vehemently opposed to Great Russian chauvinism. They had denounced the Russian Empire as the prison house of nations and called for national self-determination. Once in power, however, they were loathe to abandon territory that was critical to their might and waged a civil war to restore Russia's writ over most of the former Russian Empire, Ukraine included. They reconciled their ideology and power ambitions by nominally transforming the Empire into a federation of ethnically based socialist republics and nurturing the formation of national elites in the constituent republics under a policy known as *korenizatsiya*, or indigenization, while retaining control through the highly centralized Bolshevik party. Ukrainians were celebrated as Ukrainians and put into leadership positions in their republic. Gone was the tripartite imperial conception of the Russian nation.[22]

All that changed in the 1930s under Stalin. He abandoned world revolution in practice, if not in rhetoric, for the task of building socialism in one country. The proletariat now had a fatherland, contrary to what Marx and Engels had proclaimed in the *Communist Manifesto* and, with mounting threats from Nazi Germany and Imperial Japan, this was no time to encourage potentially centrifugal forces. To the contrary, Stalin needed to ensure the loyalty of the country's largest nationality by far, the

Russians. To that end, he reversed Bolshevik policy and began to speak positively about tsarist Russia and the role of the Russians as the core of the state.[23]

Ukrainians, however, could not be reabsorbed into the Russian nation – too much had been done to bolster them as a separate nationality and the Soviet Union remained nominally a federation of ethnically based republics. Nor could they be treated as just any other non-Russian nationality – they were too numerous and their republic too important to Soviet might. After Stalin's death, they became for all practical purposes the Russians' junior partner in running the Soviet Union.[24] Together, they formed the solid Slavic core of the country – some two-thirds of population.

Russian–Ukrainian Relations in the Post-Soviet Era

As the Soviet Union crumbled under Gorbachev, Ukrainians, whether long-standing dissident nationalists or hardcore party members, had no interest in being anyone's junior partner. They wanted full independence. With that goal in mind, they played an instrumental role in bringing down the curtain on the Soviet Union and repeatedly thwarted Russian plans to dominate the former Soviet space.

Russia's first president, Boris Yeltsin, and his allies, hailed in the West as democrats breaking with the Soviet and Russian imperial traditions, were anything but that. Initially they hoped that they could gradually take over the Soviet Union's central institutions and keep the country intact as a Russian-led federation. Ukraine's insistence on independence, declared immediately after the crushing of the putsch in August 1991 and approved overwhelmingly in a popular referendum in December, spiked those plans. Ukraine then conspired with Russia and Belarus to replace the Soviet Union with a Commonwealth of Independent States (CIS), which it saw as a tool for a "civilized divorce," while Russia hoped to use it as a platform for the political and economic reintegration of the now former Soviet space. Tellingly, Ukraine never became a full member of the Commonwealth, only an associate, and did not participate in all of its institutions.

Ukraine then refused to sign the Collective Security Treaty, which Russia saw as a means to legitimate itself as the guarantor of CIS security.

Rather, Ukraine became the first post-Soviet state to set up its own independent military. As we have seen, Ukraine hesitated before agreeing under intense American pressure to send its Soviet inheritance of nuclear weapons to Russia for dismantlement. It only did so after receiving assurances of its security and territorial integrity, codified in the Budapest Memorandum in 1994. They may have turned out to be worthless when Russia seized Crimea in 2014, but they were a clear indication of Ukraine's goals in the 1990s and afterwards.

The mutually exclusive Russian and Ukrainian ambitions made for tense relations from the last years of the Soviet Union into the post-Soviet decades. Refusing to abandon plans to restore a sphere of influence, Russia put in place policies to legitimate interference in Ukraine (and elsewhere in Eurasia) and unsettle its politics. Two have particular relevance for today's Russo–Ukrainian conflict: The concept of Russian compatriots and Crimea.

The breakup of the Soviet Union left some 25 million ethnic Russians strewn across the former Soviet space beyond the borders of the Russian Federation. More than twelve million resided in Ukraine, primarily in Crimea and the east of the country. Shortly after the breakup, Moscow declared that it had a special responsibility to guarantee the rights not only of those ethnic Russians who were now minorities in their new countries, but also of the more expansive, ill-defined group of Russian-speakers. Both groups were declared to be "compatriots," for whom a fast path to Russian citizenship was instituted. Thus emerged pockets of actual or potential Russian citizens beyond Russia's borders, which Moscow was theoretically obliged to defend. It was most attentive to the situation in Ukraine, ready to protest any infringement of the rights of Russian minorities, especially in those provinces with substantial populations of Russian speakers, which meant most of the country beyond the historical region of Galicia in the West.

Interference in Crimea was more intense. The peninsula remained home to the Soviet Black Sea Fleet, to which both Russia and Ukraine laid claim. A large share of the population was either serving Russian military or retired Soviet military. According to the 1989 census, more than two-thirds of the population were ethnic Russians, and just over a quarter ethnic Ukrainians. Although a majority of the inhabitants chose independence in the 1991 referendum, at 54 percent of the vote, it was the smallest majority by far; nowhere else was the percentage less than 80.

A substantial share of Crimeans was in fact ambivalent about remaining part of Ukraine. Even before the breakup of the Soviet Union, Crimean leaders were agitating for the restoration of the peninsula's status as an autonomous Soviet socialist republic within the Soviet Union, which it had lost in 1945. Shortly afterwards, the regional parliament adopted a constitution that declared Crimea a sovereign state joined by a federal treaty to the rest of Ukraine. That effort went nowhere in face of stiff resistance from Kyiv. Nevertheless, in 1994, Yury Meshkov, from the Russia Bloc, whose platform combined Crimean independence and pro-Russian separatism, was elected Crimean president. He named a former Russian federal minister his prime minister and worked with a loyal parliament to re-adopt the 1992 constitution. By mid 1995, however, Meshkov had lost local support; resistance from Kyiv was no less fierce than it had been earlier; and Moscow was unwilling to offer any official support. To ease tension, Kyiv granted Crimea autonomous status within Ukraine. That settled the immediate problem but did nothing to resolve the underlying sources of tension, which was to boil over again in the future.[25]

Even if the Kremlin never formally questioned the incorporation of Crimea in Ukraine in the 1990s, the Duma did, along with many leading figures, notably Moscow mayor Yury Luzhkov. They considered illegal and illegitimate the transfer of the peninsula from Russia to Ukraine in 1954 by Soviet leader Nikita Khrushchev in celebration of the 300th anniversary of the "reunification" of Russia and Ukraine. The city of Moscow provided direct support to Russian sailors in Crimea. Russians backed local efforts to enhance the peninsula's autonomy. Such efforts did not cease even after Kyiv and Moscow signed a Treaty of Friendship in 1997, under which Russia committed to respect Ukraine's borders and territorial integrity and the two sides partitioned the Black Sea Fleet, with Kyiv's agreeing to lease certain naval facilities in Crimea to Russia for twenty years.[26]

Ukraine Defies Putin

Putin's swelling great-power ambitions, fueled by Russia's rapid economic recovery during the first years of his rule, drove a more concerted campaign to anchor Ukraine in Moscow's orbit. The first test came with the Orange Revolution of 2004. Despite his high-profile public engagement (he traveled twice to Kyiv to underscore his support for Viktor Yanukovych) Putin was thwarted in his effort to make him the next president of Ukraine. It was not only Western resistance that irritated Putin. He was also shocked to discover his lack of influence over Ukrainian voters, even though the Kremlin's internal polling showed that he was very popular in that country.

In response, the Kremlin toughened the approach to Ukraine. One manifestation was Moscow's refusal to continue to heavily subsidize natural gas deliveries; it would now demand Kyiv pay market prices. It was a logical move: Why should Moscow go easy on Ukraine if it was intent on pursuing a foreign policy toward the West that was inimical to Russian interests? In a similar vein, in 2005, Gazprom, the state gas monopoly, made the final decision to move forward on the Nord Stream gas pipeline that would link Russia and Germany directly and reduce its reliance on transit through Ukraine to reach European customers. That theoretically would increase Moscow's leverage over Kyiv.

Even then, Moscow did not press Kyiv as hard as it could have; it still hoped to lure Ukraine, along with Belarus and Kazakhstan, into a larger economic arrangement that would bolster its power in Eurasia and, by extension, on the global stage. Moscow saw an opening when Yanukovych was elected president in 2010, renounced interest in NATO membership, and extended Moscow's lease of naval installations in Crimea by 20 years. But not for long. By the Summer of 2013, Ukraine was close to finalizing an Association Agreement with the European Union, which would have sharply reduced its economic and commercial ties with Russia.

But commercial ties were hardly at the top of the Kremlin's concerns. Yanukovych's flirtation with the EU was also a rejection of Putin's signature initiative, announced in 2011, to create an Eurasian Union, which was to bring all the former Soviet space into a political entity dominated by Moscow. Most importantly, it provided a non-military way of securing Russia's control over Ukraine's geopolitical orientation. It was thus the strategic, not the economic or commercial, implications of the Ukrainian president's actions that weighed heavily on the Kremlin.

In the event, Yanukovych reneged on the deal under tremendous pressure from Moscow, sparking a massive protest in Kyiv, where pro-EU sentiment prevailed. It quickly morphed into a broader movement against Yanukovych's deeply corrupt regime. Moscow eventually lost patience with his unwillingness to use sufficient force to put down the protest, but it hoped he could perform one last service as he fled Kyiv. The plan was that he would come to Kharkiv to form a government on the territory of the historical Novorossiya (roughly the eight southeastern provinces of today's Ukraine), which would declare independence from Kyiv and request reunion with Russia.

As it turned out, the deposed president refused to play the part, eventually resettling in Russia. As a second-best alternative, Moscow then seized and annexed Crimea by mid March[27] and, shortly thereafter, fomented rebellion in southeastern Ukraine. Tellingly, Putin justified these actions not because Ukraine's ties with the European Union threatened Russia but because Russia could not tolerate a NATO presence in Crimea.[28] The period of intense fighting ended with the signing of the Minsk II Agreements in February 2015 by Ukraine, the two separatist regions of Donetsk and Luhansk, the Organization for Security and Cooperation in Europe (OSCE), and Russia.[29]

The Minsk II Agreements provided for, among other things, significant autonomy for the separatist regions, which was to be codified in the Ukrainian constitution. That would serve Moscow's purposes quite well. If it had abandoned immediate hopes of bringing Ukraine solidly back into its orbit, it would now gain a powerful lever to block Kyiv's geopolitical reorientation toward the West. But Kyiv refused to implement the agreement, the West was unwilling to compel it to do so, the conflict in the East simmered, and Russia's frustration grew.

The Run-Up to the War

From Moscow's standpoint, events took an ominous turn in 2020. Inside Ukraine, President Volodymyr Zelensky cracked down on pro-Russian forces, led by the oligarch Viktor Medvedchuk, reputedly a friend of

Putin's. In February 2021, Zelensky abruptly shut down three television stations and other media outlets connected to the oligarch.[30] Shortly thereafter, Kyiv froze his assets and put him under investigation for financing terrorism by conducting business in the separatist regions.[31]

At the same time, the Ukrainian leader ratcheted up pressure on NATO countries to make good on their 2008 promise that Ukraine would become a member. The alliance was not prepared to take that step, but it did grant Ukraine the status of an enhanced opportunities partner, which provided the framework for closer military and security cooperation. One goal was to enhance the Ukrainian military's interoperability with NATO forces, which was achieved in part through more ambitious military exercises in the Black Sea region.[32]

Another step that troubled Moscow was the launching of the Crimea Platform in the Fall of 2020 with the goal of shining a light on Russia's illegal annexation of the peninsula and Kyiv's determination to regain it. Kyiv received considerable backing from Western countries; dozens attended a summit meeting of the platform in August 2021, although the G-7 countries sent ministers instead of heads of state or government to avoid unduly provoking Moscow.[33]

The deteriorating situation in Ukraine was alarming enough. For the Kremlin, however, it was only the most visible aspect of the United States' allegedly concerted drive to maintain global hegemony, directed in the first instance, the Kremlin was convinced, against Russia. As Putin put it, the United States saw Russia as an enemy, "not because of our political regime, or some other reasons, but because it simply does not need such a large, independent country, such as Russia."[34] America's original sin was breaking the promise given to Gorbachev in 1990 that NATO would not expand "an inch eastward," if he agreed to the reunification of Germany inside NATO. Thereafter, Washington simply gave no heed to Russia's concerns, as it withdrew from arms control treaties, launched military operations against Yugoslavia and Iraq without UN Security Council authorization, and supported rebel groups in Russia's North Caucasus. As the Kremlin saw it, with its NATO allies, Washington was now preparing Ukraine as a platform for further aggression against Russia. That posed an intolerable, existential threat to Russia, in Putin's view.[35]

In the Spring of 2021, Moscow's massive buildup of military forces along Ukraine's borders was intended to send a message to Kyiv to reconsider its anti-Russian policies and to Washington that it could not ignore Russia's security concerns. Moscow's maneuver did little to deter Kyiv; if anything, it only hardened the determination to resist Russia. But it did catch Washington's attention: Biden proposed an early summit to clear the air. The June meeting briefly helped ease tensions, as the two sides agreed to launch talks on strategic stability and cybersecurity.

But the Kremlin saw no evidence that Washington was prepared to deal with its broader security concerns. Quite the contrary, Washington was drawing ever closer to Ukraine, as Russia renewed its build up of forces along Ukraine's border in the Fall. In November, Washington and Kyiv signed the US–Ukraine Charter on Strategic Partnership, which articulated a framework for cooperation in security, political, and economic affairs. Stress was placed on joint efforts to bolster Ukraine's capacity to counter Russian aggression.[36] At the same time, Washington began to warn its European allies that Russia was preparing to invade Ukraine in the early months of 2022 and to share privately, and subsequently release publicly, sensitive intelligence to back up that claim. Planning with allies and Ukraine on the response to Russian aggression kicked into high gear.

In December, Moscow released two bilateral draft treaties on security guarantees, one with the United States, the other with NATO, which embedded the Ukraine crisis in the broader framework of European security architecture. Ukraine barely figured in the drafts. Rather the focus was on three key demands: that NATO expansion cease; that NATO not deploy offensive military platforms capable of striking Russian territory along Russia's borders; and that NATO withdraw its military infrastructure back to the lines of 1997, that is, the year that the NATO–Russia Founding Act was signed and two years before NATO's first post-Cold War wave of expansion. The United States and its allies were only prepared to discuss arms control measures. They categorically refused to negotiate over NATO expansion, and the demand on withdrawing infrastructure was a non-starter, as Moscow surely knew. With diplomacy at a standstill, the Kremlin had to decide what to do with its large military force along Ukraine's borders. There are limits to how long military units can remain in the field without being put into action; in a matter of weeks, the Kremlin had to decide whether to use them against Ukraine or withdraw them to the home bases. The answer came on February 24.

Putin Decides

Any Russian ruler would have viewed the developing situation in Ukraine with alarm. Many would have seen it has a mounting threat to Russian security. Most would have sought a diplomatic solution, perhaps with the help of coercive diplomacy. Putin chose war. Why?

The risks seemed obvious. The Ukrainians would surely resist; this operation would not resemble the nearly bloodless seizure of Crimea in 2014. The West would back Ukraine with increased weapons supplies. It was already threatening to levy harsh economic and financial sanctions against Russia at a time when Russia was struggling to recover from the consequences of the coronavirus pandemic. Russia would be isolated diplomatically in Europe and perhaps elsewhere, for the world would likely see a Russian military intervention as a flagrant act of aggression. Even if Russia achieved its military goals, it would take considerable time and resources to pacify the occupied territory. And NATO would likely build up its forces along the long frontier with Russia, posing a greater security challenge than had existed before the conflict. The potential losses would far outweigh the possible gains. Why then would a rational actor choose war?[37]

Putin maintained that Russia had no choice. The Ukrainian government, which, he declared, was a gang of neo-Nazis and rabid nationalists, was stepping up its campaign of genocide against Russians and Russian-speakers in the separatist regions. It had imminent plans to reconquer them by force. NATO was rapidly taking over Ukraine as a staging ground for a future assault on Russia itself. Waiting for the danger to materialize would only multiply many-fold the colossal cost Russia would pay to defend itself. That was the lesson of the Soviet effort to delay the outbreak of the Second World War. Since conflict with the collective West was inevitable, preemption would serve Russia best.[38]

That was the public justification for the war. We have little reason to doubt that Putin believed it in broad outline, even if he exaggerated certain elements for effect. But there were undoubtedly other factors that weighed in his calculation that he could discount the risks. To begin with, he had little regard for Ukraine's leaders, including his counterpart, Volodymyr Zelensky, a comic morphed into an accidental president by an electorate disgusted by the corruption and cynicism of its ruling elite. Elected with nearly three-quarters of the vote in April 2019, Zelensky's support was rapidly waning: he had a trust rating of less than 40 percent and a distrust rating of over 50 percent by late 2021.[39] (Putin's equivalent ratings were in the mid sixties and mid thirties, respectively.)[40] Internecine fighting consumed the political class, notably pitting Zelensky against his predecessor Petro Poroshenko, who was under a politically inspired investigation for treason. Poroshenko's bloc enjoyed as much popular support as Zelensky's, and a pro-Russian political party was a major player, especially in the eastern provinces, where ethnic Russians and Russian-speakers formed the majority of the population.[41] What were the chances that the elites would come together to rally the people, including ethnic Russians, against Russia?

Likewise, Putin had little respect for leaders in the West. He had seen them come and go during his twenty-plus years at Russia's helm, and the current crop did not impress. None could hope to accomplish anything close to what he had for Russia. America's chaotic exit from Afghanistan had surprised the Kremlin, but it did confirm the view that Biden's age limited his ability to lead effectively on the global stage. Putin had some respect for Germany's departing chancellor, Angela Merkel, but by December 2021 it was clear that the new chancellor, Olaf Scholz of the Social-Democratic Party, and his Green and Free Democrat coalition partners were much more interested in domestic affairs than they were in foreign policy. French President Emmanuel Macron was energetic, but never seemed able to fashion his ideas into practical policy and, in any event, he would be facing a presidential election in the Spring of 2022 that would distract his attention from foreign affairs. And the British Prime Minister, Boris Johnson, was mired in scandals.

It was not only the leaders. Putin was convinced the West, and notably the United States, was in decline, not simply relatively, but absolutely. It was not only a matter of economic and political ills. More important was the spreading decadence that sapped populations of the will to bear sacrifices to advance national goals. No matter what the leaders might decide to do, they would face insurmountable obstacles in building public support for a long-term struggle against Russia, particularly over Ukraine. Ukraine fatigue was palpable in the West; the weak response to Russia's seizure of Crimea in 2014 offered ample proof.

What's more, Russia had a powerful lever of influence in Europe – its dependence on Russian natural gas, which was critical for power generation especially in the eastern half of the continent. In 2021, Germany covered nearly half, and Italy nearly two-fifths, of its gas needs with imports from Russia. EU countries further east had even higher levels of dependence.[42] Europe was already in the midst of an energy crisis in 2021 and criticizing Russia for refusing to supply additional volumes of natural gas.[43] Would Europe really defend Ukraine if the cost was a severe reduction in, if not total cut off of, Russian gas?

The final piece of the puzzle was Russia's military capabilities. Russia had launched a concerted modernization program in 2009. In 2014, the military had operated flawlessly in seizing Crimea. The following year, it executed in good order an operationally sophisticated intervention in Syria. This was Russia's first use of force beyond the borders of the former Soviet space since the breakup of the Soviet Union. In 2018, Putin proudly announced the country's advances in the development, production, and deployment of strategic weapons that would ensure its ability to deter any strategic strike by the United States.[44] Those weapons, coupled with President Biden's public assurances that the United States would not send American forces to Ukraine and risk a direct military confrontation with Russia,[45] fed Putin's confidence that he risked little from the United States should he use force in Ukraine.

Avenging the Past, Winning the Future

There were thus reasons to see a mounting threat to Russian national security, as well as reasons to believe that Russia had the capability to act decisively to eliminate it without running undue risks of stiff Ukrainian resistance or vigorous Western retaliation. But there were also profound personal reasons for Putin's decision to invade Ukraine – he wanted to avenge past insults and burnish his legacy as the historical agent of the restoration of Russian grandeur.

During the past twenty years, Putin had suffered stinging personal setbacks in Ukraine, mainly at the hands of the West. His direct personal intervention in the 2004 presidential election failed to put in place his preferred candidate, as Ukrainian protests backed (Putin would say fomented) by the West overturned the election results, while a repeat election put the Western-favored candidate in power.[46] When Putin's desired figure, Viktor Yanukovych, was elected president in 2010, he turned out to be a disappointment, as he failed to come down firmly in the Russian camp and continued Ukraine's flirtation with the West. And in 2014 the events that resulted in Yanukovych's ouster, in which Putin once again saw a Western hand, marred the Sochi Winter Olympic Games, in which Putin had invested so much time and effort as a way of announcing Russia's return to the international stage as a respected great power. A decisive victory over Ukraine would expunge all these black marks.

Moreover, as he approached a quarter century in power, Putin was eager to seal his legacy as one of Russia's great leaders. All of them – Peter the Great, Catherine the Great, Alexander II, and Stalin – had added significant territory to Russia's domain. Putin, for his part, would not be so much adding territory as retaking land that had once been Russia's; he would be "gathering the Russian lands" once again, as the great Russian rulers had done after times of troubles in Russia. In this regard, Ukraine was of particular importance because of the many ways in which it would augment Russian power. All this was part and parcel of restoring Russia as a great power and acting like one, for all great powers cast a huge shadow beyond their borders, creating spheres of influence or annexing new lands

Putin laid out his considered views on Ukraine at length in an essay that was published in July 2021.[47] It was a manifesto for bringing Ukraine back into the Russian fold. His main point: Ukraine has never existed as an entity separate from Russia. Ukrainians and Russians are a single people who share a common religion, a common culture, and a common history. The territory of today's Ukraine was carved out of Russian lands by the communists during the course of decades, ending with the decision to transfer Crimea from Russia to Ukraine in 1954; for all practical purposes, as Putin put it, "Russia was . . . robbed." The idea of a distinct Ukrainian nationality has been historically promoted by Russia's enemies, including the Poles, Austrians, the Bolsheviks, and now the West, to weaken it. Since Ukraine gained independence in 1991, the elites – nationalists, neo-Nazis and rapacious oligarchs – have betrayed the people as a whole, working in tandem with foreign powers determined to turn that country into an "anti-Russia."

None of this augured well for Ukraine, for, in Putin's opinion, Ukraine could prosper and enjoy true sovereignty only in partnership with Russia.

It was more than just rectifying an historical injustice for Putin, however. Success in Ukraine would also send a powerful message to Washington that Russia was ready and able to defend its interests. It would put an end to the American effort to contain Russia, reversing the flow of developments since the last years of the Cold War. Russia would demonstrate emphatically that it was a great power with which the United States had to reckon.

In pursuing these goals Putin was driven by an ideological fervor that was perhaps unique among Russian rulers. In recent years, his grand strategy of restoring Russia as a great power and replacing the uni-polar American world with a multipolar one has been elevated to an ambition to save the world. He presents his Russia as *the* leader of the non-Western world fated to undo the grave injustices of a half millennium of domination by the now hopelessly decadent "collective West." Consciously or not, he is tapping into a venerable Slavophile messianism in which, to paraphrase Martin Malia, the eminent historian of Russia, one of the most humiliated of nations and peoples, Russia and Russians, become the most exalted.[48] In the face of this conviction, the hallmark of Russia's traditional realpolitik foreign policy, the sober calculation of power balances, which had marked the first years of Putin's rule, gave way.

Miscalculations Galore

And so, profound concern about Russia's security, which the elite broadly shared, combined with unique personal characteristics such as hubris, a thirst for vengeance, the determination to rectify an historical injustice, over-weening ambition, and messianic impulse, led Putin into Ukraine. He was confident his troops would be in Kyiv in a matter of days. He had told European Commission President José Manuel Barroso in 2014 that he could take Kyiv in as little as two weeks, and now he had a much more capable military.[49] He would oust Zelensky and his government and install a pro-Russian regime. Ukrainians would welcome Russia as liberators, and the West would eventually acquiesce, as they had for all practical purposes after he seized Crimea, no matter what the loud initial denunciations. The rest of the world would be supportive, starting with China, or indifferent. It would be Putin's crowning victory.

As we know, Putin miscalculated, grossly. Instead of welcoming Russian troops with flowers, the Ukrainians put up stiff resistance. In a few short weeks, Moscow abandoned the effort to seize Kyiv and Ukraine's second largest city, Kharkiv, and refocused the campaign on the Donbas region in eastern Ukraine. The drive toward Odessa, after the successful conquest of Kherson oblast, stalled. The Russian military proved incapable of executing a multi-pronged combined arms campaign. The losses in men and equipment were staggering; five months into the war, the CIA estimated Russia had suffered 15,000 deaths, with 45,000 wounded, out of an invading force of some 200,000.[50] The West united behind Ukraine, stepping up deliveries of armaments and launching a rolling series of ever more punitive anti-Russian sanctions. To be sure, much of the world, notably China and India, refused to line up behind the West against Russia, but neither were they prepared to offer it substantial material support.

The Future

By the Summer of 2022, what had been planned as a blitzkrieg had morphed into a war of attrition of uncertain outcome. How long will the acute phase of combat last? Can either side engineer a breakthrough that will yield an early victory? Can an enduring settlement be negotiated while the combatants remain on the battlefield? Will the war turn into a frozen conflict, unresolved and doomed to erupt into open warfare once again? Who will remain more resilient in the face of adversity, the Russians or the Ukrainians and their Western backers? Those are the short-term questions that bedevil policymakers.

No matter what happens, however, the critical strategic question of relations between Russia and the West will endure. Ukraine is but a small piece of that bigger equation. The issue is not new. Since at least the end of the Napoleonic era, Europe – and now the West – has faced the conundrum of how to structure relations with the huge neighbor to its east that is alien in spirit yet an inextricable part of its security equation, a country that will never be *of* Europe but will always be *in* Europe. Russia faces its own conundrum: How much does it have to be *in* Europe to feel secure *from* Europe?

The answers will prove elusive as long as war in Ukraine continues – and that means for as long as Putin remains in power, for it is his war, not Russia's, even if for the moment he seemingly enjoys both elite and popular support. Before the invasion, elite pressure for war was barely discernible, while the population as a whole preferred peace. Diplomacy had not run its course, even if negotiations were unlikely to yield near-term agreement. Putin chose war nevertheless, moving beyond the contours of Russia's traditional strategic framework to pursue personal goals. His fate is now inextricably linked to its course.

In the Summer of 2020, Putin had the Russian constitution amended so that he could serve as president at least to 2036. Many observers are convinced that he will stay in power at least that long. But the matter is not so simple, and the decision is not Putin's alone. His power still rests on his ability to protect elites from external enemies, to manage elite competition, and to maintain popular tranquility. Elite and popular confidence that he can do that, in turn, depends on successful prosecution of the war in Ukraine. And, contrary to a widespread view, he cannot simply declare victory no matter what the circumstances on the battlefield. The outraged response of right-wing forces to the stunning Russian setback in and around Kharkiv in September 2022 is a case in point.

Should the situation on the ground turn against Russia in a sustained fashion, Putin has few attractive options. Mobilizing the population for active participation in the conflict risks eroding popular support, which has been largely passive up to this point. Even a "partial" mobilization in Fall 2022 sparked widespread displeasure, as tens of thousands of Russian men fled abroad to evade conscription. Russians are fierce defenders of the homeland, as the wars against Hitler and Napoleon made abundantly clear. They are much less enthusiastic about sacrificing and, at the extreme, dying, in wars of aggression for nebulous reasons and uncertain gains. Putin will find it difficult, if not impossible, to convince the population as a whole that Ukraine is an existential issue for Russia, and not simply for himself.

Meanwhile, elite support could wane as the focus shifts to the long-term consequences of Putin's adventure. A substantial part of the elite, perhaps a majority, is not eager to abandon Europe, and those who are,

are not necessarily eager for China's embrace – they would prefer a wider range of options that would bolster Russia's strategic autonomy. Such discontent is likely to emerge most powerfully among those a generation younger than Putin and his entourage, people who already occupy positions of some responsibility who can think ahead fifteen to twenty years and see the downsides of the course Putin has chosen. They will not abandon the idea that Russia must be a great power, but they might conclude that there are more promising ways, and leaders, to ensure that future.

At a time of immense uncertainty, the challenge for the United States is to craft a policy that can help create the domestic pressures that will bring the war in Ukraine, and likely Putin's reign, to an early end, while also laying the basis for a more constructive long-term relationship with Russia. That will require both subtlety and vision. Americans need to learn the lessons of the past thirty-plus years and then apply them wisely to current circumstances. To succeed, they will need to see Russia clearly, without ideology or sentiment, and assess their own strengths, as well as the limitations on their power, honestly.

6

Washington's Blind Spots and Missteps

No American leader who has ever dealt with Russia has claimed it is easy. Even at the best of times, Russia is a vexing partner or rival. And the first post-Soviet decades were far from the best. In the midst of a profound systemic crisis in the 1990s, Russia nevertheless insisted on being treated as a great power, if not necessarily as an equal. As it recovered in the 2000s, it was ever more insistent on respect although the asymmetry in power remained yawning.

As American officials can attest, Russia has an overblown assessment of its importance in world affairs, while it is simultaneously keenly aware of its vulnerabilities. Russia's leaders can be cocky and dismissive of smaller powers, while mired in self-doubt about their own worth. They demand a seat at the table on all major global issues even when they have little to bring to their resolution. They are much better at thwarting others' initiatives than at launching something constructive themselves. They take pleasure in being feared abroad, but deny any responsibility for creating the conditions that give rise to what they denounce as other country's Russophobic policies. Imbued with a prickly pride, Russian leaders tend to see slights where none is intended, and in any negotiation they are determined to squeeze out the last drop of blood from the other side, in part to convince themselves that they have not been swindled.

No matter what the United States' post-Cold War strategy, it would have had to navigate the contradictions of Russia's character. There were times when American leaders might have preferred simply not to engage, especially given their lack of respect for Russian power, but that was never a real option. No other country except China impacts so many issues on the American foreign-policy agenda. That was true even during the turmoil of the 1990s, even if the challenge arose from Russia's weakness rather than its strength. With its vast nuclear arsenal and its experience in building weapons of mass destruction, it is critical to strategic stability and non-proliferation. Located in the heart of Eurasia, it can project power or instability into Europe, the Middle East, and Indo-Pacific region, three of the world's four major zones of strategic importance and, with the opening of the Arctic, it could eventually have easy access to the fourth, North America. It is a leading space-faring nation and one of the most creative players in cyberspace. The United States cannot afford the luxury of ignoring Russia and, as recent events in and around Ukraine dramatically demonstrate, Russia will not allow it to.

As we saw in Chapter 1, the grand strategy the United States settled on at the end of the Cold War was the integration of Russia into the Euro-Atlantic Community as a free-market democracy. Four administrations pursued it with greater or lesser vigor until Russia's seizure of Crimea in 2014 brought this course to an abrupt end. We have examined the philosophical and political underpinnings of that strategy. The question now is why it failed.

Contingency and Purpose

Russia's invasion of Ukraine has unsurprisingly infused assessments of Washington's strategy, but not for the better. Interstate relations are a matter of action and reaction, with no long or even medium-term outcome foreordained. There are always alternative paths and multiple forks in the road. Choices have consequences. But a dramatic event turns what should be a discussion of contingencies into a teleological argument for most observers; it supposedly lays bare the essence of the main actors. History becomes the unfolding of purpose.

Putin's Russia's aggressive behavior in pursuit of imperialist goals has now become for most Western observers an immutable element of its character. It easy to find evidence in the past that reinforces this judgment. Putin rose to power after all against the background of suspicious terrorist attacks on apartment complexes in Moscow and elsewhere, which many believe were in fact the work of Russia's security services, and a subsequent brutal war in Chechnya. Putin's Russia has launched large-scale cyber attacks against the West, starting with one that temporarily shut down key Estonian government websites in 2007. It fought a war against Georgia in 2008, seized Crimea and destabilized Ukraine in 2014, and joined the Syrian regime's inhumane suppression of rebel forces in 2015. Arguably, the latest invasion of Ukraine is just the logical flowering of the character of Putin's Russia.

Post-Cold War US policy is now assessed in the light of the unfolding of malign Russian purpose. Critics fault administrations for failing to take timely steps to deter Russia's aggressions. Efforts to find areas of cooperation, or hopes for constructive relations, let alone strategic partnership, are derided as woefully naive, as Russia was always laying plans for future conquest. What was needed was more vigorous measures to punish Russia for past transgressions and contain its malevolent instincts. Absent that, Russia's appetite only grew at an accelerating pace, leading naturally to the unprovoked attack on Ukraine. In this light, the effort to integrate Russia in the Euro-Atlantic Community was misguided from the start. The task was rather to build defenses against the inevitable return of an aggressive, expansionist Russia, to contain it, and to integrate Europe against Russia. In other words, the hedges should have been the core policy. This is in essence the position of many Poles, Balts, and Ukrainians today.

Defenders of American policy, often former senior administration officials, reject the accusation of naivety. Policymakers were, they argue, well aware of the noxious elements in the Russian character but, nevertheless, offered Moscow opportunities through integration to advance its interests in more legitimate, benign ways (though the American version of Russia's national interests was not necessarily Russia's). But Moscow refused America's entreaties, thus conveniently for administration backers absolving Washington of any responsibility for its rival's actions. The defenders thus agree with the critics on one essential point: Russia is the source of the problem, not the United States.[1]

There is, however, a third, very much minority, school of thought that puts the onus for the deterioration in relations and Russia's aggressions at Washington's doorstep. Despite Russia's assault on Ukraine, adherents, mostly realists, resist the notion that Russia is unusually aggressive among major powers. Rather, in their view, the original sin was the American decision at Cold War's end to expand NATO eastward up to Russia's very borders – the hedge was indeed the essence of the policy; talk of integration was little more than soothing rhetoric to conceal a power play. Any great power, the argument goes, would resist the advance of a rival power's military alliance to its borders, no matter what the latter's profession of peaceful intent. How would the United States have reacted to the Warsaw Pact's extension of membership to Canada, had the Soviet Union won the Cold War? While not justifying Russia's invasion of Ukraine, this school does argue that it is understandable as a response to American provocations.[2]

None of these three positions will do as a considered critique of post-Cold War US–Russia policy, though each captures a bit of the truth. The task is to understand how the implementation of a specific strategy interacted with Russian realities to yield the trajectory that relations have traversed in the past thirty-plus years, and to consider alternative paths that could have led to more desirable outcomes. If the goal is to improve US policy, the focus should be on identifying the flaws, or blind spots, in the original strategic design. Was there something in their mindset that caused American policymakers to conceptualize the problem of Russia inappropriately? What issues about Russia that they should have known did American leaders fail to factor into policy? What were the unknowables that would have blindsided even the most diligent policymaker? Where was execution of policy counterproductive?

This critique should not be taken as an effort to absolve Russia of its considerable share of responsibility for today's confrontation. Its actions, at times gratuitous, have undermined trust, eroded cooperation, and sharpened conflicts. But Washington's policy should not be judged by the intensity of the challenges posed by the other side or its irresponsible, malign behavior, but rather by the degree to which it advanced US interests even in the face of such adversity. The wise policymaker takes into account the other side's character, its goals and motivation, and its capabilities and plans accordingly. Strategy fails not because of the nature of the problem but because it was inappropriate, ill-designed, or poorly executed.

Integration Fails: Misconceptions and Missteps

The goal of integrating Russia into the Euro-Atlantic Community was not necessarily unrealistic, but the timeframe certainly was. Domestic US political exigencies – the constant pressure arising from short electoral cycles to produce immediate positive results – required a generational process to be compressed into a matter of years. That was not going to happen. The Soviet collapse was not the result of a democratic revolution, as the prevailing Western narrative would have it, but rather of an elite struggle that pitted Soviet leader Mikhail Gorbachev against Russian President Boris Yeltsin. Yeltsin prevailed, with the critical backing of officers in both the military and special services, and not simply on a wave of popular support.

The result was that the upper echelon of the Soviet elites was stripped away, to be replaced by Russia's second and third echelons. The latter may have avowed their desire to change Russia into a "normal country" along Western lines but, in fact, they shared the same fundamental attitude about the state as the departed upper echelon: They saw the national interest in its preservation as a great power in its traditional guise, even as newly minted "entrepreneurs" and local bosses privatized state assets, including industries critical to Russian power, such as oil and gas enterprises, steel factories, and defense industries. This stratum had little interest in integrating into the West on American terms, even if initially they hoped for Western backing in rebuilding Russia. Their influence on foreign and security policy and domestic politics was to grow steadily throughout the 1990s and then at an accelerated pace, once Putin had been elevated to the presidency.[3]

The success of America policy would have thus required the elites to abandon their political traditions and national mission, to build a new Russia liberated from its past, in short order. American leaders did not discount that possibility: Both the German and Japanese elites had done so in the process of national renewal under American tutelage at the end of the Second World War. But Russia was not a defeated country in the eyes of the elites, no matter what the prevailing view in the West, nor was it occupied and compelled to rebuild under the watchful eyes of the Western powers. Communism, admittedly, had demonstrated that it could not meet the challenges of the late twentieth century. It lost the struggle with liberal democracy. But Russia's leaders believed, not without reason, that they had played the crucial role in bringing down the communist system in Russia and elsewhere in Eastern Europe. They were thus among the victors, not the vanquished; Russia remained a great power, even if it was a bit down in its luck, going through a deep crisis as it overcame the Soviet legacy.

The crisis would eventually dissipate, in the elites' view, and Russia would reclaim its status as a great power with its fundamental character intact, as it had done repeatedly in the past. This Russia would be prepared to be a co-equal partner with the United States in managing global affairs – that was the import of Yeltsin's extending a "hand of friendship to the people of America . . . to join us in partnership in the quest for freedom and justice in the twenty-first century" in his address to a joint session of Congress in 1992.[4] What Russia would not accept is being a junior partner in backing a US-led system that it believes fails to give due account to its interests.

Nonetheless, at least until Putin's infamous address in Munich in 2007, this elite saw Russia as a part of European civilization. Integration could not be imposed on American terms, however; it would have to be negotiated in all its political, economic, and security aspects. Russia would have to be persuaded that it would benefit from any proposed arrangements – and that could only happen if Russia were integrally involved in designing them. Given the complexity of the challenges the West and Russia faced, that would take time.

But Washington was impatient to make progress; it had the power to force developments; and it saw multiplying challenges to security in Eastern Europe, particularly in the Balkans, where Serb nationalism was sparking conflict throughout the former Yugoslavia. Time was the one thing Washington believed it had in short supply. And so it pressed the pace of reform in Russia against a reluctant elite, which eventually rebelled. In 1996, Yeltsin replaced the pro-Western Andrey Kozyrev as foreign minister with Yevgeny Primakov, a veteran of the Soviet national security apparatus, who energetically promoted the idea of a multipolar world in opposition to "American hegemony."

Clinton Tarnishes Democracy

There was thus a major, perhaps fatal, flaw in the organizing concept of post-Cold War strategy. Each American administration in its own way then misstepped in executing it, discrediting the very idea of Western-styled free-market democracy inside Russia and debasing the value of integration.

The Clinton administration bears the greatest responsibility, since it launched the strategy of integration in earnest. Surveying the challenges of the transition, it decided to prioritize economic reform. Turning around the country's economic fortunes, it believed, would help build popular support for the reformist government; the institutionalization of private property and the eventual emergence of a middle class would lay a solid foundation for a future democratic polity. Operating on this assumption, the administration threw its weight behind Boris Yeltsin and a small group of "young reformers" committed to fast-paced radical economic reform, or shock therapy, as it was known at the time.

To support the reform effort, the administration funded an extensive assistance program to advise on economic and political policy and teach Russians the skills they would need to thrive in a free-market democracy. From the beginning, the effort suffered from serious flaws in design and execution, some inevitable from the way the US government manages the funding of assistance worldwide. Money did not go directly to Russians, but rather to American entities, which would design the programs and then work with Russians in implementing them. The result was that much less money was injected into Russia than the headline figures would have suggested, a major disappointment for Russian elites. Fueling further frustration in Russia, programs were often implemented by well-meaning American volunteers and professionals with an inadequate understanding of Russian conditions.

Moreover, because American organizations competed for the assistance money, the range of programs tended to reflect American concerns more closely than Russian needs. American non-governmental organizations (NGOs), pledged to overcoming the injustices in a mature free-market democracy, took their concerns and programs to a country that was in desperate need of the basic building blocks of such a polity. The programs built support for the assistance effort in the United States, but less so in Russia. In many cases, the Russian recipients of American largess became dependent on continued US funding to survive because they never developed a sufficient local constituency, so far removed were they from the immediate socio-economic challenges facing Russia.

As it supported economic reform with advice and assistance, Clinton's team not only paid less attention to promoting democracy but also took steps that they knew would jeopardize democratic reform, at least in the short run. No matter how necessary the economic reforms might be in the administration's estimation, they were deeply unpopular, not least because of the inevitable economic dislocation they initially caused.

Substantial majorities in the Congress of People's Deputies (until it was disbanded in 1993) and then the State Duma, both elected in the freest and fairest elections ever held in Russia, rejected the government's reform program.

When in 1995 Russians elected a Duma opposed to the government's policies – the prime minister's party came in a dismal third with ten percent of the vote – the prime minister and his government stayed in place and their program was left substantially unchanged. The government, with the Clinton administration's encouragement, simply circumvented the Duma in designing and implementing further reforms. The unintended message thus sent to Russians was that elections did not matter – which was indeed the case, at least as far as policy was concerned. Shortly thereafter, Washington grossly interfered in Russia's presidential election to ensure that Yeltsin defeated his communist rival, providing direct support to his campaign and turning a blind eye to its flagrant violation of spending limits and other regulations to ensure his victory. Another unintended message was thus sent: the United States cared little about Russian democracy when its own interests were at stake.

The ruble collapse in the Summer of 1998 left Clinton's strategy of integration in a shambles. Economic reform faltered, and democracy had been discredited. In the eyes of most Russians, Washington's clear and open support for Yeltsin and the young reformers linked it directly to the deep systemic crisis Russia suffered in the 1990s. Years later that made it easy for Putin to argue that the United States had never really been interested in Russia's revival as a free-market democracy but rather had advised and assisted the Russian government in pursuing policies it knew would keep Russia weak.

Bush Alienates Putin

The Bush team was much less invested in reform in Russia, certainly during its first years, even if it needed to claim that Russia was making progress to maintain public support for cooperative relations. It did not push back with much vigor, as the Kremlin requested that certain US assistance programs close up shop or cracked down on foreign-funded NGOs engaged in political activity. It was concerned by the state's reassertion of a major role in commercial enterprises, especially in strategic sectors such as oil, but expressed little displeasure and did nothing to counteract it.

While Putin's authoritarian tendencies were visible from his first days as president, it is also true that Bush's policies persuaded him to accelerate the tightening of the screws domestically and perhaps to go further than he had originally intended. Washington's vocal support for color revolutions in Georgia and Ukraine did not sit well with the Kremlin, which saw them as rehearsals for regime change in Russia itself, especially as the administration slowly, but reluctantly, began to criticize Russia for backsliding on democratic reform in some areas. The articulation of the Freedom Agenda as the key to defeating international terrorism fueled suspicions of American intent when it was applied to Russia itself, and other non-democratic members of the counterterrorism coalition, such as China. Bush's declaration that the United States' goal was to end tyranny in the world only encouraged the Kremlin to reinforce authoritarian practices it saw as essential to opposing American encroachments on its sovereignty.

Bush's war on terror served as a further impediment to Russia's integration, even as the two countries touted their counterterrorist partnership. While the Kremlin was supporting the American effort against al-Qaida and the Taliban in and around Afghanistan, it was also waging a brutal war against Chechen rebels in the Caucasus. Moscow considered all the rebels to be terrorists – terrorism, separatism, and extremism were tightly intertwined in Russian doctrine – and expected, if not direct American backing, then no efforts to thwart its campaign to crush the rebellion.

Washington, however, was at best ambivalent, arguing that some of the rebels were moderates with legitimate grievances, which should serve as the basis for negotiations. Never mind that they in fact had ties with forces the United States considered terrorists, and the mantra from Washington since 9/11 was that you are either with us or the terrorists. That the United States, and several European countries, permitted Chechen leaders in exile to operate freely and even raise funds on its territory, and refused to crack down on rebel websites on the grounds that would violate the right to free speech, was, not surprisingly, seen as an unforgivable act of betrayal by the Kremlin. Washington would have hardly countenanced such tender treatment for al-Qaida operatives. This was a Freedom Agenda the Kremlin wanted no part of.

Arguably, the United States was right to support democratic movements that ousted authoritarian regimes in the former Soviet space and to resist labeling all Chechen rebels as terrorists, particularly given the long history of Russian oppression of national minorities in the North Caucasus. But the point is that given a choice between a rigid interpretation of its principles and Russian concerns, Washington chose the former. The Kremlin was understandably outraged, since previously Washington had no qualms about compromising its democratic principles to advance its interests inside Russia or in the fight against terrorists elsewhere in the world. In its view, Washington was determined not to defend its principles, but rather to keep Russia down.

Obama Undermines Medvedev

Obama pursued integration with less energy than his two predecessors. Transforming Russia's domestic politics was not a central part of his vision, which was more focused on security matters. Moreover, Medvedev's steps to open up the political system after Putin's authoritarian measures meant there was less to criticize. The task was rather to encourage the Russian president to continue down the path he had chosen. Where Obama faltered was in not foreseeing the impact in Russia of the morphing of the UN-authorized intervention in Libya to protect civilians into a regime change operation that ended in the brutal assassination of the strongman Gaddafi. Putin had had qualms about Medvedev's decision to abstain in the UN Security Council vote authorizing the mission. The transformation of the mission and Gaddafi's fate only turned those qualms into grave doubts about Medvedev's fitness to continue serving as president. In the end, it almost certainly played a key role in Putin's decision to reclaim the presidency. His return, as we saw in Chapter 4, spelled the ultimate demise of any Russian desire to integrate into the Euro-Atlantic Community, even if it took his seizure of Crimea two years later to convince Washington that its grand strategy had failed irretrievably.

Imagination Fails: Hedging the Way to Failure

The flaws in the design and execution of the integration strategy were compounded by US policymakers' inability to imagine a Russia that wasn't either aspiring to emulate the United States or reviving the worst version of its historical self, that is, the Soviet Union. From Washington's standpoint, if Russia was not going to become a free-market democracy, then it would inevitably revert to being an authoritarian, imperial state and implacable foe. The former image was essential to the grand strategy of integrating Russia into the Euro-Atlantic Community; the latter called for rigorous hedges against Russian recidivism and its marginalization in world affairs. The former was informed by the triumphalism of the Cold War victory, by the belief in the end of history; the latter was shaped by Cold War memories and the rivalry that had defined US–Russian relations for most of the twentieth century. Excluded was a middle option between these two extremes that would have left Russia short of being fully integrated into Europe yet still an acceptable partner.

These two irreconcilable future Russias existed simultaneously in the minds of American policymakers at the dawn of the post-Soviet era and continued to coexist, albeit with the growing dominance of the malevolent historical Russia, until Washington abandoned its grand strategy of Euro-Atlantic integration. The holding of two opposing ideas in the mind while retaining the ability to function might be a sign of a first-rate intelligence, as F. Scott Fitzgerald avowed, but it makes for bad policy. Throughout, this cognitive duality gave American policy a schizophrenic cast. While Washington was loudly declaring its commitment to Russia's integration, its relentless hedging was driving Russia farther away from Europe. The Kremlin quite naturally paid less attention to the rhetoric than to the deeds.

While the Clinton, George W. Bush, and Obama administrations all suffered from this duality, they did so in varying degrees. It was most glaring in Clinton's, which at the very beginning made building an "alliance with Russian reform" its top priority and crafted an assistance program to accelerate Russia's European integration. But less than two years later, it was promoting NATO expansion as a long-term process that would end at Russia's borders, even if it did not acknowledge that publicly. In other words, it was pushing Russia out of Europe, although its declared strategy was integrating it into Europe.

Bush's team, no matter what the public record and intensity of contacts during the first years in office, tended toward the recidivist image. They too pursued practical policies at odds with their rhetoric. To be sure, unlike their predecessors, they never put Russia at the center of their foreign policy. Their goals were more limited: They wanted to keep Russia on side in the struggle against international terrorism, while working with it in securing its nuclear weapons to keep them out of the hands of terrorists. Yet that did not deter them from actively seeking to erode Russia's presence in the former Soviet space, which Moscow considered essential to its security and prosperity. The administration was unhelpful on Chechnya, backed anti-Russian forces in Georgia and Ukraine, and raised its profile in Central Asia with little regard to Russia's interests. While the declared policy continued to be one of integrating Russia, the practical policy was aimed at pushing back against Russia in Eurasia to prevent the reemergence of a threat of Soviet dimensions.

The Obama administration suffered least from this duality, perhaps because Russia mattered least to it. While it still wanted to integrate Russia into Europe, it saw no great urgency, nor was it particularly worried by Russian recidivism, in part because of Obama's own low opinion of Russian power. Of the three administrations, it initially came closest to treating Russia like just another great power, with which some cooperation was possible and competition inevitable. But the image of a malevolent Russia gained prominence when Putin reclaimed the presidency, and the duality became moot with Russia's seizure of Crimea in 2014.

Locking Russia out of Europe

Overall, the exaggerated concern about recidivism led to tougher, less flexible hedges than necessary. Whenever Russia did something that Washington found untoward – the two brutal wars in Chechnya, repeated crackdowns on opposition forces in Russia, interference in Georgia and Ukraine, and so on – pressure mounted to "lock in the gains" to consolidate the base for the further advance of American interests as opportunities presented themselves and to complicate any future reassertion of Russian power.

Locking in the gains in the waning days of the Cold War, as Secretary of State James Baker urged, might have then made sense. Gorbachev's capitulation to Soviet hardliners could have had catastrophic consequences for American interests when the anti-Soviet revolutions in Eastern Europe were far from consolidated, hundreds of thousands of Soviet troops remained stationed in the region, the Soviet Union had a vast nuclear arsenal, and the country was in turmoil. So it was critical to reunite Germany as fast as possible inside NATO and start the process of Soviet troop withdrawals from Eastern Europe. Any step that would reduce the residual power the hardliners might acquire was in America's interests. But rushing to lock in the gains in the years after the Cold War's end made less sense. Russia's glaring weakness and myriad domestic ills rendered infinitely less dangerous any communist or nationalist assumption of power in Moscow.

Nevertheless, at no point did Washington give serious thought to taking a step back and reassessing how it might help Russia deal with its legitimate interests in ways that were compatible with its own. Indeed, the United States barely acknowledged that Russia had legitimate interests, and those, it believed, could not be properly articulated by an increasingly authoritarian state. In the ultimate expression of hubris, Washington believed that it understood Russia's interests better than the Kremlin did and could more reliably identify the threats. And so Washington pressed on, despite Kremlin objections. As a former American ambassador to Russia, William J. Burns, has noted, "Restraint and compromise seemed unappealing and unnecessary, given our strength and sense of mission."[5]

This rigid, self-satisfying posture was on full display in the United States' approach to Russian interests in Europe and the former Soviet space. Here Washington erected the most formidable hedges against Russia turning bad and, in the process, radically increased the chances that it would.

In Europe, the central question was the future security architecture now that the Cold War confrontation had ended and the Soviet Union had disappeared. The United States predictably wanted to build on the foundation of NATO, the organization that anchored its presence on the continent and reduced the risk of interstate conflict. The issue of expansion was on the table from the dying days of the Cold War. Germany had been reunified in NATO, a first step in that process. The

Soviet Union's former satellites, especially the so-called Visegrad Four (the Czech Republic, Hungary, Poland, and Slovakia), were pressing for membership, as were the Baltic states and Ukraine. They all urgently sought Article 5 guarantees of their security against Russia. The Russians were adamantly opposed; moreover, they believed that they had assurances from key Western leaders that NATO would not expand eastward after German reunification.[6]

Washington debated how to reconcile the competing strategic interests, and in 1994 settled on launching the so-called Partnership for Peace. The program would enable East European countries to establish some affiliation with NATO, which would develop habits of security cooperation and interoperability, with the possibility of future membership after a prolonged period of military and political reform. No new line would be drawn in Europe to divide US-friendly states from hostile ones. The solution was not ideal, but, as the Cold War historian M.E. Sarotte has argued, it managed to minimally satisfy the East Europeans and the Balts and engaged Ukrainians in a way that did not provoke the Russians, while keeping US options open. "This is a brilliant idea, it is a stroke of genius," Yeltsin exclaimed when the partnership was first sketched out for him.[7]

But no sooner had the Partnership been announced than it began to unravel. Proponents of NATO expansion inside the bureaucracy continued to plot against it. Clumsy Russian behavior – Moscow insisted it should have a special status because of its military power and nuclear arsenal – cooled Washington's enthusiasm.[8] By the end of the year, at American urging, NATO formally opened the door to expansion. By 1997, the Alliance had issued its first invitations to Poland, the Czech Republic, and Hungary, which formally joined in 1999. Attention then quickly turned to a second wave. As for Russia, Washington promoted "an alliance with the Alliance," a clear indication that it was barred from membership. A dividing line began to emerge.

By the beginning of his second term, President Clinton had given strategic preference to Eastern Europe over Russia. The "alliance with the Alliance" predictably never achieved much. The Permanent Joint Council and its successor, the NATO–Russia Council, both intended to give Russia a voice in but not a veto over NATO decisions, never mollified Moscow; they fell far short of the key role in European affairs it aspired to. It never embraced those fora and used its mission to NATO more as an intelligence collection platform than as instruments for serious consultation and diplomacy, and that posture only further encouraged Washington to hedge against Russian recidivism. The result was a vicious circle that eroded trust and confirmed each side in its suspicions of the other.

US policy that had begun with President George H.W. Bush's aspiration to build a Europe "whole and free" ultimately sought to achieve that goal by excluding Russia from Europe. Sarotte got it right: The basic Cold War architecture for European security survived and was reinforced, with the important difference that the dividing line had moved hundreds of miles eastward from the center of Germany to Russia's own borders.[9]

Undermining Russia in the Former Soviet Space

From Moscow's perspective, NATO's eastward expansion dovetailed with an even more alarming threat – a concerted, multi-pronged American effort to erode Russia's presence in the former Soviet space. The evidence was everywhere, beginning with the admission of the Baltic states into NATO in 2004. Moscow was hardly happy, but it acquiesced – the Balts had always occupied a special place in the Russian imagination as the most European-oriented of its territories. But Washington's push to bring Ukraine and Georgia into NATO crossed a "bright red line."[10] These two states were critical to Russia's position in Europe and the Caucasus. But this step was only part and parcel of a far greater American encroachment on Russia's strategic space. Since the mid 1990s, Washington was working actively with Azerbaijan, Kazakhstan, and, to a lesser extent, Turkmenistan to construct oil and gas pipelines out of the Caspian Basin to European markets that circumvented Russian territory. In the 2000s, it abused Moscow's green-lighting of its military presence in Central Asia to prosecute the war in Afghanistan to strengthen its ties with Uzbekistan and Kyrgyzstan at Moscow's expense. It repeatedly thwarted Moscow's efforts to resolve the Transnistrian conflict in ways that would preserve, if not enhance, its influence in Moldova.

These concrete steps were a continuation of the policy that had been launched at the end of the Cold War to impede the reemergence of a threat of Soviet dimensions in Eurasia. As we saw in Chapter 1, that entailed enhancing the independence of all the former Soviet states and eroding Moscow's influence in the region. Washington was quick to recognize their independence and facilitate their admission to the United Nations, first steps in complicating any Russian effort to reassert its influence. Thereafter, Washington steadfastly refused to recognize any institutional arrangement among the former Soviet states devised in Moscow, starting with the Commonwealth of Independent States (CIS) but eventually including the Collective Security Treaty Organization (CSTO) and the Eurasian Economic Union. It made little difference to Washington that for the most part former Soviet states were not coerced into joining but rather did so voluntarily on the basis of local assessments of their interests. Ukraine and Georgia stood out as the glaring exceptions, intent on attenuating political and economic ties to Moscow and moving closer to Europe and the United States. Washington, however, wrongly generalized their discontent to the former Soviet space as a whole.

As with Europe, the issue here is not whether the United States should have abandoned its interests in the former Soviet space in deference to the Kremlin's sensitivities, but rather whether there was another way of advancing them that would not have provoked an increasingly hostile reaction from Moscow. Could Washington have nourished ties between NATO and the CSTO that would have legitimated the latter organization in return for its acceptance of a NATO and US military presence in Central Asia? Could it have encouraged US–Russian joint ventures in Central Asia that could in time serve as counterbalances to China's rapid commercial penetration of the region? Could the United States have promoted a North–South corridor from Russia through Central Asia to India that could have competed with the East–West corridor China hoped to build through the region to Europe as part of the Belt and Road Initiative? Was there a way to foster constructive political and economic ties between Russia and Ukraine that would not have eroded the latter's independence?

More broadly, was there a way of slowing down the pace of geopolitical change in the former Soviet space that would have created more time to build a solid foundation for US–Russian relations that might have been better able to withstand the inevitable stresses of a shifting geopolitical landscape? Or, if there had been the will, could Washington have used continuing Russian influence in the region to help create stable structures of peace and prosperity in Eastern Europe, the Caucasus, and Central Asia? We will never know, because Washington was not inclined to think in such terms, when the image of an imperialist, authoritarian, traditional Russia cast a dark shadow over policymaking.

Strategic Partnership a Non-Starter

American missteps in integrating Russia into the Euro-Atlantic Community and its relentless hedging in Europe and Eurasia drained the dream of strategic partnership of vitality. But, truth be told, strategic partnership was never in the cards, barring an inconceivable radical change in the way the United States or Russia thought about its security and mission in the world – inconceivable at least from the moment the end-of-history fantasy dissipated. As we showed in Chapter 2, the two powers were both inherently expansionist for reasons that put them on a collision course. Russia's search for security inevitably clashed with America's calling to spread "universal" democratic values across the globe. It would prove impossible to reconcile diverging geopolitical and ideological ambitions to agree on a broad set of shared values to undergird strategic partnership. The tension surfaced undeniably in the late nineteenth century and grew in intensity until the collapse of the Soviet Union toward the end of the twentieth. A fleeting hope for different relations vanished as Russia regained its strength in the 2000s and sought to reassert its global prerogatives.

Inherent tension did not, however, preclude constructive relations. Tension marks most great-power relationships, which are inevitably a mix of cooperation and competition. Why couldn't the United States and a resurgent Russia under Putin build such a relationship?

There were two main obstacles. First, the United States would have had to consider itself a normal great power. That would mean turning its back on the last 100 years during which it has positioned itself as a great power like no other, one that does not simply advance its own parochial national interests but works for the benefit of the world as a whole. Second, the United States would have had to put to the side its dueling images of Russia to acknowledge the possibility of a third variant, which in fact would be Russia as the normal great power its leaders consider it to be. These two steps would have opened up the possibility for trade-offs and compromises that lie at the core of constructive great-power politics.

Washington, however, has been unprepared to take either step since the end of the Cold War. The United States became the "indispensable nation" during the Clinton years and has remained so in American eyes except for a brief interlude under President Trump. And Washington's image of Russia as an aggressor nation has hardened since Putin assumed power, except for a short respite during Medvedev's presidency, granted usually in response to actual acts of Russian aggression. In these circumstances, trade-offs are seen as unacceptable compromises of principle and any concessions to Russian interests as reprehensible acts of appeasement. Moreover, the vast asymmetry in power and fortune to this day has led Washington to insist on its preferred outcomes, confident Russia would eventually relent,[11] which was generally the case, until Russia's war against Georgia in 2008.

Had the United States been prepared to treat Russia as a normal great power, a path might have opened up to more enduring constructive relations. The robust hedging in Europe and the former Soviet space would have been dispensed with, and new security arrangements could have been worked out in a less fevered atmosphere. In particular, it might have proved possible to ease the geopolitical competition over Ukraine, enabling it to build productive ties with Russia and Europe simultaneously, while focusing on its internal developments. Russia's reentry into the Middle East could have been handled in a way that reinforced a local equilibrium of power rather than exacerbated tensions, as it has in recent years. And, perhaps most important, Washington could have pursued a policy toward Russia that did not drive it into China's embrace.

Missed Opportunity

Of all the post-Cold War presidents, George W. Bush was best positioned to put relations on an enduring constructive path. During the 1990s, Russia was simply in too much disarray for Clinton to take it seriously as a partner. After Russia's war on Georgia in 2008, the path was set for the steady erosion of relations, despite Obama's efforts with Medvedev. And

Putin himself was bent on challenging American "unilateralism" and "hegemony" when he returned to the Kremlin in 2012.

But the first two to three years of the Bush administration offered a unique opportunity for better relations. Putin himself wanted to forge closer ties with the country he considered the preeminent world power by a wide margin – he saw that as the quickest path to Russia's return as a great power. He restored order to the Russian political system and engineered an economic recovery that would enable Russia to make a contribution, initially small, but real nonetheless, to resolving common problems with the United States, most importantly in the battle against international terrorism. Yet, the Bush team was never willing to make a genuine bet on Russia, to test its bona fides when it came to improved relations, despite the fact that the asymmetry in power was so great that if Russia had acted in bad faith, the United States could have easily recouped its losses.

In Afghanistan, for example, once the Taliban had been overthrown, the United States refused the Russian offer of strategic airlift to help ferry material into the Bagram airbase just outside Kabul and showed little interest in Russian engagement in restoring the country's infrastructure, much of which had earlier been built by the Soviet Union. The concern was that Russia would disrupt American initiatives, even though Moscow had earlier provided intelligence that was instrumental to the swift American victory over al-Qaida and their Taliban hosts. But, if Russia had continued to be constructive, it might have been possible to work with it to build a trade corridor from Russia through Afghanistan to India, which could have competed with China's future Belt and Road Initiative. Washington was unwilling to take the chance.

Similarly, in the NATO–Russia Council, the United States, with the support of East and Central European allies – insisted that allies agree in advance on a common NATO approach before sitting down with the Russians, although the Council had been sold to Moscow as a forum in which Russia and the allies would meet as equals. The fear was that if allies were allowed to advance national positions, Russia would see an opportunity to sow division inside the alliance. But if the United States had dropped the unanimity rule and Russia had reacted in a constructive fashion, that would have likely opened up new vistas for NATO–Russia cooperation and eased some of Moscow's concerns about expansion. But, once again, Washington was unwilling to run the risk, so engrained were the images of a malevolent Russia.[12]

Russia Policy in the Docket

After a quarter century, the grand strategy to integrate Russia into the Euro-Atlantic Community as a free-market democracy was unceremoniously jettisoned in favor of incipient containment. It had foundered on the curious contradictions in American thinking about Russia. For US policymakers, Russia was either an infinitely malleable construct or an impenetrable mass. In their hubris, they thought they could refashion a centuries-old profoundly conservative, authoritarian country into a Western liberal democracy in a relatively short historical span, while at the same time they felt helpless to prevent Russia from reverting to the most dangerous version of its historical self. They shamelessly interfered in Russian domestic politics, laying the seeds for a powerful backlash of resentment whenever Russia recovered, as it most assuredly would.[13] And they hedged so aggressively against Russia's going bad that they shattered their own effort at integration. Indeed, from Moscow's perspective, and not without reason, the hedge was Washington's genuine policy, the marginalization of Russia in Europe the true goal, only thinly veiled in soothing, but deeply hypocritical, rhetoric about partnership and integration.

Washington steadfastly refused to deal with Russia as a great power, whose interests had to be respected. It never had sufficient regard for its might, persuaded that it was in secular decline, if still a noisome troublemaker. In response to Russia's insistence that it remained a great power, Washington was prepared to mollify it with symbolic gestures. It brought it into the G-8 although it hardly measured up to the Western industrialized democratic powers. It preserved the quartet (the United States, European Union, United Nations, and Russia) for the Middle East Peace Process although Moscow had little influence in the region. And it held regular summit meetings and issued joint statements. committing the two countries to joint efforts on a range of matters. But Washington always made sure that it gained everything it needed in substance. Russia appreciated the symbolism, but its inability to effect policy in a serious way only nourished its resentment, especially as it slowly recovered.

Russia gave up on the integration project long before Washington did. It adopted a more bellicose posture, while Washington was still speaking of partnership. It thus bears a share of the responsibility for the deterioration in relations. It was nevertheless the American strategy that failed, because it could not grasp the reality of the Russia it was dealing with.

Who is to Blame?

Yet the failed integration strategy, and the increased tension in relations, still falls far short of the complete rupture that defines relations today. In the immediate aftermath of Russia's seizure of Crimea in 2014, the two countries continued to cooperate on matters of top priority to the United States – strategic stability, non-proliferation of weapons of mass destruction, and counterterrorism. European security was not in jeopardy, as Russia and the West sought ways to defuse tensions. Today, cooperation has vanished, with only minor exceptions, such as the operation of the international space station, and European security hangs in the balance as Russia wages a brutal war against Ukraine.

Was this rupture inevitable? And, if not, who or what bears responsibility – Russian and American political cultures, Putin's ambitions, or US policy?

We can easily dismiss political cultures. To be sure, geopolitical circumstances and historical experiences produced two expansionary powers, which inevitably clashed as the United States extended its geopolitical reach to the Eurasian supercontinent. Since the late nineteenth century, tension has waxed and waned, but never entirely disappeared. And it will not disappear, barring an improbable dramatic transformation in one or both countries' national character, mission, and purpose. The ardent American hope that Russia was on verge of such change at the end of the Cold War turned out to be a chimera, as the core features of historical Russia slowly but ineluctably reemerged.

This inherent tension may rule out strategic partnership, but it does not preclude constructive relations, if it is managed with skill and foresight. In this regard, US–Russian relations are no different from other great-power relationships. In short, policy matters. The choices made in Moscow and Washington either ease or exacerbate the strains and stresses.

Until Putin returned to the Kremlin as president in 2012, it was US policy that enflamed relations, even as Washington talked of integration and partnership. Putin's determination to reassert Russia's prerogatives as a great power posed serious challenges, of course, but the United States was by far the superior power. It drove relations; Russia reacted, using what power it had in an effort to compel the United States to heed its interests.

Putin's fulminations notwithstanding, it was not primarily NATO expansion that fed Russian resentment. Putin had, after all, acquiesced in the second post-Cold War wave in 2004, even though it included the former Soviet Baltic states. He only resorted to force to stymie further expansion when it threatened Russia's core interests in the former Soviet space, starting with US pressure in 2008 to bring Ukraine and Georgia into the Alliance. That US effort came after a series of steps by the Bush administration described above, which Moscow rightly considered designed to erode its influence in a region where its preeminence was essential to its geopolitical heft and standing as a great power. That was the goal of the hedge after all.

It was thus provocative US policies in the former Soviet space that poisoned relations. And they were unnecessary from the standpoint of US interests, even if Washington was right to be concerned about the Russian recidivism in the long term. In its own assessment, Russia was weak. The rest of the former Soviet space was in disarray. Even a continuing major Russian presence would do nothing to enhance its power in the short or medium term, and certainly not to a level that would threaten US interests in a region of secondary importance to the United States. Nor would it have enabled Moscow to act effectively further afield to jeopardize US goals.

In these circumstances, Washington could have moved with greater deliberation, and with more regard to Russian interests, with the goal of building trust and laying the foundation for more enduring constructive relations. If Washington had been less intent on consolidating its gains as quickly as possible and pressing its advantage at a time of Russian weakness, more attuned to Russian interests and sensitivities, it could have given Moscow more time to adjust to new geopolitical realities, to see the benefits of constructive engagement in advancing Russian well-being and security, and thus perhaps eased its concerns about its place in the world.

In practical terms, a US approach to Chechen rebels more in line with the way it treated terrorist abettors, such as the Taliban, could have fostered broader counterterrorism cooperation. Along with a less triumphalist reaction to the color revolutions in Georgia, Ukraine, and Kyrgyzstan, it could have eased Moscow's fears that Washington was intent on regime change in Russia itself. That, in turn, might have induced Moscow to refrain from a growing campaign against Russian civil society, especially those entities with good working relations with Western counterparts.

Restraint on NATO expansion into Ukraine and Georgia, which, in any event, key allies opposed, would likely have averted Russia's war against Georgia and lessened the geopolitical competition over Ukraine that only hampered that country's development. In the end, it is even conceivable that Putin would not have returned to the Kremlin, and events might not have spiraled downward to Russia's assault on Ukraine in 2014. A second Medvedev term would have likely reinforced the basis for constructive relations. But this path was not taken.

US policy thus drove relations to the estrangement of 2014. But the path forward did not inevitably lead to the war in Ukraine and a complete rupture in relations. That was more the result of Putin's burgeoning ambitions and messianic delusions.

The failure of its post-Cold War grand strategy left Washington adrift, without a well-formulated Russia policy. Russia, by contrast, moved on to the offensive and began to drive relations, as it sought to blunt and then reverse what it saw as US encroachments on its interests. Putin was encouraged by the seizure of Crimea, which proceeded almost flawlessly and caught Washington flatfooted. So did the incursion into Syria in 2015. The cost Putin paid for these actions in relations with the West was insignificant.

So, the Russian ruler pressed forward against what he saw as an increasingly decadent West. Russia flagrantly interfered in the 2016 US presidential elections. Brazen murders or attempted murders of Russian "traitors" in the West, including with banned nerve agents; widespread interference in the West's domestic affairs aimed at exacerbating societal rifts and discrediting democratic practices; cyber attacks on critical infrastructure; substantive violations of arms control agreement – all those measures only accelerated the downward spiral in relations, until Putin, with misplaced confidence, sent Russian forces into Ukraine in February 2022.

It was Putin's descent into messianic delusions, his abandonment of Russia's traditional realpolitik and his own earlier pragmatism, that produced the rupture with the United States. Washington undoubtedly could have reacted more forcefully and effectively to the mounting challenge, but it was Putin who exercised the initiative and shaped the trajectory of relations.

Implications for Containment

With the integration strategy discredited and Putin doubling down on Ukraine, the United States is challenged with developing a new approach to Russia for what promises to be a prolonged period of adversity. The measures that the Obama administration put in place – suspension of "business as usual," scaled back diplomatic contacts, economic and diplomatic sanctions, enhanced deterrence – were sharpened and expanded by Trump officials and then reinforced and reshaped into a policy of hard-edged containment by the Biden administration. But the United States still lacks a well-defined Russia strategy. In particular, it lacks a vision of future US–Russian relations toward which it is striving. Thwarting Russia's designs on Ukraine or its steps to upend the rules-based international order is a worthy goal, but it says little about the desired end state for relations in a rapidly changing world.

What that vision should be is the subject of the following chapter. The issue now is the lessons from the failure of integration that the United States should heed as it formulates a longer-term strategy for Russia.[14]

The first and most important lesson is that Russia considers itself to be a great power and will demand that the rest of the world respects it as such. This is a core element of Russian national identity, which abides in good and bad times. That was true after Russia's humiliating defeats in the Crimean War in the mid nineteenth century and the Russo-Japanese War in the early twentieth. It was true of the 1990s, even though Russia was then undergoing a profound systemic crisis unprecedented for a great power not defeated in a major (hot) war. It will assuredly remain true no matter what the outcome of the war in Ukraine or the state of the Russian economy, and no matter who leads the country. Russians, Washington needs to remember, do not believe in an arc of history stretching to some ideal. They believe in cycles of rise and fall and resurrection. After defeats, Russia always returns as some version of its historical great-power self.

A great power, by definition for Russians, is a sovereign state that governs itself free of outside interference, conducts an independent foreign policy in pursuit of its interests, and sits at the geopolitical high table on the world stage. Accordingly, Russia will be adamant in rejecting any effort by Washington to interject itself into its domestic politics; it will never agree easily to any joint course of action without presenting its own unique take on the issue at hand; and it will do what it has to do to insert itself into global issues, even if it has little to contribute. Dealing with Russia is time-consuming and taxing; ignoring it comes with its own price.

In addition, Russia will be tenacious in the defense of its interests in the former Soviet space, where its preeminence has given it the geopolitical heft to act as a great power. It is the geopolitical space that Russia has sought to dominate, at least since Peter the Great declared it an empire in 1721 and, in this space, Ukraine is Russia's top priority. This does not mean that the United States cannot engage these countries without drawing Moscow's ire. The Kremlin has, after all, reconciled itself with China's growing presence, at least for the time being. Nor does it mean that the United States has no option other than to accept Moscow's measures to limit the sovereign choices of former Soviet states. But, if Washington is not prepared to tread carefully in this region for its own reasons, it must ensure that it is prepared to respond effectively to whatever resistance Moscow might offer.

Besides understanding how great-power ambitions shape Russian conduct, US policymakers also need to accept that there will always be an inherent tension in relations that is grounded in geography, history, and values and cannot be wished away. They need to take care to prevent that tension from hardening into diametrically opposed ideologies, which would preclude any fruitful cooperation, however limited. Geopolitical competition, as a rule, is susceptible to pragmatic resolution. Ideological clashes, grounded in diverging value systems, generally are not. This has been a hard truth for Washington to accept, since it tends not to acknowledge competing geopolitical interests that are not ultimately grounded in opposing systems of values.

Certainly, the Biden administration has refused to accept this truth, with the president framing the current struggle with Russia as part of a broader, worldwide contest between democracy and autocracy for the twenty-first century. It has left little hope for improved relations, absent a fundamental shift in Russian attitudes. Its hard-edged containment is aimed at eroding Russia's standing as a great power in a definitive fashion. In short, its Russia strategy is an extreme version of America's Cold War strategy, pursued in a world that has moved far beyond that era in the structure of global affairs and the nature of the challenges the world faces. That is not a recipe for success.

The final lesson applies not only to Russia but more broadly to the conduct of US foreign policy: The need for strategic patience. The Cold War triumph left the United States as the undisputed, and unchallenged, sole superpower, fostering the belief that it could force the pace of global developments toward a world remade in its image. Since then, the evolution of US–Russian relations, along with the persistent challenges the United States has faced around the world and on transnational matters, should have disabused the country of illusions of rapid success. Indeed, the goal of foreign policy should not be immediate, irreversible total victory on each and every matter of interest, but rather the slow accumulation over time of advantage that moves developments in directions that favor American principles and interests. That is how the country triumphed in the Cold War. Recapturing that patience is critical to its further success, including in relations with Russia.

7

What is to be Done?

What is to be done? That is one of those "accursed questions" that have agonized Russian thinkers for centuries, as they consider how to reorder their own country to promote prosperity and justice, while sustaining it as a major presence on the world stage. It is a question that has tested Western leaders for decades as they contemplate how to manage relations with Russia, that huge country to the East that is alien in spirit yet critical to the West's security. It is not about to go away, no matter how and when the war in Ukraine ends.

That war is only part of a greater struggle between Russia and the West over the new world order that, at least in the minds of Russian leaders, will emerge in the years to come, as the US-led liberal, rules-based order loses its appeal to vast portions of the globe and the overwhelming US power that has underwritten it dissipates. More specifically, the European security order is at stake. Russia launched the war in large part to revise the Cold War settlement in Europe, which the Kremlin firmly believes the West imposed on it in the 1990s, as it suffered through a time of painful strategic weakness. As we saw in Chapter 5, the draft treaties on security guarantees with NATO and the United States that the Kremlin released in December 2021 barely mention Ukraine. The key demands were that NATO not expand further or deploy in Eastern Europe offensive weapons capable of striking Russian territory, and that it withdraw its infrastructure to the lines of 1997, when the NATO–Russia Founding Act was signed.[1] Win, lose, or draw in Ukraine, Russia will not be easily reconciled to a settlement it considers unjust.

What the post-conflict Russia will look like, how well it will be positioned to challenge the rules-based order, is an open question. Much will depend on how the conflict ends. But two scenarios – one that drives the hopes of many in the West, and one that carries untold pitfalls – are the least probable: a democratic breakthrough or the collapse of the Russian Federation.

The Kremlin has eviscerated the democratic opposition in the past few years. Its leading figure, Alexey Navalny, sits in a Siberian prison camp; his organization, which once spanned the country, even if it barely registered with the larger population, has been systematically dismantled and its leaders imprisoned or hounded into exile. There is as a result no organizational basis for a democratic breakthrough and little evidence of either elite or popular support for one.

A military defeat would undoubtedly produce a period of instability, especially if Putin were forced out and a new leader or leaders struggled to consolidate power. It is even conceivable that Russia might lose territory that is internationally recognized as Russian – the Kaliningrad exclave in the Baltic region, for instance, or Chechnya or another ethnic republic in the North Caucasus. But that would be a far cry from the collapse of the Russian state, which would still occupy a vast territory in the heart of Eurasia. Moreover, unlike the Soviet Union in its agony, Russia is held together by powerful centripetal forces, including patriotism and xenophobia, supply chains and critical infrastructure, not to mention the powerful security services that want to draw on the resources of the entire country. Although there are substantial minorities, notably the Tatars in the Volga region, and whiffs of separatism, the country remains overwhelmingly ethnic Russian (70–75 percent of the total population), and countries that are ethnically homogenous rarely, if ever, break up from internal causes.[2]

Barring extraordinary developments, post-conflict Russia, with or without Putin at the helm, is most likely to be some recognizable version of its historical self, authoritarian in domestic structure, expansionist in impulse, economically and technologically lagging, yet determined to play the role of a great power. Its nuclear arsenal will command attention; its vast natural resources will attract investment; and its geographical location will enable it to project power or pathologies into regions of strategic importance across the Eurasian landmass. The question is whether its political leaders will have the necessary will, and the state apparatus sufficient capacity, to mobilize shrinking assets to field a capable military and the world-class space, counter-space, cyber, informational, grey-zone, and other instruments it needs to punch above its weight on the global stage.

The answer is unknowable. Various scenarios are plausible with a stronger or weaker Russia as a more or less dangerous competitor to the

United States. This is hardly surprising, given the complexity of Russia and the many forces at play. But uncertainty is no excuse for avoiding the rigors of policymaking. As noted in the Introduction, policy is made, as a rule, in the absence of certainty. The moment of maximal influence often comes when knowledge is scant; influence wanes as certainty emerges. This is as true of strategic choices as it is of tactical decisions.

Consequently, American policymakers should set Russia policy now based on their best assessment of its future. Prudence would dictate that flexibility be built in and that hedges be erected against initial errors in judgment. What the policymaker should not do is avoid crafting a coherent, substantive Russia policy, on the argument that a Russia in decline does not now, or soon will not, matter. Rather, Washington should proceed on the assumption that Russia will be a major geopolitical actor well into the future, whether or not that turns out to be the case. Adjusting to Russian weakness will prove far easier and less fraught with peril than adapting to unexpected Russian strength.

The Foundations of Policy

Washington has two tasks: to craft policy to deal with the urgent issue of Russia's invasion of Ukraine and challenge to European and world order, and to create a strategic framework for the longer-term management of relations. Ideally, the framework would guide decisions on dealing with Russia in the current crisis. To the greatest extent possible, Washington should want to ensure that the steps it takes to counter the current threat do not contradict what it hopes to do with Russia over the long run. The reality, however, is that the long term is usually neglected in the rush to deal with the immediate; the urgent drives out the important. The long-term policy emerges as an accumulation of short-term measures, rather as a consequence of conscious design.

Outside observers do not have the excuse of urgency. They can consider policy in the proper sequence and start with the strategic framework. Constructing one requires examining three issues: What is the trajectory of global developments; that is, where are we headed? What should the United States' goals be as the world evolves; that is, what do we want to, and what can we, achieve? And what can Russia do to help or thwart the United States; that is, how does Russia matter? The answers provide the grist for determining where Russia lies among US foreign-policy priorities and what goals the United States should pursue in relations with it.

The Historical Pivot

It is now a commonplace that we have reached an historical inflection point. The Biden administration's *National Security Strategy* starts from that assumption, declaring that we are in the first years of "the decisive decade" that will determine the shape of the global order for generations to come.[3]

It is hard to overstate the dimensions of the change we are witnessing. It far exceeds the change that was ushered in with the end of the Cold War and the collapse of the Soviet Union some thirty years ago. In retrospect, those developments were not nearly as far-reaching as they appeared at the time. The collapse of the Cold War bipolar world into a unipolar moment did not produce a dramatic shift in the direction of global geopolitical, political, or economic developments. The United States did not change course; it just proceeded more rapidly down the path it was on in the absence of a countervailing superpower. Today's change is also of a different quality from that of the 1930s, which witnessed worldwide depression and the rise of murderous ideologies that erupted in the horrors of the Second World War. The crisis of the capitalist system and the ideologies were not so much unique effusions of their time as the offspring of developments of the prior half century.

It is that prior half century, the late nineteenth and early twentieth centuries, that offers the better analogy to today's circumstances. It was an era when the dimensions of change, geopolitical, political, techno-logical, economic, and philosophical, outran human imagination. The geopolitical landscape was shifting quickly as a rising Germany chal-lenged the reigning hegemon, Great Britain, and a young country of extraordinary power and potential, the United States, was waiting in the wings. The sharpening competition disrupted the balance-of-power system that had largely spared Europe devastating great-power wars since the end of the Napoleonic era in 1815. The major wars – the Crimean War of 1854–1856, which pitted France, Great Britain, and the Ottoman Empire against Russia, and the wars of German unification in the 1860s and 1870s – were short, with limited losses of life and property compared to twentieth-century warfare, even if the geopolitical consequences were far-reaching.

Meanwhile, the technological innovations that accompanied the industrial and scientific revolutions changed unalterably the way societies communicated, traveled, and manufactured, producing the first wave of globalization. They fueled social developments that reshaped relations between the state and society and the individual, as they shattered religious beliefs in God and the natural order of things in favor of secularism and social engineering. And they produced weapons of ever greater lethality that raised exponentially the costs of war, even if European statesmen were slow to grasp the implications and hewed to an all-too-easy resort to the force of arms as a tool of policy.[4] The momentous change laid the foundations for the spreading global prosperity that came at the end of the twentieth century and raised the quality of life for billions. But it also gave birth to the philosophical ideas and political movements that shattered the global order and made the twentieth century the bloodiest in history.

Something similar is unfolding today. China's rise has reshaped the geopolitical landscape. Washington now recognizes it as the sole strategic competitor, with growing political, economic, and technological capabilities and political ambitions to erect a new order in place of the US-led, rules-based order. Russia, no matter what its ills, remains a major presence and challenge to American global leadership. Elsewhere, other centers of power are emerging – Brazil, India, Indonesia, Iran, South Africa, and Turkey, for example – with the capacity to alter regional dynamics in ways that diminish the influence of the liberal Western world.

As in the late nineteenth century, technological innovation, especially in information and communications, is revolutionizing the way the world communicates, travels, and manufactures, producing a second wave of globalization, which probably peaked a decade ago, even though the world continues to grow ever more interconnected. Robotics, artificial intelligence, and bioengineering are challenging concepts of what it means to be human, while radically altering relations between state and society and the individual. As before, technology is applied to producing ever more destructive weapons and multiplying the means by which nations can attack one another. While great powers are careful to avoid war with one another, and the risk of a nuclear cataclysm that would entail, they nevertheless vigorously deploy measures short of war to undermine rivals.[5]

Moreover, continuing industrialization based on fossil fuels has made climate change an existential threat, while global interconnectedness has amplified a raft of transnational threats: pandemics, proliferation of weapons of mass destruction, international terrorism, and organized crime. Meeting those challenges requires some level of cooperation among major countries, which proves elusive as they increasingly see one another as rivals. This situation adds an element of complexity and danger, which the first era of globalization lacked.

Taken together, these developments have eroded the foundations of the US-led liberal, rule-based order. Liberal values have lost their appeal in much of the world outside the West. The margin of superiority of US power is rapidly narrowing, as China in particular closes the economic and technological gap. The international agencies founded in the wake of the Second World War and grounded in liberal values – the United Nations and its affiliates and the Bretton Woods institutions – are losing their legitimacy and capacity to deal with the security and financial problems for which they were created. The largely US–Russian bipolar arms control architecture that fostered strategic stability and restraint is crumbling as the strategic landscape becomes increasingly multipolar, new technologies give conventional weapons strategic capabilities, and cyberspace and space become ever more contested strategic realms.

What order will replace the crumbling US-led system is far from certain. Will China push aside the United States as the global hegemon to lead a world according to rules written in Chinese characters? Will the world become bipolar, divided between two more or less rigidly defined blocs led by the United States and China? Will a genuinely multipolar world emerge based on several states or coalitions of more or less equal strength? Will a far messier world of multiple centers of uneven power and capabilities take shape, in which coalitions rise and fall in rapid succession as ad hoc responses to a shifting set of national priorities, regional dynamics, and international challenges? Or will a technological breakthrough redefine the nature of power and abruptly overturn the global hierarchy that now exists or appears to be emerging?

Whatever the answer, perhaps the critical issue is whether the new order can congeal without the general war or other convulsion that has historically served as the midwife. Can the world today enjoy the prosperity that modern technology promises without enduring devastation akin to that that followed a similar era in the late nineteenth and early twentieth centuries? That question should weigh heavily on policy deliberations in Washington.

Retrenchment, Restoration, or Reinvention?[6]

At a time of immense uncertainty, and after the four disruptive years of the Trump administration, the United States is challenged to reassess its global role. Even if its margin of superiority is diminishing, the United States nevertheless remains the dominant world power across all dimensions. Its economy is the world's most complex and largest in nominal terms (China's is larger in purchasing power party terms), and its capital markets the deepest. Its military is the most sophisticated, capable, and battle-hardened – the failings in Afghanistan, Iraq, and elsewhere were not military defeats but the unraveling of flawed political strategies. The United States remains the center of technological innovation, with the world's leading network of research institutions, still capable of attracting the best minds from around the globe. And it retains tremendous soft power and cultural appeal, even though its image has been badly tarnished by growing polarization and political dysfunction. In this light, the challenge is to align American ambitions with its still great, yet limited, power.

Two schools dominate the public debate. One advocates retrenchment, a selective withdrawal from global commitments to focus on domestic priorities. While many in this school are isolationists, more thoughtful proponents understand that Fortress America is not a viable option in today's interconnected world. But they insist that the United States should limit its engagement abroad to defend a more narrowly defined set of truly vital interests and not squander its power in a broader effort to police the world or actively spread liberal democratic values. Like John Quincy Adams, they believe that the United States should "not go abroad in search of monsters to destroy."

The other school is intent on restoring the United States as *the* global leader of a liberal, rules-based order after Trump's abdication. This is the clear intent behind the Biden administration's declaration that "America is back," its promise to restore the integrity and purpose of America's alliances, and the president's Manichean framing of the current era as an existential struggle between democracy and autocracy. This school advocates an activist, interventionist, internationalist foreign policy in defense of the liberal order, to include spreading democratic values and supporting democratic forces in authoritarian states. Its adherents are convinced that no other country is capable of replacing the United States as the defender of the global commons and builder of multilateral coalitions to confront international challenges.

Neither school is adequate to today's circumstances, however, as William Burns, a prominent US diplomat, has noted.[7] The proponents of retrenchment have yet to provide a satisfying answer to the question of which country or coalition is capable of filling the vacuum in the management of the global commons that would be created by the withdrawal of American power. Europe does not have the hard power to do so. Neither does China at the moment but, if it does in the future, how would that advance American interests? Because of the vital importance of the global commons to a trading nation lacking land corridors to the world's other zones of economic significance, the United States started to play a large role in defending the commons, once Great Britain was no longer capable of doing so. Similarly, it is unclear how the United States would prevent a hostile power from dominating Europe or East Asia, a longstanding requirement of US security and prosperity. The United States raised its presence in these regions precisely to reduce the risk of such eventualities and to spare itself from having to fight major wars, hot or cold, to defeat aspiring hegemons, as it did three times during the twentieth century.

Meanwhile, the restorers ignore all the developments noted above that are eroding the rules-based order. Their hope is that America's alliances can compensate for the limitations on US power to recreate the dominant global position that American power on its own once guaranteed. But they neglect the continuing doubts European and East Asian allies have about the endurance of American commitments after four years of Trump. How certain can the allies be of continued American support after the 2024 or any subsequent presidential election? Buoyed by the unexpectedly strong and unified Western response to Russia's invasion of

Ukraine, the restorationists also underestimate the fissiparous forces that stress the West's unity and some states' internal stability.

How then should the United States position itself in world affairs? How can it stay loyal to its democratic traditions, while ensuring its access to global markets and guarding against the rise of a peer-hostile power or coalition of hostile powers? And how can it perform those tasks, cognizant of the limits of its still tremendous power?

A necessary first task is putting its own house in order. The list of domestic matters that have far too long been neglected or remain the victims of political dysfunction is well known – modernization of critical infrastructure; reduction of runaway national debt; development of an effective immigration system; renovation of the educational system at all levels; elaboration of a sustainable, climate-friendly energy policy; improvement in public health; alleviation of poverty, and so on. All this will require the overcoming of the acute polarization that has riven American politics in recent decades. Without a restored national unity and a renewed sense of national purpose, the United States cannot elaborate and execute an effective long-term policy.[8]

As the United States deals with its domestic ills, it needs to fashion a global role that is consistent with the country's character and aligns goals and means. That role should contain three key elements. First, the United States, along with a few other major powers, must play a large role in policing the global commons. Second, it must maintain a significant security presence in the world's strategic zones on the periphery of Eurasia, including Europe, the Persian Gulf, the Indo-Pacific region, and the Arctic. And, third, it must promote American values while respecting the right of other countries to govern themselves as they see fit.

The United States can, and should, continue to support a liberal rules-based order, but it needs to recognize that that order will be limited geographically to what we now call the West and a few other states, much as was the case during the Cold War. It will no longer span the globe; one or more regional orders will coalesce around other centers of power, starting with China. In this environment, Washington will have no choice but to lay the foundation for peaceful coexistence. It will nevertheless want to create and sustain balances of power that favor American interests in the world's strategically important regions. To do that, the United States would ideally have constructive relations with all the major centers of power, no matter what the character of their domestic regimes, to ensure that it can forge shifting, ad hoc coalitions to deal with the numerous and unpredictable challenges that will arise in the decades ahead. Flexibility will have to be combined with principle to advance American interests. The goal should be to carve out a secure space in which the United States and its allies and partners can prosper.

Russia to Remain a Great Power

Among those centers of power will almost certainly be Russia. Because of its large nuclear arsenal, cyber and space capabilities, and military potential, Russia will continue to be a key factor in strategic stability, even if stability will no longer be solely, or even primarily, a matter of finding the right balance between US and Russian strategic capabilities. Any code of conduct for cyberspace would be incomplete if it did not include Russia. Multilateral efforts to prevent the spread of weapons of mass destruction and contain Iranian and North Korean nuclear ambitions will be more effective if Russia and the United States are working in tandem and not at cross-purposes.

Beyond strategic matters, Russia will remain a critical component of European security. The immediate question is whether Europe's security architecture needs to be designed to protect the continent from Russia over the long term, or whether it might prove possible to build that architecture in cooperation with it, especially once the acute phase of the war in Ukraine has passed. Russia's long coastline and extensive continental shelf in the Arctic makes it a key player in that region's future, as rapid warming opens it up to the exploration and development of its vast natural resources and lucrative maritime trade, while encouraging geopolitical competition.

Elsewhere, Russia's role will be less prominent, but still important to US interests. In the Middle East, its effort to build constructive relations with all the region's major powers – Egypt, Iran, Israel, Saudi Arabia, and Turkey – gives it influence over the regional balance of power. Its cooperation with Saudi Arabia is critical to the evolution of the world's oil markets. And its naval and air bases in Syria enable it to play an active role in the Eastern Mediterranean. In the Indo-Pacific region, Russia's vast, mineral rich, sparsely populated territories can help ensure

China's further robust economic growth, while its relations with other key regional actors – India, Japan, and South Korea – could provide a basis for constraining Chinese ambitions.

Finally, with regard to transnational challenges, as one of the top four emitters of greenhouse gases, Russia is an unavoidable partner in mitigating the risks of climate change. Its long tradition of expertise in the hard sciences could enable it to play a large role in the development of renewals if Moscow were inclined to devote resources to such an effort. Similarly, Russia has the scientific foundations to become a significant player in dealing with deadly pandemics – it has a rich history in the development of vaccines, for example – if Moscow saw political advantage in cooperating.

In short, even a Russia in decline should matter to the United States. Its opposition can complicate, and its cooperation facilitate, the United States' achievement of its goals. The challenge to Washington, then, is to harness Russian power to its own advancement in the global arena.

The Way Forward

Today, the Biden administration has set its goal, in broad terms, as laying the foundations for a "free, open, secure, and prosperous world" during a decade marked by geopolitical competition among major powers and the prevalence of the cross-border challenges that require a modicum of cooperation among those very powers. But, for all practical purposes, it sees no positive role for Russia or room for constructive US–Russian relations, at least as long as Putin is at the helm. Russia's massive invasion of Ukraine has drained any hope the administration might have had when it entered office of seeking "stability and predictability and areas of constructive work with Russia, where it is in our interest to do that," as a senior administration official put it.[9] The *National Security Strategy* released in October 2022 describes Putin's Russia as "an immediate and persistent threat to international peace and stability."[10]

The *Strategy* states that the United States is prepared to engage in the "pragmatic modes of interaction" with Russia to handle matters, where dealing with it could bring mutual benefit, but there is no hint as to what those matters might be. Even on the issues of strategic stability and European security, usually core issues in US Russia policy, the strategy leaves open the possibility that stability will have to be pursued without Russia – even if the administration is seeking ways to continue arms control measures and talks with it despite the war in Ukraine – and European security would be designed as protection against Russia. It is a bleak and unforgiving assessment of relations with Russia.[11]

And so to the extent that the administration speaks about Russia, it is about what it will do with allies and partners to constrain Russia's malign behavior. Never since the end of the Cold War has the United States held out so little hope for relations with Russia and so thoroughly rejected it as a possible, albeit limited, partner. Indeed, for extensive periods during the Cold War, the United States and the Soviet Union cooperated in multiple ways, ways that the Biden administration appears to believe are now beyond reach without a radical change in Russian conduct, which would require new leaders in Russia, as far as Washington is concerned.

The Russia We Need

Nevertheless, it is imperative to think beyond the current moment to longer-term relations with Russia. Despite the administration's assessment, the three tasks that have defined relations with Russia for the past half century, if not longer, should continue to inform American policy. First is the pursuit of peaceful coexistence to reduce to the minimum the risk of a nuclear cataclysm – an imperative for the two rivals that between themselves control slightly less than 90 percent of the world's nuclear weapons. Second is the responsible management of the inevitable competition to avoid a direct confrontation, which could escalate to nuclear war, especially in Europe, the Middle East, and the Arctic, where Russia plays prominent roles. And third is mutually beneficial cooperation to meet urgent transnational threats, such as climate change, the proliferation of weapons of mass destruction, international terrorism, and pandemics. In current circumstances, a fourth should be added: structuring relations with Russia to best position the United States to deal with its major strategic rival, China, in an increasingly multipolar world.

To accomplish those tasks, Washington should bear in mind three considerations that run counter to conventional wisdom within the expert community.

To begin, while there is good reason to seek to weaken Russia to a degree that prevents it from invading again any European country, a goal Defense Secretary Lloyd Austin identified early in the Ukraine conflict,[12] seeking to cripple the Russian economy at some point jeopardizes American interests. Most important, as the United States well understood during the final days of the Soviet Union, it needs a Russia strong enough to reliably control its arsenal of weapons of mass destruction, the vehicles to deliver them, and the materials and knowledge needed to build them. It also needs a Russia strong enough to govern its own territory effectively and to prevent domestic destabilization that would inevitably spill over into neighboring regions. Today, to deal with climate change, it also needs a Russia strong enough to negotiate and then implement agreements to reduce the production of greenhouse gases and to mitigate the damaging consequences of the rapid warming of the Arctic region.

Beyond that, Washington has an interest in a Russia strong enough to play a role in sustaining stable balances of power in the regions along its long periphery in Eurasia. An overly weak Russia would enable China to gain excessive influence over the exploitation of Russia's natural resources, especially in Eastern Siberia and the Far East, substantially enhancing its own power at little cost. It would also jeopardize stability in the Arctic and management of the Northern Sea Route through its Arctic waters, perhaps encouraging a greater Chinese presence. And, ironically, it would threaten to erode the West's unity, which is preserved to a great degree by a continuing fear of Russian power, or even enhanced, as we have seen since Russia's invasion of Ukraine.

In addition, while Russia has long since lost the centrality it once had in American foreign policy, due to its weakness and shifting geopolitical realities, Washington still needs to engage it in a serious fashion. Russia's own conduct has made it an outcast in the Western world, but turning it into an *international* pariah and isolating it diplomatically will ultimately make it impossible to advance American interests with regard to such priority issues as strategic stability, European security, and climate change. As the acute phase of the war in Ukraine abates, Washington should slowly restore severed channels of communication. But it should also bear in mind that most of the issues of concern in relations with Moscow are no longer strictly, or even primarily, bilateral; their management or resolution requires multilateral effort. For that reason, bilateral relations need to be embedded in a multilateral framework. Deft management of relations with other countries will thus become a critical factor in managing relations with Russia.

Finally, while a democratic Russia is much to be preferred, that is not the Russia Washington will be dealing with. Given the onrush of urgent matters, the United States does not have the luxury of waiting for a reformed Russia to engage. Constructive relations are possible even with authoritarian regimes, where interests overlap, if not with excessively aggressive ones, as is the case with today's Russia. The challenge for Washington is to seize the moment when Russia's conduct has changed sufficiently to allow for serious negotiations, and not hold out for even further change, which is unlikely or far in the future, thus forfeiting the near-term opportunity to make progress on issues of vital importance to the United States.

The Critical Issues

Three issues will dominate US relations with Russia in the years ahead. Two are old perennials – strategic stability and, despite each country's professed pivot to Asia, European security. The third is a consequence of the shifting geopolitical landscape – managing China's power.

Strategic Stability

The era of strategic stability based on a set of interlocking US–Russian bilateral nuclear arms control treaties has ended irretrievably. Critical elements, such as the Anti-Ballistic Missile (ABM) and the Intermediate-Range Nuclear Forces (INF) Treaties, have been abandoned, and the last central element, the new START, which regulates US and Russian strategic arsenals, is set to expire in 2026. Even though Washington claims to retain interest in "developing a more expansive, transparent, and verifiable arms control infrastructure to succeed New START,"[13] that treaty is likely to be the last of its kind. There is not sufficient time to work out a follow-on treaty before it expires, and, even if one were unexpectedly negotiated, the chances of its gaining the two-thirds majority in the Senate needed for ratification approach is zero.

Nevertheless, the US–Russian nuclear relationship will long remain central to strategic stability, and the United States has a deep interest in reaching agreements regulating both countries' nuclear arsenals. Monitoring, through on-site inspections and national technical means, has been critical to assuring each side that it has adequate insight into the other's forces to retain confidence in its strategic deterrent and should continue in some fashion. Agreements short of treaties could provide the basis for limiting the numbers or the deployment of certain weapons systems. For instance, as part of the process of promoting European security, both sides have expressed an interest in banning intermediate-range nuclear forces in the European theater, while allowing their deployment in Asia and elsewhere, in effect reviving the INF Treaty solely with regard to Europe. Parallel unilateral measures, such as the United States and the Soviet Union undertook in the Soviet Union's final days to increase the security of non-strategic nuclear weapons, could also be applied to certain weapons systems, although the total breakdown in trust between the two sides probably precludes such arrangements in the near future.

Agreements between the United States and Russia will not, however, suffice to reliably preserve strategic stability in an increasingly multipolar strategic landscape. In particular, China's expansion and modernization of its nuclear forces, which could approach parity with Russia's and the United States' this decade, mean that it will have to be part of any nuclear arms control arrangement, with hopes of stabilizing the strategic environment in the years ahead. But matters extend far beyond China. More countries could seek nuclear weapons to enhance their security. Iran is almost certainly moving in this direction. Doubts about America's commitment to extended deterrence, that is, its willingness to extend its nuclear umbrella to allies in Europe and East Asia, could persuade some US allies to develop their own nuclear deterrent. These doubts are not new, but four years of Trump's dismissive attitudes toward allies, profound uncertainty about America's future direction in foreign policy, and China's mounting ambitions, could persuade Japan and South Korea, for example, to develop their own nuclear deterrent. Both countries have the technological capability to build a nuclear weapon in a matter of months.

Meanwhile, technological advance is changing the strategic environment, multiplying the number of players, and thereby complicating the equation for strategic stability. Precision-guided conventional weapons that can perform tasks that only nuclear weapons once could are in the arsenals of a growing number of states. Space is only growing in importance to strategic communications, guidance systems, and monitoring capabilities, while more and more states and now private actors are engaged in that realm. And the increasing centrality of cyberspace to political and socio-economic processes and the low threshold for the development and deployment of cyber weapons allow middle and lesser powers to play a strategic role once beyond their reach.

In this environment, strategic stability will have to be based on an interlocking network of bilateral and multilateral arrangements, understandings, and codes of conduct and unilateral initiatives undertaken in the hope that other states will emulate them. No two states have deeper experience in conceptualizing strategic stability than Russia and the United States, and their joint efforts will be critical to developing a future framework for it. That should be reason enough for Washington to revive and sustain strategic stability talks with Moscow.

European Security

Until Russia's invasion of Ukraine, Europe's security was grounded in states' adherence to ten principles laid out in the 1975 Helsinki Accords: sovereign equality, territorial integrity, inviolability of frontiers, peaceful settlement of disputes, refraining from the threat or use of force, non-interference in internal affairs, respect for human rights and fundamental freedoms, self-determination, cooperation among states, and good-faith fulfillment of obligations under international law. Those principles, supplemented by arms control agreements, the most important of which was the Conventional Forces in Europe (CFE) Treaty, had helped to stabilize the frontier between NATO and the Warsaw Pact during the last years of the Cold War, and between NATO and Russia in the post-Soviet era. Russia's suspension of its participation in the CFE Treaty in 2007, and mounting disregard for other arms control measures, had already stressed Europe's security architecture before its invasion of Ukraine put an emphatic end to European security as a cooperative effort by all European states, including Russia.

The long-term US goal should be the resurrection of a security system based on cooperation with Russia but, perhaps paradoxically, the path to it runs through a near-term effort to secure Europe against Russia. Washington's initial focus should be on further enhancing NATO's deterrence posture and defensive capabilities, building on the steps taken during the first months of the Ukraine conflict. It needs to hold European members, especially Germany, to their commitments to spend more on defense, and it should encourage them to do a better job in coordinating defense and security policies so that duplication of effort is minimized. In this way, an effective European conventional deterrent force could be built over time, backed up by a continuing American strategic deterrent. Such an arrangement would undergird security in Europe while allowing the United States to shift resources to meeting the challenge of China in the Indo-Pacific region.

A core element of this effort should be nourishing the development of a genuine European pillar inside the Alliance, which would bear greater responsibility for alliance management and to some extent diminish the US role. Finnish and Swedish membership provides the basis for such a step – all those European states with significant military capabilities are now inside NATO, as is most of the European Union (Austria, Cyprus, Ireland, and Malta, not noted for their military prowess, are the hold-outs). A European pillar would necessarily encourage a modicum of European strategic autonomy, which would shield the continent from the vicissitudes of American politics and wavering commitment. While Washington will resist, as it always has when the issue of European strategic autonomy has surfaced, such a development would actually be good for the United States. A countervailing European voice would help discipline the use of American power and enhance the West's flexibility in dealing with the broader range of strategic challenges global trends adumbrate. Indeed, one of Washington's goals should be to assist Europe to become a genuine pole in a multipolar world.

Ukraine would not be included directly in this process. Indeed, NATO should put on hold for an indefinite period any further expansion eastward into the former Soviet space to avoid further provoking Russia at a time when Europe's energies should be focused on consolidation within NATO and the EU, as a way of deterring Russian adventurism. Nevertheless, arrangements would have to be made to guarantee Ukraine's security and remove it to the greatest extent possible as a focal point of geopolitical competition between Russia and the West.

Some form of armed neutrality might provide the answer. To this end, the West would maintain close defense and security cooperation with Ukraine, helping it to build a competent military adept at territorial defense and reconstructing and modernizing its defense-industrial sector so that it could adequately equip the country's armed forces. Much effort would also have to be placed in rebuilding Ukraine's economy after the devastation of the current war. All this would be undertaken in the belief that a strong, prosperous Ukraine would deflate Russia's expansionary impulses – throughout history Russia's expansion has ended whenever it has encountered countervailing power in the form of well-ordered, prosperous, capable states.

Building a European pillar and creating the conditions for armed neutrality for Ukraine could easily occupy the rest of this decade and beyond. Success will require close continuing American engagement, not an abrupt withdrawal or abandonment of commitments. But it is critical that the direction be set now, and that the United States, its allies, and Ukraine coordinate the steps toward this long-term vision.

These arrangements would provide a solid foundation for European security in the face of Russian hostility. But, as was the case during the Cold War, there will be no enduring security without Russia's participation, and Europeans will eventually grow tired of the stress and strain of the constant need to be on their guard against their eastern neighbor. Pressure will inevitably mount to engage Russia in a cooperative effort to reduce tensions and the risk of war.

The major challenge will be reconciling Russia to a situation in which for all practical purposes it is no longer *inside* Europe but rather compelled to deal *with* a more or less politically consolidated Europe. As we saw in Chapter 4, this is precisely the situation Russia wants to avoid. In Moscow's view, this arrangement denies it the strategic depth it sees as essential to its security, deprives it of an arena in which it could demonstrate its prowess as a great power, and creates on its borders a state-like entity that dwarfs it in population, wealth, and power potential, much as the United States does today. The great irony of course is that it is precisely Russia's invasion of Ukraine, intended to enhance its security, that accelerated movement toward this outcome, creating a strategic conundrum in the West not dissimilar to the one it faces today in the East with China.

How could the West reconcile Moscow with these arrangements? Arms control and confidence-building measures akin to those developed during the Cold War to ease tensions would be critical. Something analogous to the CFE Treaty will be needed to regulate military activities along the NATO/Russia frontier. US–Russian agreement to ban the deployment of intermediate-ranged ballistic missiles in the European theater would reduce the risk of a nuclear confrontation, as the INF Treaty once did. Confidence-building measures identified in the Vienna Documents could be resurrected and updated to deal with current realities.

Strong consultative mechanisms would also be essential. The NATO–Russia Council and the EU–Russian Partnership and Cooperation Agreement obviously did little to retard serious deterioration in relations; the Organization for Security and Cooperation in Europe (OSCE) slowly became a point of contention rather than platform for building consensus. But Moscow would likely see greater utility in consultations with NATO and the EU, if Europe had some strategic autonomy and the EU had a higher profile in security matters. At a minimum, Moscow could tell itself that it is no longer dealing with a "collective West" managed by a single center, Washington, a situation that would open up more room for bargaining.

The final element would be a Helsinki-2, but this time not negotiated by all European states plus the United States and Canada, but by North America, Europe, and Russia. One focus would be the updating and reinterpretation of the ten original Helsinki principles to take into account current geopolitical realities and technological capabilities.

Even with such arrangements, tensions would remain, as would US–Russian competition, including to some extent for Europe's support. But there would be a framework that would set parameters for constructive competition and limit the risk of another outbreak of violence in Europe along the lines of what is occurring in and around Ukraine today.

China

Russia has been developing a close strategic alignment with China for the past decade. That alignment has grown more intimate in the past two years, as both countries come under greater pressure from Washington, culminating in Putin's and Xi's declaration in February 2022 that friendship between their two countries was "without limits." That does not augur well for the United States. As my colleague Robert Legvold and I have warned, "a central pillar of US grand strategy since the beginning of the twentieth century . . . [has been] preventing an adversary or coalition of adversaries from dominating the Eurasian supercontinent or its strategically critical subregions, Europe, the Middle East and East Asia. Today that means preventing the emergence of a hard Russia–China alliance, which would wed Chinese dynamism with Russian natural resources into a potent threat to dominate Eurasia."[14]

Nevertheless, Russia has historically valued its strategic autonomy. Underlying frictions could resurface quickly as China's robust economic growth and rapid technological advance widen the asymmetry in power and fortune between the two countries, and Beijing's geopolitical ambitions further impinge on Russia's influence in the fora Soviet space. Russia is already hedging against an excessive reliance on its giant Asian neighbor, in part by seeking to embed it in multilateral fora that constrain its ambitions. Russia's effort will accelerate as the disparity widens.

This growing asymmetry provides the United States with an opportunity to attenuate Russia's strategic alignment with China. To succeed, Washington must recognize that it cannot undo the alignment – Moscow has good strategic reasons for not wanting to alienate a powerful neighbor – and it must act with subtlety and patience.

At the moment, Washington is understandably engaging China in an effort to deter it from providing material support to Russia in its war on Ukraine. But over the long run, it makes no strategic sense to use the stronger party, the strategic competitor, against the weaker one, which is no more than a "persistent threat." Rather, Washington should be considering how once the acute phase of the Ukraine conflict has passed, to engage Russia to constrain China's options in its rivalry with the United States.

The guiding principle should be to provide Russia with alternatives to China to enhance its bargaining position and ensure that deals, both political and commercial, tilt less favorably toward Beijing. A first step would be the normalization of diplomatic relations as soon as possible, once the situation in and around Ukraine provides an opening. As the United States, along with its partners and allies, considers sanctions relief, it should look to easing those that would enable Western firms to reenter projects in Eastern Siberia and the Far East to reduce the chances that the vast resources of these territories will become captive to China's markets at marked down prices.

In addition, Washington should consider how it might bolster Russia's position in Central Asia as a counterweight to China, as the latter builds up its commercial and security presence there. Opening up the possibility for Western companies to enter into joint ventures with Russian companies in the region would be one step. Encouraging America's regional allies and partners, Japan, South Korea, and India, which have interests in Central Asia, to engage with Russia constructively would be another step. In particular, the United States should work with these three countries and Russia to develop infrastructure projects that could effectively compete with China's Belt and Road Initiative. Building a North–South transportation corridor that links Russia to India through Central Asia and Afghanistan is one grand project worth considering.

While seeking to work with Russia to constrain China, the United States should also keep in mind the possibility of nourishing trilateral cooperation with those two countries to deal with urgent transnational challenges. Indeed, a more balanced Russia–China relationship should open up opportunities for such cooperation. At the top of the list would be joint work on sustaining strategic stability, as China joins the United States and Russia as the world's leading nuclear powers. As three of the top four emitters of greenhouse gases, the three are indispensable to efforts to mitigate the consequences of climate change. And, as the world's three most active geopolitical actors, they will have to play the leading roles if a new global equilibrium is to be reached and sustained.[15]

Ukraine in the Strategic Context

The vision for US–Russian relations outlined above should provide the strategic framework within which Washington approaches the war in Ukraine. With the war still raging and its course unpredictable, it makes little sense to offer a detailed prescription for US policy. The best that can be offered are guidelines.

The United States has two interrelated interests: Thwarting Russia's strategic goals and deterring vertical or horizontal escalation to lay a firmer foundation for peace and security in Europe, while still holding open the possibility of more constructive great-power relations in the long run.

To that end, the United States should mix war and diplomacy. Along with its allies and partners, it should continue to provide Ukraine with weapons to fight the war, intelligence to improve Ukraine's military performance, and funds to bridge Kyiv's budgetary gaps. NATO needs to ensure a robust deterrence posture in Eastern Europe to reassure allies and reduce the risks of the war spreading.

At the same time, the United States needs to expand diplomatic contacts with Moscow to reduce the risk of the conflict escalating. Contacts are particularly critical to preventing the use of nuclear weapons and, even as the war rages, Washington has an interest in working with Moscow on follow-on arrangements to the new START, to sustain strategic stability beyond the treaty's expiration date in 2026. At the appropriate moment, the contacts can also be used to explore a negotiated resolution of the conflict.

It should also be clear by this time that the United States will have to engage in direct, substantive negotiations with Moscow to end the conflict; this is not something that can be left to bilateral talks between Kyiv and Moscow. The realities of power in Europe and the nature of the conflict dictate that approach. To begin with, in Moscow's eyes, the conflict is part of a broader struggle with the West over the post-Cold War settlement, which it seeks to revise. Only Moscow and Washington wield sufficient power to alter the balance in Europe, and only they can guarantee the implementation of any agreement.

Moreover, Moscow is convinced that Washington is directing the conflict, and that European states and Ukraine are little more than its vassals. It will only negotiate in earnest with the country it believes is calling the shots on the West's side. In the end, Washington will have to talk to Moscow about Ukraine and Europe without Ukrainians and Europeans in the room, despite rhetoric to the contrary. Admittedly, it will have to take great care to consult with them so that they will support any deal it negotiates, but it will have to do the serious talking.

As the United States pursues the dual track of war and diplomacy, it should also do what it can to encourage more constructive voices in Moscow. While polls show widespread support for the war, and there have been few examples of elite defection, there is also reason to believe that discontent with Kremlin policy is widespread. The Kremlin's crackdown on dissent has played the main role in encouraging the discontented to keep their views private, but harsh Western policies and rhetoric have also played their part.

Washington, however, has an interest in nourishing this discontent, and it has means to do so. It can start by pushing back against the widespread popular tendency to demonize Russia and Russians by keeping its own wrath focused on Putin and others in the Kremlin responsible for the conflict, while reiterating that it has no quarrel with the Russian people. But it can go farther than that with reassurances that it is prepared to deal with Russia's legitimate security concerns and that it has no interest in widespread instability in Russia, let alone its collapse. In these ways it can send a message to the discontented that there is a way forward to better times, if only Russia's war against Ukraine can be brought to an end.

Elements of a Negotiated Settlement

Any negotiated end to the war, if it is to offer more than a temporary respite from bitter conflict, must meet three criteria. It must produce a firm foundation for peace and security; it must appear to be just – to Ukrainians, Russians, and Westerners – in the way it deals with territorial issues and war crimes; and it must provide for the reconstruction of the Ukrainian lands devastated by the war.

The first task could be accomplished in part through the arms control agreements and confidence-building measures outlined above. Those steps would have to be applied to Ukrainian–Russian relations to stabilize their common border. In particular, agreements to refrain from basing troops and conducting exercises within a certain distance from the border could ease concerns in both Moscow and Kyiv. In line with a pledge of neutrality, Kyiv would ban any foreign military bases on the territory it controls at the end of the war. Appropriate monitoring and verification measures would have to be developed, in which the United States and other Western countries could participate as part of a broader effort along the entire NATO/Russia frontier.

The territorial disputes should be resolved with an eye to setting principles and precedents for the resolution of similar conflicts elsewhere in Europe, including in particular those in the Balkans and South Caucasus.

The fundamental principle should be local democracy, that is, the population of the disputed territory should decide on the basis of a referendum or similar procedure, certified as free and fair by international monitors, whether it wants to be independent or included in one or another state. The details would have to be worked out – what territory should be subject to the referenda, who has the right to vote, what are the procedures for voting and determining the result, and so on. Consideration should be given to the establishment of interim international administrations in certain areas, to ensure that the referenda do not take place under the intimidating eyes of Russian or Ukrainian military forces. If any territory should decide to join Russia, provisions would have to be made to handle property and other issues that would arise in any transfer of territory from one jurisdiction to another.

Crimea will undoubtedly turn out to be a particularly thorny issue, since it has been integrated into the Russian political and administrative system since 2014, and Moscow, if, as likely, it still controls the territory, would resist the conduct of a referendum. Diplomats will be challenged to come up with a procedure that Moscow will allow and Kyiv, and Western capitals, would accept as legitimate to ascertain the will of Crimeans. If they decide to remain with Russia, arrangements will have to be negotiated to deal with all the technical issues that would have arisen if the transfer of sovereignty had occurred through peaceful negotiations, including compensation for property, provision for maritime transportation through the Kerch Strait, rights to offshore resources, and so on.

Provisions will also have to be made for the investigation of possible war crimes. The overwhelming bulk have been committed by Russian forces, and getting Moscow to take these investigations seriously is an impossible task. It will fall to the Ukrainians and their Western backers, with the help of the relevant international organizations, to conduct thorough investigations of the alleged crimes. At a minimum, sanctions should be levied against concrete Russians found guilty, while suspects, both Russian and Ukrainian, in Ukrainian custody should receive proper trials to determine guilt and punishment.

As for reconstruction, massive funding will be required after the devastation caused by the fighting and the Russian assault on infrastructure far from the battlefield. Moscow should pay a considerable amount, and sanctions relief should be keyed to its contribution. But the amounts that will be needed will be far beyond Russia's resources, and it will be impossible to compel it to pay the full cost since the settlement will almost certainly not result as a consequence of Moscow's capitulation. The West will also have to provide considerable resources, and it should, in coordination with Kyiv, take advantage of the devastation of what in many instances was obsolete infrastructure to modernize it and lay the foundation for a more prosperous Ukraine.

The post-conflict situation will also mark the time of maximum Western influence in Ukraine, and the United States and its allies should use the moment to insist that Ukraine put in the past the corrupt oligarchic political and economic system that has condemned the country to economic stagnation since the end of the Cold War. Kyiv has, rightly, said that it is fighting for freedom and defending Western democratic values. Victory, Washington should stress, will come not by defeating Russia but with the emergence of a strong, prosperous, democratic Ukraine, anchored in Europe.

Getting Russia Right

Nearly two centuries ago, the French aristocrat Alexis de Tocqueville prophesied that America and Russia were each destined to sway the destinies of half the globe. For much of the second half of the twentieth century his words held true as the two countries were locked in a bitter, bipolar, existential struggle across the globe, which ended with the exhaustion of Russia in the guise of the Soviet Union. There followed a quarter century during which the United States sought to integrate Russia into the Euro-Atlantic community as a free-market democracy, hoping to transform a once bitter foe into a junior partner in support of an American-led liberal, rules-based order. The American project ran aground on Russia's determination to regain its status as a great power and preserve what Russian rulers saw as their country's unique character in the face of American universalism.

With Russia's invasion of Ukraine in February 2022, US–Russian relations entered one of the darkest periods in their history with no obvious exit. Eager to focus on China, Washington dismissed Russia as a declining power, a "persistent threat." Along with allies and partners, it has sought to turn Russia into an international pariah, to isolate it diplomatically, and to cripple its economy. Whether it will succeed in thwarting Russia's strategic ambitions in Ukraine remains to be seen.

No matter what happens in Ukraine, however, the United States is not about to rid itself of Russia. Russia, even when it is weak, has an uncanny ability to make its presence felt on the global stage, and opportunities to do so will multiply as the US-led world order comes under increasing stress and slowly gives way to a new one, which may not be strictly multipolar, but in which power will be more defused. In this emerging order, the challenge for the United States is not to defeat Russia, as much of the American foreign-policy establishment would now have it, but rather to skillfully exploit relations with a rival to construct a new global equilibrium that advances American interests. To do that, the United States needs to see Russia plainly and without sentiment. Getting Russia right, as so often in the past, still remains critical to America's future.

Epilogue

On March 31, 2023, Vladimir Putin approved a new *Foreign Policy Concept* for the Russian Federation, the fifth that has appeared on his watch. This one was profoundly different in tone and substance. As the Russian president said, "cardinal changes in international affairs required us to seriously correct the key documents of strategic planning."[1] Left unsaid was that he had precipitated or accelerated many of those changes with his massive invasion of Ukraine.

Yet he was right. The concept had to change if it was to provide the elites with a clear articulation of the ambitions, ideas, and perspectives that were now guiding his, and Russia's, conduct on the world stage. The earlier ones, from 2000, 2008, 2013, and 2016,[2] were lifeless bureaucratic products, nearly indistinguishable from one another in structure and content; they failed to capture the ferment in the Kremlin's thinking in past years as it sought to assert Russia as a great power.

Those past concepts all began with pedestrian descriptions of a world in flux, driven by geopolitical shifts and technological advances, but with no clear sense of direction. That view hardly conveyed the true dynamic of the current moment, in Putin's view. The new concept now speaks of "revolutionary changes" leading to a more just, multipolar world and ending a long era of domination by "colonial" powers at the expense of the non-Western world. The turmoil is imbued with an historic purpose.

No matter what the objective state of Russia's power might have been at the time of publication, all the earlier concepts asserted that it remained an "influential center of power," thanks to its permanent seat on the UN Security Council, participation in other leading international organizations, vast resources, and active interaction with other major powers. That still holds true, but is much too modest a description for Putin's swelling ambition. In the new concept, Russia is portrayed as a leading global power. To the factors that undergird that status, the concept adds those that truly make Russia stand out, at least in Putin's mind. It is one of the two great nuclear powers; it played a decisive role in the victory over fascism in the Second World War, in the formation of the current international system, and in the liquidation of colonialism. Those past achievements, he believes, augur well for Russia's potential to fashion a more just world order out of the current disarray.

Similarly, past concepts blandly stated that Russia pursued an independent foreign policy to advance its national interests, while helping to preserve a global equilibrium. That description may have been adequate for a power that prized pragmatism in foreign policy, but it no longer sufficed for a country that now had a mission in the world beyond its own survival and progress. As the new concept proclaims, Russia "fulfills a unique, historically grounded mission in support of a global balance of power and the formation of a multipolar international system." It is a critical voice for justice in a world for much too long subjected to the West's depredations.[3]

Finally, the prior concepts all ranked Russia's regional priorities in the same way, with a clear Western orientation: the former Soviet states topped the list, followed by Europe and the United States; then came Asia, with mention of China and India, and the Middle East. Latin America and Africa were mere afterthoughts. That ranking might have been a true reflection of Putin's priorities in his first two presidential terms in the 2000s, but it failed to grasp the new directions in which he had steered Russia since returning to the Kremlin in 2012, let alone his current mental map of the world.

The near abroad still ranks first in the new concept: it remains Russia's strategic backyard, the indispensable foundation of its geopolitical heft. Reflecting Putin's pivot to the East, there follows the Eurasian continent, with specific mention of China and India, two "friendly sovereign centers of global power and growth" that broadly share Russia's approach to world order; the Asia–Pacific, a region of "dynamically growing multifaceted potential"; and the Islamic World, "an emerging independent center of global development," where Russia has increasingly reliable partners. Next are Africa, with the potential to become "a unique center of global growth," and Latin America, where, the concept asserts, key countries are seeking to escape US domination. At the bottom is Europe, portrayed as a continent of hostile powers under America's thumb, followed by the

United States and "other Anglo-Saxon states," presented as the bastion of Russophobia in today's world.

Clash of Civilizations

In unvarnished, unapologetic language, the new concept thus aims to prepare Russia for a period of prolonged confrontation with the West, as a multipolar world slowly takes shape. This is more than the era of great-power competition invoked in American national security documents, however. It is rather a monumental clash of civilizations along the lines of Samuel Huntington's provocative article on the driving forces of conflict in the post-Cold War world, which appeared in *Foreign Affairs* in 1993.[4] Putin would hardly cite an American political scientist as his source of inspiration, and there is no evidence that he is. But Putin was aware of the thesis – in 2001 he told an interviewer it was "harmful."[5] He has since changed his mind, adopting a similar design to illuminate Russia's mission in world affairs.

Huntington envisioned a world of seven or eight civilizations. While in theory conflict was possible between any two, he foresaw a future in which the West, as the dominant civilization, would find itself fending off challenges from all the others. It was the "West against the Rest." This is Putin's vision as well, although the concept does not explicitly identify any civilizations other than Russia – but there is a twist. For him, the critical fault line lies between the United States as the leader of the "collective West" and Russia as one of the two key leaders of the Rest. As Putin and Chinese President Xi Jinping agreed at their meeting in March 2023, "Right now there are changes – the likes of which we haven't seen for 100 years – and we are the ones driving these changes together."[6]

Echoing Putin's recent rhetoric, the new concept underscores Russia's role as "a unique state-civilization, a vast Eurasian and Euro-Pacific power, uniting the Russian people and other peoples who form the cultural–civilizational community of the Russian world."[7] The enemy is the United States, "an influential world power" that is also "the chief inspirer, organizer, and executor of the aggressive anti-Russian policies of the collective West, the source of the primary risks to Russia's security, international peace, and the balanced, just, and progressive development of humanity."[8]

Despite the deep-seated anti-American animus, the concept does not suggest that Russia's goal is to defeat the United States or to replace it as the global leader. Rather it is to compel it to treat Russia as an equal, that is, to respect it as a great power. For that to happen, the concept concludes, the United States will have to abandon its hegemonic designs and anti-Russian course. It is cooperation on Russia's terms or no cooperation at all – the mirror image of the US position presented in the most recent *National Security Strategy*. Meanwhile, Russia remains interested in maintaining strategic parity with the United States and it ultimately seeks peaceful coexistence on the basis of a balance of interests; amid the call to arms, there is still room for a dose of prudence in a chaotic world.

Messianic Detour

Although Putin rejected the formulation of a state ideology when he rose to power twenty-plus years ago,[9] and the Russian constitution explicitly forbids one, the new concept lays the foundation for one in the realm of foreign policy.[10] A civilizational clash implies ideological conflict; it can't simply be a matter of geopolitical competition; values and worldviews matter. In this way, the concept diminishes the role of realpolitik in the formulation and execution of foreign policy, a role that has historically undergirded Russia's conduct at the times of its greatest success.

Indeed, the concept has a powerful whiff of messianism. Russia is no ordinary great power. It is leading the worldwide crusade against the decadent, hegemonic West toward a new, just, "democratic" world order. Such messianism, as we saw in Chapter 2, has often seized the imagination of educated Russians, but rarely has it penetrated into state counsels and, whenever it has, the consequences have been ruinous for the Russian state. Putin nevertheless set Russia upon this path as he laid the grounds for the invasion of Ukraine, and he has now codified it as state doctrine, even though the battle over Ukraine, at least for the moment, appears to be a strategic disaster.

In this messianic miasma, the new foreign-policy concept presents a strategic vision that is divorced from current realities. While many countries in the global South might, for example, chafe at Western domination and harbor deep-seated resentment of European colonialism, there are few signs that they are prepared to fall in behind Russia in a crusade against the West. Their resentment preceded Russia's break with the West by many years, in some cases by decades. India is a prime example, a proud country that has led the anti-colonial movement since the end of the First World War. Non-Western countries will, of course, exploit Russia's challenge to the West to advance their own interests, and they will work with like-minded states to that end. But few, if any, are seeking a rupture in relations as the pathway to a more just world order. Even if they seek membership in organizations that Russia played a key role in founding – the Shanghai Cooperation Organization and the BRICS, for instance – what attracts them is not Russia's self-declared leading role but rather China's towering presence.

To be sure, many non-Western countries have refrained from joining the West in levying sanctions against Russia – something the Kremlin repeatedly crows about. Yet, consistently, in UN General Assembly votes, overwhelming majorities of non-Western states have refused to condone Russia's assault on Ukraine. Quite the contrary. Of the 193 member states, more than 140 (including close to one hundred non-Western states) voted for, and fewer than ten against, resolutions condemning the invasion shortly after the war began and on its first anniversary. The others (just over thirty, all from the global South, including China and India) either abstained or did not vote.[11]

And so Russia is claiming to lead a movement, which may not exist and in any event it did not create, among countries that are not looking to it for leadership. Moreover, Putin's vision exaggerates Russia's own capabilities to head a worldwide crusade, as messianic delusions characteristically do, thus preparing the ground for disappointment and, at the extreme, ruin. Chapter 3 examined the dim prospects Russia has in the next ten to fifteen years for economic growth, technological advance, and demographic revival – all necessary for the success of the crusade Putin now envisages.

He thus confronts a dilemma. Changing Russia's fortunes will almost certainly require him to abandon his messianic fervor in favor of traditional realpolitik, with its focus on preserving Russia's strategic autonomy by deftly maneuvering among major powers, not by launching crusades against some of them. Similarly, Russia needs to rebuild its ties with the West in order to realize its economic potential and to ensure it has an effective counterbalance to excessive dependence on China. In other words, Russia can seek to lead an anti-Western crusade or it can grow its future power, but it cannot do both. Putin is betting otherwise, however, and nothing suggests that he will change his mind, as long as he retains power.

Putin's War Becomes Russia's

To what extent the elites share Putin's dreams and calculations is an open question. Despite the pervasive public avowals of loyalty, occasional leaks of private conversations and anecdotal evidence suggest that some elite figures, especially from the business world, believe he is leading the country to a disaster.[12]

What is clear, nevertheless, is that a war Putin launched against the prevailing wishes of the elites and in the absence of any significant public pro-war sentiment has over time absorbed ever greater numbers of elite figures in its prosecution. Government technocrats responsible for managing the economy and blunting the impact of Western sanctions, no matter what their personal views, have done a remarkable job in keeping the economy afloat, replenishing state coffers to continue the war effort, while precipitating a sharp debate in the West about the efficacy of sanctions.[13] The dissension that erupts from time to time among officers in the military and special services and the bloggers close to them is over how the war is being conducted, not over the war as such, which they support. Finally, those who oppose the war and refuse to flee abroad have gone to ground in order to survive in an increasingly repressive environment. In this way, the elites have enabled Putin's war to become Russia's.

The situation with the broader population is more complicated. Despite some protests in Moscow and other large cities in the initial weeks of the invasion, which received widespread coverage in the West, ordinary Russians have been largely supportive. From the beginning, polls have consistently recorded that over 70 percent of the population backs the war. Popular support has not wavered, despite mounting casualities and obvious setbacks, such as the retreats from Kharkiv and Kherson in the Fall of 2022. This was true even after the Kremlin announced a partial military mobilization in September 2022, contrary to the widespread perception in the West, which focused on the tens of thousands of young men who fled abroad to avoid conscription, while ignoring the equally large numbers who filled the military's depleting ranks in Ukraine.[14] This support should perhaps not be surprising. As the Russian political analyst Andrey Kolesnikov has pointed out, the overwhelming majority of Russians are dependent on the state for their standard of living, through direct employment or monetary transfers. They are in no position to defy the state, and most see it as their duty to defend it when called.[15]

At the same time, popular attitudes turned sharply against the United States once Putin launched the invasion, much as they had eight years earlier after he seized Crimea. On the eve, fewer than half of Russians had negative feelings about the United States; the share soared to about three-quarters shortly thereafter and has stayed there ever since.[16] Again, this is not surprising, given the steady diet of anti-American vitriol spewed out by the Kremlin.

Polling results indicating support for the Kremlin should not, however, be taken as signs of great enthusiasm. Despite anecdotal evidence of Russians helping the local boys being sent to the front, the impression is that most Russians would prefer that the war simply not intrude on their daily lives. Instead of volunteering for the war, most men with family support actively seek ways to avoid being conscripted. In short, the non-elites are not as deeply involved in the war as the elites are. Even if vanishingly few are prepared to oppose it openly, Putin's war is not truly theirs. It remains far from being a patriotic war, in which the people are prepared to accept extraordinary deprivations in pursuit of victory.

With the elites implicated and the people quiescent, Putin's position would appear to be solid. And yet, so much depends on what happens on the battlefield and how the economy holds up in the face of ever-stiffer sanctions. Glaring military setbacks have fueled elite infighting, especially among those directly involved in the combat. In the Spring of 2023, for example, the head of the Wagner private military company, Evgeny Prigozhin, bitterly accused the leadership of the Ministry of Defense of treason for failing to provide adequate supplies to his forces on the front lines, as the effort to seize the eastern Ukrainian city of Bakhmut appeared to stall.[17] Thus far, such attacks have not been directed explicitly at Putin, but they can do nothing to improve the morale of front-line troops and the overall coherence of the military effort.

Nevertheless, the question remains for how long Putin can maintain domestic control. His impressive tools of repression would suggest that he can for a long time. But deteriorating conditions on the front, the need for additional rounds of mobilization, and further economic decline, all likely developments in the months ahead, could rapidly and unexpectedly change the political dynamics. The prevailing tranquility in Moscow, so critical to regime stability, could be shattered if the Kremlin can no longer spare the city the gravest consequences of war and, reversing course, finds it necessary to conscript for duty on the front lines ever greater numbers of Muscovites, many of whom then return home in coffins.[18] The forces of repression could change loyalties in the face of humiliating setbacks. Those pragmatically seeking an end to the war and improved ties with the West could be emboldened.

What Putin has made Russia's war could thus become solely his once again, should Russians ever begin to cast about for someone to blame. If his messianic ambitions go awry, he is the obvious culprit.

The Reality of Separateness

No matter what happens in the immediate aftermath of Putin's departure, whenever that might occur and under whatever circumstances, realism will eventually reemerge as the foundation of Russian foreign policy, as it has after earlier fits of messianism. Its return will allow for the restoration of more normal interaction between Russia and the United States, and the West in general, but the inherent tension that has infused relations since the end of the nineteenth century will not disappear.

This is particularly so because Russia has for an extended period abandoned the effort to join Europe that Peter the Great launched some three centuries ago. In 2018, reflecting on events after Russia's seizure of Crimea in 2014, Vladislav Surkov, who once managed domestic politics for Putin, spoke of "a hundred years of solitude," after Russia failed to find its place in the West (which, in his telling, followed an equally long, unsuccessful effort to become part of Asia).[19]

But one corrective is in order. For the past three hundred years, Russia has sought not so much to become European as to become "modern," that is, to catch up to the economic, industrial, and military standards of contemporary European, and now Western, great powers, so that Russia could hold its own on the battlefield. And the goal was always to ensure that Russia, or more properly the Russian state, could survive in what its rulers considered to be its unique characteristics, which deviated ever further from European norms as the continent advanced along its historical liberal democratic trajectory, accelerating the pace after the Napoleonic era.

Nevertheless, as is their wont, Russians have argued that it was Europe, and now the West, that refused to accept Russia as one of its own, not that Russia was disinclined to become fully European or Western. That sentiment infuses Putin's rhetoric – the West, he insists, cannot abide a powerful, independent Russia, so it has always endeavored to contain it and erode its power. His view reflects that of a broad segment of the elites.

This view is not entirely without foundation. Europeans might have considered Russia an integral part of the balance-of-power system from the mid-eighteenth century to the beginning of the Second World War, but their attitude toward Russian power shifted dramatically after the Napoleonic era. Earlier, Russia was seen as a European state in large part because its autocratic system did not differ in fundamental ways from its European counterparts.[20] European nobles from across the continent could feel comfortable at the Gallicized court in St. Petersburg – and that was all that mattered for Europe's rulers. How closely the state of Russia beyond the court hewed to European standards – and the answer is not much – was irrelevant. With this mindset, European powers did not panic in reaction to Catherine the Great's seizure of vast territories in Eastern Europe. Rather, their attitudes varied depending on a rational assessment of the threat that expansion posed to their own interests. Austria and Prussia were little concerned, in part because they also expanded into Eastern Europe and the Balkans, at times in coordination with Russia, while France was disturbed by the loss of allies in the East to Russia's expansion.[21]

When liberal democratic ideas began to sweep across Europe in the post-Napoleonic era, and Russia clung stubbornly to its autocratic principles, Russia was metaphorically steadily driven out of Europe. Any accumulation of Russia's power alarmed European rulers, because it came to be seen as a fundamental threat to European values, to Europe's essence, even if they needed to deal with Russia to maintain a stable equilibrium on the continent. Russia was in Europe but not of Europe, an alien force that had to be managed with care because it was an essential factor in Europe's power equation. This was not containment, contrary to Putin's claims, but it did bespeak a mounting unease with Russian power.

This history repeated itself in a truncated form during the initial post-Cold War decades. The United States sought to integrate Russia into the Euro-Atlantic community on the condition that it become a free-market democracy, and it made an effort, no matter how misguided, to help Russia in that transition. Russia, for its part, avowed interest in integration, but on the condition that the West accept it as it was. After briefly committing itself to democratic reforms, the Kremlin slowly took Russia down the path toward authoritarianism, seemingly not understanding that, to join the West, it had to become Western.

When it became clear that the integration project had failed, the United States reverted to a policy of containment in the face of what it saw as the resurrection of the historically imperialist, authoritarian Russia. Russia meanwhile accused Washington of bad faith. The reality was more prosaic. As Surkov pointed out, for all the similarities, Russia and the West have "different software and incompatible connectors." Or, as this book has argued, American and Russian political imperatives and national missions are fundamentally incompatible. Integration was always something of a mirage.

And so, after a short quarter-century interlude, Russia and the West returned to the status quo of the past two hundred years as two separate polities grounded in clashing worldviews that share a continent – or, in the case of Russia and the United States, as two expansionary powers with colliding ambitions across the entire Eurasian landmass, with the conflict centered today on Ukraine. Tension is unavoidable.

This situation need not inevitably yield a clash of civilizations, however, and certainly not the one of Putin's imagination. It only turns hopes for strategic partnership into delusions, while leaving open space for constructive great-power competition. Admittedly, this is a profound disappointment after the great expectations at the end of the Cold War. But it is the reality the United States faces, and, in truth, it is sufficient for American purposes. The question is what the United States might do to advance toward such relations with Russia. The answer is this book's other central theme: treat Russia as a great power.

Dealing with Russia as It Is and Will Be

No matter how the war in Ukraine might end, the United States is going to be left with Russia as a major player on the global stage, perhaps greatly diminished, but a player nonetheless. Relations will be competitive, if not necessarily adversarial, for reasons that we have already explored. That condition will last long into the future, through leadership changes in both countries. For it to be otherwise, either Russia or the United States would have to abandon the worldview, mission, and sense of purpose that have defined its national character for centuries. That is not impossible, but improbable, to say the least.

In the face of irreconcilable differences, the critical necessity is to avoid war, which would have cataclysmic consequences for both sides given the destructiveness of modern weaponry, while still engaged in competition. In other words, the task is to compete responsibly.

In that spirit, Chapter 7 laid out a framework for dealing with some key issues that Washington will confront in coming years: strategic stability, European security, Russia–China strategic alignment, and the war in Ukraine. The details will obviously depend on how events actually unfold in the years ahead. We close with reflections on the general posture the United States should adopt in order to foster responsible competition, which entails showing respect for Russia as a great power, without jeopardizing the advance of America's own long-term interests or compromising its basic principles. None of what follows is particularly novel, much is simply commonsensical. But American administrations have been reluctant to adopt wholeheartedly such a posture because it would necessarily rein in the exceptionalist or messianic impulses that have driven American foreign policy from the very beginning.

Accept Russia's Regime as Legitimate

Accepting the Russian regime and its leaders as legitimate and avoiding any appearances of seeking regime change is an essential element of respecting Russia as a great power. As a practical matter, it is impossible to have constructive talks with Russian leaders, or leaders of any other country for that matter, if they are convinced that the US goal is to overthrow them. Moreover, Washington cannot afford to wait for the emergence of more desirable leaders, given the urgency of global challenges, in which Russia is part of either the problem or the solution. Nor does Washington have the means to change Russia's domestic trajectory – the failings of the first post-Soviet decades offer ample proof. It thus has little choice but to deal with Russia as it is; nothing is gained by claiming that its rulers are illegitimate.

Establish the Limits of Acceptable Interference in Domestic Affairs

Alleviating the Kremlin's suspicions that the US goal is regime change is not a simple task. Interference in Russian domestic affairs is unavoidable, given the state of modern communications technology and its likely evolution and, of course, Russia routinely interferes in American domestic affairs. In these circumstances, the task is to forge an agreement with Moscow on the limits of acceptable interference, or, to put it contrariwise, to reach an understanding as to the point beyond which interference constitutes a direct threat to the regime's integrity. Could the two countries, for example, agree that routine commentary critical of the other's domestic policies is tolerable, while efforts to tamper with electoral processes and results clearly cross the line? Could they agree on what level of backing for opposition forces is acceptable and what level threatens regime stability? We do not know. What we do know is that coming to an agreement on where to draw the line, and how to monitor adherence to it, will prove arduous. Washington needs to seek one with Moscow, nonetheless.

Accommodate Russia's Legitimate Interests When Possible

Like any great power, Russia has geopolitical and security interests, especially with regard to its immediate neighbors, which will often run contrary to American goals. Refusing to acknowledge any of them as legitimate is inconsistent with treating Russia like a great power. This is not a call for Washington to defer to Moscow's legitimate preferences, but rather for it to seek to accommodate them to the extent that that does not risk the long-term advancement of its own goals and interests. It is also a call for Washington to make sure it is prepared to counter effectively whatever steps Moscow might take to defend its interests, legitimate or not, if it must for its own reasons cross Moscow's red lines.

Harness Russian Power to US Interests

The United States needs to accept the reality of Russian power and influence. Both will wax and wane over time, but they most likely will never diminish to such an extent that Moscow no longer has the ability to complicate or facilitate the success of a significant range of American policies. In that light, Washington should resist the temptation to see Russia's exercise of power and influence as essentially malign, as it has for the greater part of the last one hundred years. The task is not to blindly counter, or to contain, Russian power, but rather to harness it to the achievement of American goals. That should be obvious when it comes to issues of strategic stability, the non-proliferation of weapons of mass destruction, international terrorism, and climate change, for example. But Russian power could also be harnessed to the creation of regional balances of power that serve American interests, especially along Russia's long periphery in Asia and the Arctic.

Eschew Ideology and Moralism

The United States gains nothing by turning relations with Russia into a morality play, a contest between democracy and autocracy or, at the extreme, between good and evil. Because it cuts to the heart of a country's values and identity, ideological confrontation, unlike geopolitical competition, feeds the demonization of competitors, precluding the compromises and trade-offs that are necessary to advance American interests in an increasingly complex and multifaceted world. It complicates efforts to forge relations with other countries that the United States will need as partners in dealing with various geopolitical challenges, in part because it will find that they do not neatly fall into the bipolar schema it has fashioned, particularly in regions outside Europe, where democracy as a rule is not flourishing.

Strategic Patience

To reiterate one lesson the United States should have learned from the failed effort to integrate Russia into the Euro-Atlantic community, strategic patience is a virtue. The Russia challenge is not going to vanish magically, no matter what policies the United States pursues in the years ahead. The best it can hope for, to which it should also aspire, is the transformation of the current adversarial relationship, which is fraught with the risk of direct military confrontation and the escalation to nuclear catastrophe that could foreshadow, into a competition reasonably managed in the spirit of peaceful coexistence. The path to that goal will be laid by a series of small steps to resolve or constructively manage the points of tension that have accumulated in recent years and the new ones that will inevitably arise in the future, starting with the war in Ukraine.

Success will be measured by the extent to which the United States can harness Russian power to its purposes and limit the damage of the unavoidable setbacks through periodic leadership changes in both countries and the shifting global geopolitical and technological environment. To succeed, American leaders will need strategic vision. They will need to be clear-eyed about American power and its limits. They will need to be unsentimental, unblinkered, and non-ideological in their assessment of Russia. And they will need to be patient in pursuit of their vision, as their predecessors were during the Cold War.

Russia will never be the strategic partner the United States once hoped for. But neither must it remain the unrelenting adversary it is today. With skillful American diplomacy, and, granted, good fortune, it could become a constructive rival. Whatever the regrets might be over the failure to achieve the loftier aspirations nourished by the Cold War's end, such a Russia would be adequate for American purposes in the new world that is taking shape before our eyes. Fashioning and then sustaining constructive rivalry should thus be counted as a great success.

Notes

Introduction

1 Robert Legvold, *Return to Cold War* (London, United Kingdom: Polity, 2016), 28–31.

2 White House, *National Security Strategy of the United States of America* (Washington, DC: The White House, October 2022), 25, https://www.whi tehouse.gov/wp-content/uploads/2022/10/Biden-Harris-Administrations-Nati onal-Security-Strategy-10.2022.pdf.

3 Edward L. Keenan, "Muscovite Political Folkways," *Russian Review* 45, no. 2 (April 1986): 118–19.

1 The Foundations of America's Russia Policy

1 George H.W. Bush, "Address Before a Joint Session of the Congress on the State of the Union" (State of the Union, Washington, DC, January 28, 1992), https://www.presidency.ucsb.edu/documents/address-before-joint-session-the -congress-the-state-the-union-0.

2 Michael Wines, "Bush and Yeltsin Declare Formal End To Cold War; Agree to Exchange Visits," *New York Times*, February 2, 1992, sec. World, https://www .nytimes.com/1992/02/02/world/bush-and-yeltsin-declare-formal-end-to-cold -war-agree-to-exchange-visits.html. The text of the declaration can be found at "Presidents Bush and Yeltsin: 'Dawn of a New Era,'" *New York Times*, February 2, 1992, sec. World, https://www.nytimes.com/1992/02/02/world/presidents -bush-and-yeltsin-dawn-of-a-new-era.html.

3 "Russian Federation–United States: Charter for Partnership and Friendship," *International Legal Materials* 31, no. 4 (July 1992): 782–9, https://www.jstor .org/stable/20693708#metadata_info_tab_contents.

4 The stabilization fund was never set up.

5 James A. Baker, III, *The Politics of Diplomacy* (New York, NY: G.P. Putnam's Sons, 1995), 654–8.

6 The treaty was signed on January 3, 1993, but never entered into force. The US Senate ratified it in 1996. The Russian State Duma followed in 2000 but

only on the condition that the United States did not withdraw from the Anti-Ballistic Missile (ABM) Treaty. Russia withdrew from the Treaty in 2002 in response to the US exit from the ABM Treaty.

7 Baker, III, *Politics of Diplomacy*, op. cit., 625–33.

8 George Bush and Brent Scowcroft, *A World Transformed* (New York, NY: Alfred A. Knopf, 1998).

9 Strobe Talbott, "The End of the Beginning: The Emergence of a New Russia" (Address, Stanford University, September 19, 1997), https://1997-2001.state .gov/regions/nis/970919talbott.html.

10 Bill Clinton, "Remarks to the American Society of Newspaper Editors in Annapolis" (Address, United States Naval Academy, April 1, 1993), https:// www.presidency.ucsb.edu/documents/remarks-the-american-society-newspa per-editors-annapolis.

11 Strobe Talbott, *The Russia Hand* (New York, NY: Random House, 2002), 10; See also William J. Burns, *The Back Channel* (New York, NY: Random House, 2019), 104–5.

12 Clinton, "Remarks," op. cit. See also Bill Clinton, *My Life*, 1st edn. (New York, NY: Alfred A. Knopf, 2004), 502–8.

13 Talbott, *The Russia Hand*, op. cit., 43.

14 James M. Goldgeier and Michael McFaul, *Power and Purpose* (Washington, DC: Brookings Institution Press, 2003), 92.

15 Matthew Rojansky, "Indispensable Institutions: The Obama–Medvedev Commission and Five Decades of US–Russia Dialogue" (Carnegie Endowment for International Peace, 2010).

16 Goldgeier and McFaul, *Power and Purpose*, op. cit., 95–8.

17 Talbott, "The End of the Beginning," op. cit.

18 Angela Stent, *The Limits of Partnership* (Princeton, NJ: Princeton University Press, 2014), 42–5; M.E. Sarotte, *Not One Inch: America, Russia, and the Making of the Post-Cold War Stalemate* (New Haven, CT: Yale University Press, 2021), 316–19.

19 See Condoleezza Rice, "Campaign 2000: Promoting the National Interest," *Foreign Affairs* (January/February 2000), https://www.foreignaffairs.com/print /node/1110090.

20 Russia and the former Soviet space were reabsorbed into the European Directorate of the National Security Council apparatus. Central Asia and the Caucasus were paired with the Aegean region, and the post-Soviet European

states – Belarus, Moldova, and Ukraine – were treated as part of Eastern Europe. Russia stood alone.

21 Press Conference by President Bush and Russian Federation President Putin, Brdo Pri Kranju, Slovenia, June 16, 2001, https://georgewbush-whitehouse.ar chives.gov/news/releases/2001/06/20010618.html

22 Peter Baker and Susan Glasser, *Kremlin Rising*, updated edn. (Washington, DC: Potomac Books, Inc., 2007), 132–4.

23 White House, *National Security Strategy of the United States of America* (Washington, DC: White House, 2002), https://history.defense.gov/Portals /70/Documents/nss/nss2002.pdf?ver=oyVN99aEnrAWijAc_O5eiQ%3d%3d. See also Condoleezza Rice, "Campaign 2000," op. cit.

24 George W. Bush and Vladimir Putin, "Joint Statement on New US–Russian Relationship" (Crawford, Texas, November 13, 2001), https:// georgewbush-whitehouse.archives.gov/news/releases/2001/11/20011113-4. html.

25 Text of Joint Declaration, Moscow, May 24, 2002, https://georgewbush-white house.archives.gov/news/releases/2002/05/20020524-2.html

26 Condoleezza Rice, *No Higher Honor* (New York, NY: Crown Publishers, 2011), 324–6.

27 George W. Bush, "Second Inaugural Address of George W. Bush" (Washington, DC, January 20, 2005), https://avalon.law.yale.edu/21st_ century/gbush2.asp.

28 "US–Russia Strategic Framework Declaration" (April 6, 2008), https://george wbush-whitehouse.archives.gov/news/releases/2008/04/20080406-4.html.

29 Barack Obama and Dmitry Medvedev, "Joint Statement by President Dmitry Medvedev of the Russian Federation and President Barack Obama of the United States of America" (Washington, DC, 2009).

30 Rojansky, "Indispensable Institutions," op. cit., 29–34.

31 Dmitry Medvedev, "Go Russia!," Russian President, September 10, 2009, http://en.kremlin.ru/events/president/news/5413.

32 Nikolaus von Twickel, "Biden 'Opposes' 3rd Putin Term," *Moscow Times*, March 10, 2011, https://www.themoscowtimes.com/2011/03/10/biden-oppo ses-3rd-putin-term-a5538.

33 Francis Fukuyama, "The End of History?," *The National Interest*, Summer 1989, 12.

34 Samuel P. Huntington, "Democracy's Third Wave," *Journal of Democracy* 2, no. 2 (Spring 1991).

35 Algimantas Jankauskas and Liutauras Gudzinskas, "Reconceptualizing Transitology: Lessons from Post-Communism," *Lithuanian Annual Strategic Review*, November 18, 2008, 181–99.

36 John Williamson, ch. 2, "What Washington Means by Policy Reform," in *Latin American Adjustment: How Much Has Happened?* (Washington, DC: Institute for International Economics, 1990).

37 George H.W. Bush, "A Whole Europe, A Free Europe" (Mainz, Germany, May 31, 1989), https://voicesofdemocracy.umd.edu/bush-a-whole-europe-spe ech-text/.

38 "Russia GDP 1988–2022," Macrotrends, n.d., https://www.macrotrends.net /countries/RUS/russia/gdp-gross-domestic-product.

39 "U.S. GDP 1960–2022," Macrotrends, n.d., https://www.macrotrends.net/co untries/USA/united-states/gdp-gross-domestic-product.

40 GDP (Constant 2015 US$) - Russian Federation, United States" (World Bank, n.d.), https://data.worldbank.org/indicator/NY.GDP.MKTP.KD?lo cations=RU-US;%20https://data.worldbank.org/indicator/NY.GDP.MKTP .PP.KD?locations=RU-US.

41 "GDP Growth (Annual %) - Russian Federation" (The World Bank, n.d.), https://data.worldbank.org/indicator/NY.GDP.MKTP.KD.ZG?end=2021&l ocations=RU&name_desc=false&start=2002.

42 Nickolas Roth, "US–Russian Nuclear Security Cooperation: Rebuilding Equality, Mutual Benefit, and Respect," *Deep Cuts*, no. 4 (June 2015), https:// deepcuts.org/files/pdf/Deep_Cuts_Issue_Brief4_US-Russian_Nuclear_Secur ity_Cooperation1.pdf.

43 Talbott, *The Russia Hand*, op. cit., 78–82, 111–14; Sarotte, *Not One Inch* op. cit., 158–60, 203–4; Steven Pifer, "The Trilateral Process: The United States, Ukraine, Russia and Nuclear Weapons," Arms Control (Brookings Institution, May 9, 2011), https://www.brookings.edu/research/the-trilateral-process-the -united-states-ukraine-russia-and-nuclear-weapons/. To persuade Kyiv to send the nuclear weapons to Russia, the United States, United Kingdom, and Russia provided Ukraine with "assurances" of its security, independence, and territo-rial integrity, codified in the 1994 Budapest Memorandum. Russia of course failed to honor its commitment when it seized Crimea from Ukraine in 2014, not to speak of when it invaded Ukraine for a second time in February 2022.

44 See the argument laid out by Talbott in 1995: Strobe Talbott, "Why NATO Should Grow," *New York Review*, August 10, 1995, https://www.nybooks.com /articles/1995/08/10/why-nato-should-grow/?lp_txn_id=1359478.

45 Ibid.

46 Michael A. Allen, "The US Military Presence in Europe Has Been Declining for 30 Years – the Current Crisis in Ukraine May Reverse That Trend," *The Conversation*, January 25, 2022, https://theconversation.com/the-us-military -presence-in-europe-has-been-declining-for-30-years-the-current-crisis-in-ukra ine-may-reverse-that-trend-175595.

47 The formal title is "Founding Act on Mutual Relations, Cooperation and Security between NATO and the Russian Federation." For the text, see "Founding Act on Mutual Relations, Cooperation and Security between NATO and the Russian Federation" (Paris, France: NATO, 1997), https://www.nato.int/cps /en/natohq/official_texts_25468.htm.

48 Sarotte, *Not One Inch*, op. cit., 219–27. In 2002, NATO replaced the Permanent Joint Council with the NATO–Russian Council, where Russia would sit down not with NATO as an organization but with NATO members in their national capacities for discussion of a limited, but expandable, range of issues that could result in parallel or joint operations. Russia would presumably have a greater voice in, but still no veto over, NATO decisions.

49 Condoleezza Rice, *No Higher Honor*, op. cit., 667.

50 On the Russian elite attitude toward Ukrainian and Georgian NATO member-ship during the Bush administration, see Burns, *The Back Channel*, op. cit., 233.

51 George W. Bush, *Decision Points* (New York, NY: Crown Publishers, 2010), 430–1; Condoleezza Rice, *No Higher Honor*, op. cit., 671–5.

52 Stephen Blank, "Commentary: Russia Versus NATO In The CIS," RadioFreeEurope/RadioLiberty, May 14, 2008, https://www.rferl.org/a/1117 479.html; Condoleezza Rice, *No Higher Honor*, op. cit., 675–6.

53 Zbigniew Brzezinski, "The Premature Partnership," *Foreign Affairs*, March/ April 1994, https://www.foreignaffairs.com/articles/russian-federation/1994 -03-01/premature-partnership.

54 Steven Pifer, "Ukraine, Russia and the US Policy Response," Brookings Institution, June 4, 2014, https://www.brookings.edu/testimonies/ukraine-rus sia-and-the-u-s-policy-response/.

55 After the war in Georgia, Russia quickly recognized the independence of Abkhazia and South Ossetia, but it never moved to annex them. Moreover, what Russia did was not radically different from many Western countries' recognition of Kosovo's independence after the war against the former Yugoslavia, although the period between the war and recognition was measured

in years, not days, as was the case with Russia and Georgia's two separatist regions.

56 Julian Borger, "Barack Obama: Russia Is a Regional Power Showing Weakness over Ukraine." *Guardian*, March 25, 2014. https://www.the guardian.com/world/2014/mar/25/barack-obama-russia-regional-power-ukraine-weakness.

57 Joseph Biden, "Remarks by the Vice President at the Munich Security Conference" (Munich, Germany, February 7, 2015), https://obamawhiteh ouse.archives.gov/the-press-office/2015/02/07/remarks-vice-president-munich-security-conference.

58 That is, the five permanent members of the UN Security Council, China, France, Great Britain, Russia, and the United States, plus Germany.

59 John Bolton, *The Room Where It Happened* (New York, NY: Simon & Schuster, 2020), 156–7; Fiona Hill, *There Is Nothing for You Here* (New York, NY: Harper Books, 2021), 231–5.

60 Burgess Everett and Rachel Bade, "Trump Sparks Republican Rift on Russia," Politico, July 11, 2018, https://www.politico.com/story/2018/07/11/trump-russia-republicans-713537.

61 "Summary of the National Defense Strategy of The United States of America" (Department of Defense, 2018), 2, https://dod.defense.gov/Portals/1/Docu ments/pubs/2018-National-Defense-Strategy-Summary.pdf.

62 Cited in Colm Quinn, "Biden Issues His First Russia Sanctions – But Not His Last." Foreign Policy, March 3, 2021. https://foreignpolicy.com/2021/03/03 /biden-issues-his-first-russia-sanctions-but-not-his-last/.

63 Joseph R. Biden Jr., "Interim National Security Strategic Guidance" (White House, March 2021), https://www.whitehouse.gov/wp-content/uploads/2021 /03/NSC-1v2.pdf.

64 "War in Europe: Responding to Russia's Invasion of Ukraine," Statement (International Crisis Group, February 24, 2022). https://www.crisisgroup.org /europe-central-asia/eastern-europe/ukraine/war-europe-responding-russias-in vasion-ukraine.

65 Joseph Biden, "Remarks by President Biden on the United Efforts of the Free World to Support the People of Ukraine" (Warsaw, Poland, March 26, 2022). https://www.whitehouse.gov/briefing-room/speeches-remarks/2022/03/26/re marks-by-president-biden-on-the-united-efforts-of-the-free-world-to-support -the-people-of-ukraine/.

66 Ibid. See also Joseph Biden, "President Biden: What America Will and Will Not Do in Ukraine," *New York Times*, May 31, 2022, sec. Opinion, https://www.nytimes.com/2022/05/31/opinion/biden-ukraine-strategy.html.

67 Biden, "Remarks by President Biden," op. cit.

2 *The Clash of Worldviews*

1 Norman E. Saul, *Distant Friends: The United States and Russia, 1763–1867* (Lawrence, KS: University of Kansas Press, 1991).

2 John Lewis Gaddis, *Russia, the Soviet Union, and the United States: An Interpretive History* (New York, NY: John Wiley and Sons, Inc., 1978), 25–6.

3 Ibid., 55–6.

4 William Appleman Williams, *American–Russian Relations 1782–1947* (New York, NY: Octagon Books, 1971), 3.

5 V.O. Klyuchevsky, "Kurs russkoy istorii: Lecture 3," http://www.spsl.nsc.ru/history/kluch/kluch03.htm; Klyuchevsky, "Kurs russkoy istorii: Lecture 4," http://www.spsl.nsc.ru/history/kluch/kluch04.htm; Dominic Lieven, *Empire: The Russian Empire and Its Rivals* (New Haven, CT: Yale University Press, 2000), 201–6.

6 The Geopolitics of the United States, Part 1: The Inevitable Empire" (Stratfor, July 4, 2016), https://worldview.stratfor.com/article/geopolitics-united-states-part-1-inevitable-empire.

7 Ibid.

8 Ibid.

9 Adam B. Ulam, "Nationalism, Panslavism, Communism," in *Russian Foreign Policy: Essays in Historical Perspective*, ed. Ivo J. Lederer (New Haven, CT: Yale University Press, 1962), 39–40.

10 James H. Billington, *The Icon and the Axe: An Interpretative History of Russian Culture* (New York, NY: Vintage Books, 1966), 52–9. The quotation from Philoteus's letter to Vasily III is on page 58. See also V.O. Klyuchevsky, "Part II," in *Kurs russkoy istorii*, 3rd edn. (Moscow, Russia: P.P. Rubinshinsky, 1912), 172–3.

11 Michael Cherniavsky, "'Holy Russia': A Study in the History of an Idea," *The American Historical Review* 63, no. 3 (April 1958): 617–37. See also Liah Greenfeld, *Nationalism: Five Roads to Modernity* (Cambridge, MA: Harvard University Press, 1992), 260–74.

12 Martin Malia, *Alexander Herzen and the Birth of Russian Socialism* (New York, NY: Grosset & Dunlap, 1961), 281–9. The quotation is on page 289.

13 Ibid., 395–406; According to Paul Bushkovitch's personal email on August 1, 2021, the populists eventually decided that Marxism was appropriate for Europe, but not for Russia, where they were convinced their ideology provided the right guide to the future.

14 Billington, *The Icon and the Axe*, op. cit., 395–97; Geoffrey Hosking, *Russia and the Russians: A History* (Cambridge, MA: Harvard University Press, 2001), 313–14.

15 Ibid., 107. See also Donald Ostrowski, "'Moscow the Third Rome' as Historical Ghost," in *Byzantium: Faith and Power (1261–1557): Perspectives on Late Byzantine Art and Culture*, ed. Sarah T. Brooks (New Haven, CT: Yale University Press, 2006), 177. For a review of the sources, see pages 170–7, which demonstrate that "Moscow the Third Rome" had little influence in the tsarist court.

16 Aleksandr Filyushkin, "Proyekt 'Russkaya Livoniya,'" *Quaestio Rossica* 2 (2014): 97, https://elar.urfu.ru/bitstream/10995/27746/1/qr_2_2014_07.pdf.

17 Hosking, *Russia and the Russians*, op. cit., 99–107,117–19; Orlando Figes, *The Story of Russia* (New York, NY: Metropolitan Books, 2022), 70–1.

18 William Fuller, Jr., *Strategy and Power in Russia 1600–1914* (New York, NY: The Free Press, 1992), 131–3.

19 Mark Jarrett, *The Congress of Vienna and Its Legacy: War and Great Power Diplomacy after Napoleon* (London, United Kingdom: I.B. Tauris, 2016), 152–3.

20 Marie-Pierre Rey, *Alexander I: The Tsar Who Defeated Napoleon* (DeKalb, IL: Northern Illinois University Press, 2012), 289–91.

21 Nicholas Riasanovsky, "Official Nationality: Foreign Policy," in *Nicholas I and Official Nationality in Russia 1825-1855* (Berkeley, CA: University of California Press, 1959), 236–65.

22 David Gillard, *The Struggle for Asia, 1828-1914* (New York: Holmes and Meier Publishers, Inc. 1977), 79–91.

23 Hosking, *Russia and the Russians*, op. cit., 289-300; Richard Pipes, The *Russian Revolution* (New York: Alfred A. Knopf, 1990), 38–9.

24 Cyril E. Black, "The Pattern of Russian Objectives," in *Russian Foreign Policy: Essays in Historical Perspective*, ed. Ivo J. Lederer (New Haven, CT: Yale University Press, 1962), 26–7, and Alexander Dallin, "The Use of International Movements," in *Russian Foreign Policy: Essays in Historical Perspective*, ed. Ivo J. Lederer (New Haven, CT: Yale University Press, 1962), 316–18; and Hosking, *Russia and the Russians*, op. cit., 313–17.

25 Ibid., 386–8.

26 Fuller, Jr., *Strategy and Power in Russia*, op. cit., 369–77.

27 Ulam, "Nationalism, Panslavism, Communism," op. cit., 46–60.

28 Adam B. Ulam, *Expansion and Coexistence: The History of Soviet Foreign Policy 1917–1967* (New York, NY: Praeger Publishers, 1968), 243–5.

29 Ibid., 247–50.

30 Geoffrey Hosking, *Russia: People and Empire 1552–1917* (Cambridge, MA: Harvard University Press, 1997), 4. with my substituting "state" for Hosking's "empire." See also Alexander Yanov, ch. 8, in *The Origin of Autocracy: Ivan the Terrible in Russian History* (Berkeley, CA: University of California Press, 1981).

31 Dale Carter, "American Exceptionalism: An Idea That Will Not Die," *American Studies in Scandinavia* 29, no. 2 (1997): 76–84; Jason A. Edwards, "An Exceptional Debate: The Championing of and Challenge to American Exceptionalism," *Rhetoric & Public Affairs* 13, no. 2 (Summer 2012): 351–67.

32 Hilde Eliassen Restad, "Old Paradigms in History Die Hard in Political Science: US Foreign Policy and American Exceptionalism," *American Political Thought* 1, no. 1 (May 2012): 53–76. https://www.jstor.org/stable/10.1086/664586 ?seq=1#metadata_info_tab_contents; Robert Kagan, *Dangerous Nation* (New York, NY: Vintage Books, 2007), 7–10.

33 Bernard Bailyn, *The Ideological Origins of the American Revolution*, 50th Anniversary edn. (Cambridge, MA: Harvard University Press, 2017), 32–3.

34 Ibid., 26–30.

35 Restad, "Old Paradigms in History," op. cit., 53–76, https://www.jstor.org/st able/10.1086/664586?seq=1#metadata_info_tab_contents.

36 Ibid.

37 Peter S. Onuf, *Jefferson's Empire: The Language of American Nationhood* (Charlottesville, VA: University Press of Virginia, 2000), 1–10; Thomas R. Hietala, *Manifest Design: American Exceptionalism and Empire,* revd. edn. (Ithaca, NY: Cornell University Press, 1985), 193–208.

38 Henry Kissinger, *Diplomacy* (New York, NY: Simon & Schuster, 1994), 18–19.

39 John Quincy Adams, "Address Delivered at the Request of the Committee for Arrangements for Celebrating the Anniversary of Independence" (Address, Washington, DC, July 4, 1821), https://www.libertarianism.org/essays/addre ss-delivered-request-committee-arrangements-celebrating-anniversary-indepen dence.

40 Charles A. Kupchan, *Isolationism: A History of America's Efforts to Shield Itself from the World* (Oxford University Press, 2020), 102–6.

41 Henry Kissinger, *Diplomacy*, op. cit., 38–9.

42 Kupchan, *Isolationism*, op. cit., 189, 193–7. See also Kagan, *Dangerous Nation*, op. cit., 416.

43 Stephen Wertheim, "Reluctant Liberator: Theodore Roosevelt's Philosophy of Self-Government and Preparation for Philippine Independence," *Presidential Studies Quarterly* 39, no. 3 (September 2009): 497–8.

44 Kupchan, *Isolationism*, op. cit., 197–200.

45 Ibid., 206–8; Wertheim, "Reluctant Liberator," op. cit., 505–9.

46 Kissinger, *Diplomacy*, op. cit., 45. See also Kupchan, *Isolationism*, op. cit., 219–22.

47 Ibid., 244–53.

48 Madeleine K. Albright, Interview on NBC-TV "The Today Show" with Matt Lauer, Television, February 19, 1998, https://1997-2001.state.gov/statements /1998/980219a.html.

49 "Excerpts from 'Tales of Times Gone By' [Povest' vremennykh let]," *Russian Chronicles*, n.d., https://pages.uoregon.edu/kimball/chronicle. htm. This paragraph contains lightly rewritten material originally included in Thomas E. Graham, "The Sources of Russian Conduct," *The National Interest*, August 24, 2016, https://nationalinterest.org/feature/the-sou rces-russian-conduct-17462.

50 Keenan, "Muscovite Political Folkways," op. cit., 128–36, 156–72.

51 For a description of this dilemma in the eighteenth century, see Fuller, Jr., *Strategy and Power in Russia*, op. cit., 94–8.

52 For a detailed description and analysis of Russian expansion from 1700 to 1917, see John P. LeDonne, *The Russian Empire and the World, 1700-1917: The Geopolitics of Expansion and Containment* (New York, NY: Oxford University Press, 1997). See also Fuller, Jr., *Strategy and Power in Russia*, op. cit., 132–9; Lieven, *Empire*, op. cit., 262–8; Black, "The Pattern of Russian Objectives," op. cit., 3–38.

53 Lieven, *Empire*, op. cit., 262.

54 Fuller, Jr., *Strategy and Power in Russia*, op. cit., 220–30.

55 As William Fuller notes, writing about the period after the Crimean War, "The tsarist regime was reluctant to display any signs of weakness in its dealings abroad and was therefore reluctant to accept any diminution in Russia's international standing and prestige." Fuller, Jr., *Strategy and Power in Russia*, op. cit., 462.

56 Lieven, *Empire*, op. cit., 249–50.

57 Robert D. Kaplan, *The Revenge of Geography* (New York, NY: Random House, 2012), 159.

58 Joseph Biden, "Remarks by President Biden on America's Place in the World" (Washington, DC, February 4, 2021), https://www.whitehouse.gov/briefing -room/speeches-remarks/2021/02/04/remarks-by-president-biden-on-americas -place-in-the-world/.

59 "Yeltsin Addresses Russian Parliament on 25th December," BBC, December 28, 1991, SU/1264/C3/1.

60 Boris Yeltsin, "Zapiski prezidenta," *Ogonek*, 1994, 150–3. The quotations can be found on page 152.

61 "Speech by Andrei Kozyrev," BBC, April 20, 1992, SU/1359/C1/1.

62 Vladimir Putin, "Ob istoricheskom yedinstve russkikh i ukraintsev," President of Russia, July 12, 2021, http://kremlin.ru/events/president/news/66181.

63 Vladimir Putin, "Vstrecha s molodymi predprinimataelyami, inzhenerami i uchenymi," President of Russia, June 9, 2022, http://kremlin.ru/events/presi dent/news/68606.

3 The Paradox of Russian Power

1 Paul Kennedy, *The Rise and Fall of the Great Powers* (New York, NY: Vintage Books, 1987), 232–41.

2 Robert B. Zoellick, *America in the World* (New York, NY: Twelve, 2020), 260–5; see also John Lewis Gaddis, *Strategies of Containment*, revd. and exp. edn. (Oxford University Press, 2005), 22–3.

3 James Risen and Ken Klippenstein, "The CIA Thought Putin Would Quickly Conquer Ukraine. Why Did They Get It so Wrong?," *The Intercept*, October 5, 2022, https://theintercept.com/2022/10/05/russia-ukraine-putin-cia; Farida Rustamova and Maxim Tovkaylo, "How Putin Pumped Money into Russia's Army for More than Two Decades, and What Came of It," *Faridaily* (blog), August 30, 2022, https://faridaily.substack.com/p/how-putin-pumped-money -into-russias.

4 Martin Malia, *Russia under Western Eyes: From the Bronze Horseman to the Lenin Mausoleum* (Cambridge, MA: The Belknap Press, 1990), 7–8.

5 Scott Wilson, "Obama Dismisses Russia as 'Regional Power' Acting out of Weakness," *Washington Post*, March 25, 2014, https://www.washingtonpost .com/world/national-security/obama-dismisses-russia-as-regional-power-acting -out-of-weakness/2014/03/25/1e5a678e-b439-11e3-b899-20667de76985_sto ry.html.

6 Biden Jr., "Interim National Security Strategic Guidance," op. cit.

7 Ibid., 8.

8 White House, *National Security Strategy*, op. cit., October 2022.

9 John D. Negroponte, "Annual Threat Assessment of the US Intelligence Community" (Office of the Director of National Intelligence, January 11, 2007), https://www.dni.gov/files/documents/Newsroom/Testimonies/200701 11_testimony.pdf.

10 Dennis C. Blair, "Annual Threat Assessment of the US Intelligence Community" (Office of the Director of National Intelligence, March 10, 2009), https://www.dni.gov/files/documents/Newsroom/Testimonies/200903 10_testimony.pdf.

11 See, for example, James R. Clapper, "Annual Threat Assessment of the US Intelligence Community" (Office of the Director of National Intelligence, February 9, 2016), https://www.dni.gov/files/documents/SASC_Unclassified _2016_ATA_SFR_FINAL.pdf; and "Annual Threat Assessment of the US Intelligence Community" (Office of the Director of National Intelligence, April 9, 2021), https://www.dni.gov/files/ODNI/documents/assessments/ATA -2021-Unclassified-Report.pdf.

12 Daniel R. Coats, "Statement for the Record Worldwide Threat Assessment of the US Intelligence Community" (Washington, DC: Senate Select Committee on Intelligence, January 29, 2019), https://www.dni.gov/files/ODNI/docu ments/2019-ATA-SFR---SSCI.pdf.

13 "Annual Threat Assessment of the US Intelligence Community" (Office of the Director of National Intelligence, February 7, 2022), 10–13, https:// www.dni.gov/files/ODNI/documents/assessments/ATA-2022-Unclassified- Report.pdf.

14 See Nabi Abdullaev and Simon Saradzhyan, "Measuring National Power: Is Vladimir Putin's Russia in Decline?," Russia Matters, May 4, 2018, https:// www.russiamatters.org/analysis/measuring-national-power-vladimir-putins-rus sia-decline.

15 On China's global ambitions, see Elizabeth Economy, "Xi's New World Order," *Foreign Affairs*, January/February 2022, https://www.foreignaffairs .com/articles/china/2021-12-09/xi-jinpings-new-world-order?utm_medium= promo_email&utm_source=pre_release&utm_campaign=pre_release_06072 2&utm_content=20221010&utm_term=all-special-send; Kevin Rudd, "The World According to Xi Jinping," *Foreign Affairs*, November/December 2022, https://www.foreignaffairs.com/china/world-according-xi-jinping-china-ideo

logue-kevin-rudd?utm_medium=promo_email&utm_source=pre_release&u
tm_campaign=pre_release_060722&utm_content=20221010&utm_term=all
-special-send.

16 "Soviet Economy: Assessment of How Well the CIA Has Estimated the Size of
the Economy" (United States General Accounting Office, September 1991), 2,
16, https://www.gao.gov/assets/nsiad-91-274.pdf.

17 Vladimir   Putin,   "Poslaniye   Prezidenta   Federal'nomu   Sobraniyu"
(Moscow, Russia, March 1, 2018), http://www.kremlin.ru/events/president/ne
ws/56957.

18 "GDP (Constant 2015 US$)- China, Russian Federation, United States" (The
World Bank, n.d.), https://data.worldbank.org/indicator/NY.GDP.MKTP
.KD?end=2021&locations=CN-RU-US&start=2008; "GDP, PPP (Constant
2017 International $) - China, Russian Federation, United States" (The World
Bank, n.d.), https://data.worldbank.org/indicator/NY.GDP.MKTP.PP.KD?en
d=2021&locations=CN-RU-US&start=2008.

19 "Prognoz dolgosrochnogo sotsial'no-ekonomicheskogo razvitiya Rossiyskoy
Federatsii na period do 2030 goda" (Moscow, Russia: Ministry of Economic
Development, March 2013), http://static.government.ru/media/files/41d4575
92e04b76338b7.pdf.

20 Evgeny Gontmakher, "Russia's Import Substitution: Effects and Consequence"
(Geopolitical Intelligence Services, December 2, 2021), https://www.gisreports
online.com/r/import-substitution/: "Proizvoditeli perechislili pomekhi impor-
tozameshcheniyu," *Kommersant*, October 5, 2021, https://www.kommersant
.ru/doc/5018091.

21 Richard Connolly, "Russia's Economic Pivot to Asia in a Shifting Regional
Environment" (Royal United Services Institute for Defence and Security
Studies, September 2021), 5–14, https://static.rusi.org/297_EI_RFE.pdf.

22 For a book length discussion of the implications of climate change for Russia's
standing as a great power, see Thane Gustafson, *Klimat: Russia in the Age of
Climate Change* (Cambridge, MA: Harvard University Press, 2021).

23 Soumitra Dutta et al., *Global Innovation Index 2022*, 15th edn. (Geneva,
Switzerland: World Intellectual Property Organization, 2022), 19–20, https://
www.wipo.int/edocs/pubdocs/en/wipo-pub-2000-2022-section1-en-gii-2022
-at-a-glance-global-innovation-index-2022-15th-edition.pdf.

24 Vladimir Putin, "O strategii nauchno-tekhnologicheskogo razvitiya Rossiyskoy
Federatsii" (Prezident Rossiyskoy Federatsii, December 1, 2016), http://static
.kremlin.ru/media/acts/files/0001201612010007.pdf.

25 Medvedev, "Go Russia!", op. cit.

26 Sam Klebanov, "Skolkovo: The Story of Russia's Failed Attempt to Build Its Own Silicon Valley," The Business of Business, April 27, 2022.

27 "Research and Development Expenditure (% of GDP) - United States, Russian Federation" (The World Bank, n.d.), https://data.worldbank.org/indicator/GB.XPD.RSDV.GD.ZS?locations=US-RU.

28 Putin, "O Strategii," op. cit., December 1, 2016, 10007.

29 Putin, "Poslaniye Prezidenta Federal'nomu Sobraniiu," op. cit., March 1, 2018, 56957.

30 James Byrne et al., "Silicon Lifeline: Western Electronics at the Heart of Russia's War Machine" (Royal United Services Institute for Defence and Security Studies, August 2022), 5, https://static.rusi.org/RUSI-Silicon-Lifeline-final-updated-web_1.pdf.

31 "Rosstat Predicts a Decline in Russia's Population over the next Two Decades" (The Bank of Finland Institute for Emerging Economies (BOFIT), January 17, 2020), https://www.bofit.fi/en/monitoring/weekly/2020/vw202003_5/; see "Russian Federation: Total Population" (The United Nations, 2022.), https://population.un.org/wpp/Graphs/Probabilistic/POP/TOT/643; and Eugeniu Han, "Appendix C," in *The Future of the Russian Military: Russia's Ground Combat Capabilities and Implications for US–Russia Competition*, by Andrew Radin et al. (Santa Monica, CA: RAND Corporation, 2019), https://doi.org/10.7249/RR3099.

32 "Russian Federation: Population (65+)" (The United Nations, 2022), https://population.un.org/wpp/Graphs/Probabilistic/POP/65plus/643.

33 Michael Kofman, "Russian Demographics and Power: Does the Kremlin Have a Long Game?" War on the Rocks, February 4, 2020, https://warontherocks.com/2020/02/russian-demographics-and-power-does-the-kremlin-have-a-long-game/.

34 See Vladimir Putin, "Poslaniye Federal'nomu Sobraniyu Rossiyskoy Federatsii" (Moscow, Russia, April 25, 2005), https://www.prlib.ru/item/438195, and Vladimir Putin, "Poslaniye Federal'nomu Sobraniyu Rossiyskoy Federatsii" (Moscow, Russia, May 10, 2006), http://kremlin.ru/events/president/transcripts/23577.

35 "Current Health Expenditure (% of GDP) – Russian Federation, OECD Members" (The World Bank, n.d.), https://data.worldbank.org/indicator/SH.XPD.CHEX.GD.ZS?locations=RU-OE.

36 "Life Expectancy at Birth, male (years) – Russian Federation" (The World

Bank, n.d.), https://data.worldbank.org/indicator/SP.DYN.LE00.MA.IN?loca
tions=RU.

37 "Education" (Organization for Economic Co-operation and Development,
n.d.), https://data.oecd.org/education.htm.

38 "QS World University Rankings 2023: Top Global Universities" (Quacquarelli
Symonds, June 8, 2022), https://www.topuniversities.com/university-rankings
/world-university-rankings/2023.

39 "U21 Rankings" (UNIVERSITAS 21, 2020), https://universitas21.com/wh
at-we-do/u21-rankings/u21-ranking-national-higher-education-systems-2020
/comparison-table.

40 OECD data available at "U21 Rankings" (UNIVERSITAS 21, 2020), https://
universitas21.com/what-we-do/u21-rankings/u21-ranking-national-higher
-education-systems-2020/comparison-table.

41 Tat'yana Stanovaya, "Russia's Elites Are Starting to Admit the Possibility of
Defeat," Carnegie Endowment for International Peace, September 29, 2022,
https://carnegieendowment.org/politika/88072; Andrey Pertsev, "Pered nim
strakh do usrachki. No strakh bez uvazheniya," Meduza, October 7, 2022,
https://meduza.io/feature/2022/10/07/pered-nim-strah-do-usrachki-no-strah
-bez-uvazheniya.

42 "SIPRI Military Expenditure Database" (Stockholm International Peace
Research Institute, n.d.), https://milex.sipri.org/sipri.

43 Dmitri Trenin, "The Revival of the Russian Military: How Moscow Reloaded,"
Foreign Affairs, May/June 2016, https://www.foreignaffairs.com/articles/russia
-fsu/2016-04-18/revival-russian-military.

44 "Chto ostalos' ot rossiyskoy armii k sed'momu mesyatsu voyny," Vazhnyye
Istorii, September 29, 2022, https://istories.media/stories/2022/09/29/chto-os
talos-ot-rossiiskoi-armii-k-sedmomu-mesyatsu-voini/.

45 Fabian Burkhardt, "Foolproofing Putinism," Riddle, March 29, 2021, https://
ridl.io/foolproofing-putinism/#.

4 Russian National Interests and Grand Strategy

1 Max Seddon and Polina Ivanova, "Russia's Melancholy Oligarchs," Financial
Times, September 7, 2022, https://www.ft.com/content/daee2387-6d96-4f2e
-9a80-5cc70cd8cc67?fbclid=IwAR2fisAICDFAjC5MQoXCf9GqMb28qsq1t
WHpj-zqtYcveuXUgdFLdTEYDFM.

2 Pjotr Sauer, "'We Have Already Lost': Far-Right Russian Bloggers Slam
Military Failures," Guardian, September 8, 2022, https://www.theguardian

.com/world/2022/sep/08/we-have-already-lost-far-right-russian-bloggers-sl am-kremlin-over-army-response; Anton Troianovski, "As Russians Retreat, Putin Is Criticized by Hawks Who Trumpeted His War," *New York Times*, September 10, 2022, https://www.nytimes.com/2022/09/10/world/europe/rus sia-ukraine-retreat-putin.html?smid=nytcore-ios-share&referringSource=articl eShare.

3 "Global Wealth Report 2013" (Credit Suisse, October 2013), 53, https://www .files.ethz.ch/isn/172470/global_wealth_report_2013.pdf.

4 See, for example, Karen Dawisha, *Putin's Kleptocracy* (New York, NY: Simon & Schuster, 2014).

5 Kimberly Marten, "Russia's Use of Semi-State Security Forces: The Case of the Wagner Group," *Post-Soviet Affairs* 35, no. 3 (2019): 181–204, https://doi .org/10.1080/1060586X.2019.1591142.; Candace Rondeaux, "Decoding the Wagner Group: Analyzing the Role of Private Military Security Contractors in Russian Proxy Warfare" (New America, November 7, 2019), https://www.ne wamerica.org/international-security/reports/decoding-wagner-group-analyzing -role-private-military-security-contractors-russian-proxy-warfare/.

6 Vladimir Putin, "Rossiya na rubezhe tysyacheletiy," *Nezavisimaya Gazeta*, December 30, 1999, https://www.ng.ru/politics/1999-12-30/4_millenium.html.

7 Dmitry Medvedev, "Stenograficheskiy otchet o vstreche s predstavitelyami obshchestvenniykh organizatsiy" (Moscow, Russia, September 19, 2008), http://kremlin.ru/events/president/transcripts/1467.

8 Putin, "Rossiya na rubezhe tysyacheletiy," op. cit.

9 Thomas Graham Jr., "World Without Russia?," *The Wall Street Journal*, August 30, 1999, https://www.wsj.com/articles/SB935781632337847057. For the complete text of the article, see Thomas Graham Jr., "World Without Russia?" (Jamestown Foundation Conference, Washington, DC, 1999), https://carnegi eendowment.org/1999/06/09/world-without-russia-pub-285.

10 Thomas E. Graham Jr., *Russia's Decline and Uncertain Recovery* (Washington, DC: Carnegie Endowment for International Peace, 2002), 47–8.

11 Ibid., 48–9.

12 C.J. Chivers, "Kremlin Puts Foreign NGO's on Notice," *New York Times*, October 20, 2006, https://www.nytimes.com/2006/10/20/world/europe/20r ussia.html.

13 Vladimir Putin, "Obrashcheniye Prezidenta Rossii Vladimira Putina" (Moscow, Russia, September 4, 2004), http://kremlin.ru/events/president/transcripts /22589.

14 Vladimir Putin, "Speech at a Conference in the Jawaharhal Nehru Memorial Foundation" (New Delhi, India, December 3, 2004), http://en.kremlin.ru/eve nts/president/transcripts/22720.

15 Vladimir Putin, "Speech and the Following Discussion at the Munich Conference on Security Policy" (Munich, Germany, February 10, 2007), http://en.kremlin.ru/events/president/transcripts/24034.

16 Trenin, "The Revival of the Russian Military," op. cit., 23–9; Keir Giles, "Russia's 'New' Tools for Confronting the West: Continuity and Innovation in Moscow's Exercise of Power" (London, United Kingdom: Chatham House, March 2016), 12–26, https://www.chathamhouse.org/sites/default/files/pub lications/2016-03-russia-new-tools-giles.pdf.

17 Vladimir Putin, "Rossiya i menyayushchiysya mir," *Moskovskiye Novosti*, February 27, 2012, https://www.mn.ru/politics/78738.

18 "Population, Total – China, Russian Federation, United States" (The World Bank, n.d.), https://data.worldbank.org/indicator/SP.POP.TOTL?locations= CN-RU-US.

19 Calculated from World Bank data, "GDP (Constant 2015 US$) - World, United States, Russian Federation, China" (The World Bank, n.d.), https://da ta.worldbank.org/indicator/NY.GDP.MKTP.KD?locations=1W-US-RU-CN &name_desc=false.

20 See Richard Connolly, "Russian Military Expenditure in Comparative Perspective: A Purchasing Power Parity Estimate" (CNA Analysis and Solutions, October 2019), https://www.cna.org/reports/2019/10/russian-military-expend iture; and Michael Kofman and Richard Connolly, "Why Russian Military Expenditure Is Much Higher than Commonly Understood (as is China's)," War on the Rocks, December 16, 2019, https://warontherocks.com/2019/12 /why-russian-military-expenditure-is-much-higher-than-commonly-understo od-as-is-chinas/. See also Sam Perlo-Freeman et al., "Trends in World Military Expenditure, 2012" (Stockholm International Peace Research Institute, April 2013), https://www.sipri.org/sites/default/files/files/FS/SIPRIFS1304.pdf, which, using current prices and exchange rates, estimates the military expenditure of Russia, the United States, and China in 2012 at $90 billion, some $680 billion, and more than $165 billion, respectively.

21 "Research and Development Expenditure (% of GDP) - China, United States, Russian Federation" (The World Bank, June 2022), https://data.worldbank.org /indicator/GB.XPD.RSDV.GD.ZS?view=chart&locations=CN-US-RU.

22 "List Statistics" (TOP500, n.d.), https://www.top500.org/statistics/list/.

23 "QS World University Rankings 2012" (Quacquarelli Symonds, n.d.), https://www.topuniversities.com/university-rankings/world-university-rankings/2012.

24 "World Nuclear Forces," in *SIPRI Yearbook 2012* (Stockholm International Peace Research Institute, 2012), https://www.sipri.org/yearbook/2012/07.

25 Vladimir Basov, "Top 10 Oil and Gas Producing Countries in 2012," MINING.COM, June 14, 2013, https://www.mining.com/top-10-oil-and-gas-producing-countries-in-2012-24585/.

26 "Oil and Petroleum Products Explained" (The US Energy Information Administration), https://www.eia.gov/energyexplained/oil-and-petroleum-products/imports-and-exports.php for oil imports and "Natural Gas Explained" (The US Energy Information Administration), https://www.eia.gov/energyexplained/natural-gas/imports-and-exports.php for natural gas imports. The figures represent net imports as a share of total consumption.

27 "China" (The US Energy Information Administration, May 14, 2015), https://www.energy.gov/sites/prod/files/2016/04/f30/China_International_Analysis_US.pdf.

28 Vladimir Putin, "Rossiya i menyayushchiysya mir," op. cit.

29 "GDP (Constant 2015 US$) - European Union" (The World Bank, n.d.), https://data.worldbank.org/indicator/NY.GDP.MKTP.KD?locations=EU.

30 Marta Domínguez-Jiménez and Niclas Frederic Poitiers, "An Analysis of EU FDI Inflow into Russia," *Russian Journal of Economics* 6, no. 2 (June 30, 2020): Figure 1, https://doi.org/10.32609/j.ruje.6.55880.

31 Vladimir Putin, "Vstupitel'noye slovo na soveshchanii 'O perspektivakh razvitiya Dal'nego Vostoka i Zabaykal'ya,'" (Blagoveshchensk, Russia, July 21, 2000), http://kremlin.ru/events/president/transcripts/21494.

32 D. Medvedev, "Russian Federation's Policy for the Arctic to 2020," *Rossiyskaya Gazeta*, March 30, 2009, http://www.arctis-search.com/Russian+Federation+Policy+for+the+Arctic+to+2020.; 645; Vladimir Putin, "O Strategii razvitiya Arkticheskoy zony Rossiyskoy Federatsii i obespecheniya natsional'noy bezopasnosti na period do 2035 goda" (The President of the Russian Federation, October 26, 2020), http://publication.pravo.gov.ru/Document/View/0001202010260033?index=0&rangeSize=1.

33 Gaddis, *Strategies of Containment*, op. cit., ix. In the original edition, completed as the Reagan administration took over, Gaddis identified five geopolitical codes. The revised edition added the sixth, Reagan's and George H.W. Bush's.

34 Vladimir Putin, "Vystupleniye v bundestage FRG" (Berlin, Germany, September 25, 2001), http://kremlin.ru/events/president/transcripts/21340.

35 A.V. Lukin and D.P. Novikov, "Bol'shaya Yevraziya: ot polyusa konfrontatsii k soobshchestvu razvitiya," *Vostok (Oriens)* 6 (2019): 175, https://elibrary.ru /item.asp?id=41507292.

36 Vladimir Putin, "Rossiya i menyayushchiysya mir," op. cit.; Maxim Tkachenko, "Putin Points to US Role in Gadhafi's Killing," CNN, December 15, 2011, https://www.cnn.com/2011/12/15/world/europe/russia-putin-libya.

37 von Twickel, "Biden 'Opposes' 3rd Putin Term," op. cit.

38 Elise Labott, "Clinton Cites 'Serious Concerns' about Russian Election," CNN, December 6, 2011, https://www.cnn.com/2011/12/06/world/europe /russia-elections-clinton.

39 Vladimir Putin and Dmitry Medvedev, "Speech at a Rally in Support of Presidential Candidate Vladimir Putin" (Moscow, Russia, March 4, 2012), http://en.kremlin.ru/events/president/news/14684.

40 Vladimir Putin, "Obrashcheniye Prezidenta Rossiyskoy Federatsii," (Moscow, March 18, 2014), http://kremlin.ru/events/president/news/20603.

41 See, for example, Vladimir Putin, "A Plea for Caution From Russia," *New York Times*, September 11, 2013, https://www.nytimes.com/2013/09/12/opinion /putin-plea-for-caution-from-russia-on-syria.html.

42 Lionel Barber and Henry Foy, "Vladimir Putin: liberalism has 'outlived its purpose'," *Financial Times*, September 17, 2019, https://on.ft.com/3h8H0fq.

43 See Tania Marocchi, "EU–Russia Relations: Towards an Increasingly Geopolitical Paradigm," Heinrich Böll Stiftung, July 3, 2017, https://eu.boell .org/en/2017/07/03/eu-russia-relations-towards-increasingly-geopolitical-para digm.

44 The Kremlin took former German Chancellor Angela Merkel's remark in December 2022 that the Minsk Agreements had been an attempt to "give Ukraine time" to build up its defenses against Russian aggression as irrefutable evidence that Germany and France had acted in bad faith. See "Putin: Russia May Have to Make Ukraine Deal One Day, but Partners Cheated in the Past," Reuters, December 9, 2022, https://www.reuters.com/world/putin-russia-may -have-make-ukraine-deal-one-day-partners-cheated-past-2022-12-09/.

45 See Dmitry Trenin, "From Greater Europe to Greater Asia?" (Moscow, Russia: Carnegie Moscow Center, April 2015), https://carnegieendowment.org/files /CP_Trenin_To_Asia_WEB_2015Eng.pdf; A.V. Lukin and D.P. Novikov, "Ot Bol'shoy Yevropy k Bol'shoy Yeverazii: chto neset miru korennoy

geopoliticheskiy sdvig," *Vostok (Oriens)* 5 (2019): 60–76, https://publications
.hse.ru/mirror/pubs/share/direct/322655137; Lukin and Novikov, "Bol'shaya
Yevraziya," op. cit., 173–88.

46 Vladimir Putin, "Pervyy Yevraziyskiy ekonomicheskiy forum" (Moscow,
Russia, May 26, 2022), http://kremlin.ru/events/president/news/68484.

47 "In Their Own Words: Joint Statement of the Russian Federation and the
People's Republic of China on the International Relations Entering a New Era
and the Global Sustainable Development" (China Aerospace Studies Institute,
2022), https://www.airuniversity.af.edu/Portals/10/CASI/documents/Transl
ations/2022-02-04%20China%20Russia%20joint%20statement%20Internati
onal%20Relations%20Entering%20a%20New%20Era.pdf.

48 Lindsay Maizland, "China and Russia: Exploring Ties Between Two
Authoritarian Powers," Council on Foreign Relations, June 14, 2022, https://
www.cfr.org/backgrounder/china-russia-relationship-xi-putin-taiwan-ukraine.

49 Chen Aizhu, "China May oil imports from Russia soar to a record, surpass
top supplier Saudi," Reuters, July 6, 2022, https://www.reuters.com/markets
/commodities/chinas-may-oil-imports-russia-soar-55-record-surpass-saudi-sup
ply-2022-06-20/.

50 Victoria Zaretskaya and Faouzi Aloulou, "As of 2021, China Imports More
Liquefied Natural Gas than Any Other Country," Today in Energy (US Energy
Information Agency, May 2, 2022), https://www.eia.gov/todayinenergy/detail
.php?id=52258.

51 Trenin, "From Greater Europe to Greater Asia?" op. cit.

5 *The Putin Factor*

1 "Net Putina – net rossii: prezident v otsenkakh chinovnikov i biznesmenov,"
RBK, October 23, 2014, https://www.rbc.ru/photoreport/23/10/2014/54491
408cbb20f72ecea58db.

2 Timothy Frye, *Weak Strongman: The Limits of Power in Putin's Russia* (Princeton,
New Jersey: Princeton University Press, 2021) makes a compelling case for the
political limitations on Putin's power.

3 This widespread English rendering of Putin's remark is in fact a misleading
mistranslation. A more accurate translation appears on the Kremlin website:
"The collapse of the Soviet Union was *a major* [that is, not "the greatest"]
geopolitical disaster of the [20th] century." Emphasis added. See Vladimir
Putin, "Poslaniye Federalnomu Sobraniyu Rossiskoi Federatsii" (Moscow,
Russia, April 25, 2005), 438195.

4 Fiona Hill and Clifford G. Gaddy, *Mr. Putin: Operative in the Kremlin*, 2nd edn. (Washington, DC: Brookings Institution Press, 2015), 39–43.

5 Putin, "Rossiya na rubezhe tysyacheletiy," op. cit.

6 Putin, "Vstrecha s molodymi predprinimatelyami, inzhenerami i uchenymi," op. cit. 9,

7 Hill and Gaddy, *Mr. Putin*, op. cit., 63–4.

8 V.V. Putin, "75 let Velikoy Pobedy: obshchay otvetstvennost' pered istoriey i budushchim" (Moscow, Russia, 2020), http://static.kremlin.ru/media/events/fi les/ru/hOAWB1GRwEMuVtAAGREjC8Vvl3VxqiW4.pdf.

9 Putin, "Ob istoricheskom yedinstve russkikh i ukraintsev," op. cit.

10 For a recent Putin statement on the need to honor all of Russian history, see Vladimir Putin, "Torzhestvennyy kontsert, posvyashchennyy 1160-letiyu zarozhdeniya rossiyskoy gosudarstvennostie" (Velikiy Novgorod, Russia, September 21, 2022), http://kremlin.ru/events/president/news/69397.

11 Keenan, "Muscovite Political Folkways," op. cit., 132. Emphasis added.

12 Vladimir Tomsinov, *Arakcheev* (Moscow, Russia: Molodaya gvardiya, Moscow, 2003), 84. For a similar observation about Putin's decision-making, see Aleksey Venediktov, "Ot konflikta na Ukraine vyigrala i kolumbiyskaya narkomafiya," *Delovoy Peterburg*, May 22, 2015, https://www.dp.ru/a/2015/05/22/U_nih _ponti_dorozhe_deneg.

13 Timothy Frye, *Weak Strongman*, op cit., 66–9, who makes a slightly different but complementary point about the importance of elections.

14 Ibid., 50–2.

15 V.O. Klyuchevsky, "Kurs Russkoi istorii, Lecture 9," http://www.spsl.nsc.ru /history/kluch/kluch09.htm and Klyuchevsky, "Kurs Russkoi istorii, Lecture 10," http://www.spsl.nsc.ru/history/kluch/kluch10.htm.

16 Klyuchevsky, "Kurs Russkoi istorii, Lecture 76," http://www.spsl.nsc.ru/histo ry/kluch/kluch76.htm.

17 Dominic Lieven, *The End of Tsarist Russia* (New York, NY: Viking, 2015), 52.

18 Ibid., 1.

19 Orysia Kulick, "Global Arms Production and Ukraine's Unpredictable Soviet Inheritance," Jahrbuch für Wirtschaftsgeschichte / Economic History Yearbook, 60, no. 2 (2019): 409–32.

20 Lieven, *The End of Tsarist Russia*, op. cit., 52–3.

21 Serhii Plokhy, "Killing the Language," in *Lost Kingdom: The Quest for Empire and the Making of the Russian Nation* (New York, NY: Basic Books, 2017).

22 Ibid., 228–30.

23 Ibid., 245–50.

24 Ibid., 281–4.

25 Gwendolyn Sasse, *The Crimea Question: Identity, Transition, and Conflict* (Cambridge, MA: Harvard University Press, 2007), 155–73.

26 Ibid., 222–35.

27 There is evidence that Putin took this decision over the objections of many members of the Russian Security Council. See Venediktov, "Ot konflikta na Ukraine," op. cit.

28 Putin, "Obrashcheniye Prezidenta Rossiyskoy Federatsii," op. cit., March 18, 2014, 20603. See also Daniel Treisman, "Why Putin Took Crimea," *Foreign Affairs*, May/June 2016, https://www.foreignaffairs.com/print/node/1117090.

29 This account of the events of early 2014 is based on a Russian source who worked closely with the Kremlin on Ukraine policy during that time, email of September 20, 2022.

30 Dan Peleschuk, "Ukraine's President Finally Flexes His Muscles," *Foreign Policy*, February 12, 2021, https://foreignpolicy.com/2021/02/12/ukraine-vo lodymyr-zelensky-russia-propaganda-media-medvedchuk-euromaidan-kremlin -hybrid-war/.

31 Natalia Zinets, "Ukraine Sanctions Kremlin Ally Medvedchuk, Says Will Take Back Fuel Pipeline," Reuters, February 19, 2021, https://www.reuters.com/ar ticle/us-ukraine-sanctions-idUSKBN2AJ28O.

32 "NATO Recognises Ukraine as Enhanced Opportunities Partner," North Atlantic Treaty Organization, June 12, 2020, https://www.nato.int/cps/en/na tohq/news_176327.htm.

33 See "Crimea Platform," n.d., https://crimea-platform.org/en/about.

34 Vladimir Putin, "Obrashcheniye Prezidenta Rossiyskoy Federatsii" (Moscow, Russia, February 21, 2022), http://kremlin.ru/events/president/news/67828.

35 Putin, "Obrashcheniye Prezidenta Rossiyskoy Federatsii," op. cit., February 21, 2022, 67828.; Vladimir Putin, "Obrashcheniye Prezidenta Rossiyskoy Federatsii" (Moscow, Russia, February 24, 2022), http://kremlin.ru/events /president/news/67843.

36 Antony J. Blinken and Dmytro Kuleba, "US–Ukraine Charter on Strategic Partnership," November 10, 2021, https://www.state.gov/u-s-ukraine-charter -on-strategic-partnership/.

37 Ivan Timofeyev, "Pochemu eksperty ne verili v veroyatnost' vooruzhennogo konflikta c Ukrainoy," Rossiickii sovet po mezhdunarodnym delam, March

2, 2022, https://russiancouncil.ru/analytics-and-comments/analytics/pochemu
-eksperty-ne-verili-v-veroyatnost-vooruzhennogo-konflikta-s-ukrainoy/.

38 Putin, "Obrashcheniye Prezidenta Rossiyskoy Federatsii," op. cit., February 24, 2022, 67843.

39 Mariya Makukha, "Reyting Zelenskogo vyros: yemu doveryayut pochti 40% ukraintsev – opros," The Page, November 16, 2021, https://thepage.ua/politics/rejting-zelenskogo-vyros.

40 See the Public Opinion Foundation data at "Kliuchevye indikatory obshchestvenogo mneniya" (FOMnibus, September 1, 2022), https://media.fom.ru/fom-bd/d34pi2022.pdf.

41 See the polling data of the Kyiv International Institute of Sociology at "Dynamics of Party Rating in the Elections to the Verkhovna Rada of Ukraine and Candidates in the Election of the President of Ukraine: Results of the Telephone Survey, Conducted on February 5–13, 2022." (Kyiv International Institute of Sociology, 2022), https://www.kiis.com.ua/?lang=eng&cat=reports&id=1100&page=1.

42 "Share of Gas Supply from Russia in Europe in 2021, by Selected Country" (Statista, July 2022), https://www.statista.com/statistics/1201743/russian-gas-dependence-in-europe-by-country/.

43 Yana Popkostova, "Europe's Energy Crisis Conundrum" (European Union Institute for Security Studies (EUISS), January 28, 2022), https://www.iss.europa.eu/content/europes-energy-crisis-conundrum.

44 Vladimir Putin, "Poslaniye Prezidenta Federal'nomu Sobraniyu," op. cit., March 1, 2018, 56957.

45 Jeff Mason, "Biden says putting US troops on ground in Ukraine is 'not on the table'," Reuters, December 8, 2021, https://www.reuters.com/world/us/biden-says-putting-us-troops-ground-ukraine-is-not-table-2021-12-08/.

46 Philip Short, *Putin* (New York, NY: Henry Holt and Company, 2022), 391–8.

47 Putin, "Ob istoricheskom yedinstve russkikh i ukraintsev," op. cit.; see also Eugene Rumer and Andrew Weiss, "Ukraine: Putin's Unfinished Business," Carnegie Endowment for International Peace, November 12, 2021, https://carnegieendowment.org/2021/11/12/ukraine-putin-s-unfinished-business-pub-85771.

48 See, for example, Vladimir Putin, "Podpisaniye dogovorov o prinyatii DNR, LNR, Zaporozhskoy i Khersonskoy Oblastey v sostav Rossii" (Moscow, Russia, September 30, 2022), http://kremlin.ru/events/president/news/69465; Zasedaniye Mezhdunarodnogo diskussionnogo kluba "Valday", Moscow

Oblast, Russia, October 27, 2022), http://kremlin.ru/events/president/news /69695.

49 "U Putina zayavili, chto yego fraza o 'vzyatii Kieva za 2 nedeli' neverno inter-pretirovana," RBK-Ukraina, September 2, 2014, https://www.rbc.ua/rus/ne ws/u-putina-zayavili-chto-ego-fraza-o-vzyatii-kieva-za-2-nedeli--0209201411 2500.

50 Phil Stewart, "CIA Director Estimates 15,000 Russians Killed in Ukraine War," Reuters, July 20, 2022, https://www.reuters.com/world/europe/cia-di rector-says-some-15000-russians-killed-ukraine-war-2022-07-20/.

6 Washington's Blind Spots and Missteps

1 See, for example, Michael McFaul, *From Cold War to Hot Peace* (Boston, MA: Houghton Mifflin Harcourt, 2018), 409–28.

2 See, for example, John J. Mearsheimer, *The Great Illusion* (New Haven, CT: Yale University Press, 2018), 178–9; John J. Mearsheimer, "Why the Ukraine Crisis Is the West's Fault," *Foreign Affairs* (September/October 2014), 1–12, https://www.foreignaffairs.com/articles/russia-fsu/2014-08-18/why-ukraine-cr isis-west-s-fault

3 See Olga Kryshtanovskaya and Stephen White, "From Soviet *Nomenklatura* to Russian Elite," *Europe–Asia Studies* 48, no. 5 (July 1996): 711–33, https://www.jstor.org/stable/152994; Yevgenia Albats, "The Great Illusion of 1991," *Moscow Times*, August 21, 2001; and Tomas Grekhem [Thomas Graham], "Novyy rossiyskiy rezhim," *Nezavisimaya Gazeta*, November 23, 1995.

4 "Russian President's Address to Joint Session of Congress," *Washington Post*, June 18, 1992, https://www.washingtonpost.com/archive/politics/1992/06/18 /russian-presidents-address-to-joint-session-of-congress/303246d0-5ecf-43b6 -b39b-264e651c78b1/.

5 Burns, *The Back Channel*, op. cit., 242.

6 Sarotte, *Not One Inch*, op. cit., provides a detailed assessment of the evolu-tion of the United States' NATO policy, on which the following paragraphs draw.

7 Ibid., 173–80.

8 Ibid., 189–96.

9 Ibid., 341–2.

10 Burns, *The Back Channel*, op. cit., 413.

11 Ibid., 227.

12 See Thomas Graham, "Russia," in *Hand-Off: The Foreign Policy George W. Bush Passed to Barack Obama*, ed. Stephen J. Hadley et al. (Washington, DC: Brookings Institution Press, 2023), 412–14.

13 Although I argued otherwise in the late 1990s. See Graham, "World Without Russia?" op. cit.

14 The following discussion builds on ideas first laid out in Thomas Graham, "Russia," in *Hand-Off*, op. cit., 414–15.

7 *What is to be Done?*

1 See "Soglashenye o merakh obespechenia bezopasnosti Rossiyskoy Federatsii i gosudarstv-chlenov Organizatsii Severoatlanticheskogo dogovora" (Ministerstvo inostrannykh del Rossiyskoy Federatsii, December 17, 2021), https://mid.ru/ru/foreign_policy/rso/nato/1790803/?lang=ru.; and "Dogovor mezhdu Rossiyskoy Federatsii i Soedinennymi Shtatami Ameriki o garantiyakh bezopasnosti" (Ministerstvo inostrannykh del Rossiyskoy Federatsii, December 17, 2021), https://mid.ru/ru/foreign_policy/rso/nato/1790818/?lang=ru.

2 See Aleksandr Kynev, "Pochemu raspada Rossii ne budet," Vazhnyye Istorii, November 15, 2022, https://storage.googleapis.com/istories/opinions/2022/11/15/pochemu-raspada-rossii-ne-budet/index.html.

3 White House, *National Security Strategy*, op. cit., October 2022, 6.

4 See Barbara W. Tuchman, *The Guns of August, The Proud Tower* (New York, NY: Literary Classics of the United States, 2012), 562–3.

5 On the current challenges facing world order, Henry Kissinger, *Leadership: Six Studies in World Strategy* (New York, NY: Penguin Press, 2022), 409–14.

6 I borrow these terms from William J. Burns, "The United States Needs a New Foreign Policy," *The Atlantic*, July 14, 2020, https://www.theatlantic.com/ideas/archive/2020/07/united-states-needs-new-foreign-policy/614110/. The rest of this section draws on the argument he lays out in that essay.

7 Burns, "The United States Needs a New Foreign Policy," op. cit.

8 For an extended discussion of this issue, which also underscores how long it has been in the making, see Richard N. Haass, *Foreign Policy Begins at Home: The Case for Putting America's House in Order* (New York, NY: Basic Books, 2013).

9 Cited in Quinn, "Biden Issues His First Russia Sanctions," op. cit.

10 White House, *National Security Strategy*, op. cit., October 2022, 25.

11 Ibid., 25–6.

12 Missy Ryan and Annabelle Timsit, "US Wants Russian Military 'Weakened' from Ukraine Invasion, Austin Says," *Washington Post*, April 25, 2022, https://

www.washingtonpost.com/world/2022/04/25/russia-weakened-lloyd-austin
-ukraine-visit/.

13 White House, *National Security Strategy*, op. cit., October 2022, 26.

14 Thomas Graham and Robert Legvold, "It's Better to Deal with China and
Russia in Tandem," February 4, 2021, https://www.politico.com/news/magaz
ine/2021/02/04/china-russia-tandem-policy-465616.

15 Ibid.

Epilogue

1 *Soveshchaniye s postoyannymi chlenami Soveta Bezopasnosti*, March 31, 2023,
http://kremlin.ru/events/president/news/70810.

2 The concepts can be found at "Kontseptsiya vneshey politiki Rossiyskoy
Federatsii, June 28, 2000, https://docs.cntd.ru/document/901764263.;
"Kontseptsiya vneshey politiki Rossiyskoy Federatsii," July 15, 2008, http://
kremlin.ru/acts/news/785; "Kontseptsiya vneshey politiki Rossiyskoy Federatsii,"
March 1, 2013, https://docs.cntd.ru/document/499003797; and "Ob utverzhdenii Kontseptsiyi vneshey politiki Rossiyskoy Federatsii," November 30, 2016,
http://static.kremlin.ru/media/acts/files/0001201612010045.pdf.

3 "Ob utverzhdenii Kontseptsiyi vneshey politiki Rossiyskoy Federatsii," March
31, 2023, 2, http://static.kremlin.ru/media/events/files/ru/udpjZePcMAycLX
OGGAgmVHQDIoFCN2Ae.pdf.

4 Samuel P. Huntington, "The Clash of Civilizations?," *Foreign Affairs*, Summer
1993, 22–49, https://www.jstor.org/stable/20045621.

5 Vladimir Putin, Interv'yu nemetskoy gazete "Bil'd," September 18, 2001,
http://kremlin.ru/events/president/transcripts/21334.

6 "China's Xi Tells Putin of 'Changes Not Seen for 100 years,'" Al Jazeera, March
22, 2023, https://www.aljazeera.com/news/2023/3/22/xi-tells-putin-of-chan
ges-not-seen-for-100.

7 "Ob utverzhdenii Kontseptsiyi vneshey politiki Rossiyskoy Federatsii," op. cit.,
1–2, March 31, 2023.

8 Ibid., 38.

9 Putin, "Rossiya na rubezhe tysyacheletiy," op. cit. https://www.ng.ru/politics
/1999-12-30/4_millenium.html.

10 See Andrey Kolesnikov, "Nauchnyy putinizm. Kak v Rossii oformlyaetsya
ofitsial'naya ideologiya," Carnegie Endowment for International Peace,
November 1, 2022, https://carnegieendowment.org/politika/88295.

11 "UN General Assembly Demands Russian Federation Withdraw All Military

Forces from the Territory of Ukraine," European External Action Service, March 2, 2022, https://www.eeas.europa.eu/eeas/un-general-assembly-demands-russi an-federation-withdraw-all-military-forces-territory-ukraine_en.; "UN General Assembly Calls for Immediate End to War in Ukraine," UN News, February 23, 2023, https://news.un.org/en/story/2023/02/1133847.

12 See, for example, the conversations from early 2023 between the musical produce Iosif Prigozhin (no relation to Yevgeny Prigozhin, the head of the private military company Wagner) and the businessman Farkhad Akhmedov at https://www.youtube.com/watch?v=RwSTW8seAPE and between business-men Roman Trotsenko and Nikolay Matushevskiy at https://www.youtube .com/watch?v=ran0iemlI3k

13 See, for example, Noah Berman and Anshu Siripurapu, "Are Sanctions Against Russia Making a Difference?," PBS NewsHour, February 21, 2023, https:// www.pbs.org/newshour/politics/are-sanctions-against-russia-making-a-differen ce; Maria Snegovaya et al., "Russia Sanctions at One Year" (Center for Strategic and International Studies, February 23, 2023), https://www.csis.org/analysis /russia-sanctions-one-year.

14 See "Conflict with Ukraine: Assessments for March 2023" (Levada-Center, April 7, 2023), https://www.levada.ru/en/2023/04/07/conflict-with-ukraine-as sessments-for-march=2023/.

15 Andrey Kolesnikov, "Poza embriona. Pochemu rossiyskoye obshchestvo smiri-los' s proiskhodyashchim," Carnegie Endowment for International Peace, January 26, 2023, https://carnegieendowment.org/politika/88886.

16 See "Attitude to Countries: February 2023" (Levada-Center, April 5, 2023), https://www.levada.ru/en/2023/04/05/attitude-to-countries-february-2023/.

17 See, for example, Yelizaveta Fokht and Pavel Aksenov, "Shoygu! Gerasimov! Gde boyepripasy? Posmotrite na nikh, suki". Prigozhin poobeshchal, chto ChVK 'Vagner' pokinet Bakhmut," BBC News, May 5, 2023, https://www .bbc.com/russian/features-65501087; "Prigozhin obvinil Shoygu i Gerasimova v izmene Rodine za popytku unichtozhit' yego ChVK," EADaily, February 21, 2023, https://eadaily.com/ru/news/2023/02/21/prigozhin-obvinil-shoygu-i-g erasimova-v-izmene-rodine-za-popytku-unichtozhit-ego-chvk. For an analysis of Putin's ties to Prigozhin, see Andrei Soldatov and Irina Borogan, "Why Putin Needs Wagner," *Foreign Affairs*, May 12, 2023, https://www.foreignaffa irs.com/russian-federation/why-putin-needs-wagner?utm_medium=newsletter s&utm_source=fatoday&utm_campaign=Why%20Putin%20Needs%20Wag ner&utm_content=20230512&utm_term=FA%20Today%20-%20112017.

18 See, for example, Valerie Hopkins, "'Nothing Has Really Changed': In Moscow, the Fighting Is a World Away," *New York Times*, September 6, 2022, https://www.nytimes.com/2022/09/06/world/europe/moscow-war-ukraine-mood.html; "Gorod, v kotorom net voyny. Moskva i moskvichi cherez god posle vtorzheniya," BBC News, February 26, 2023, https://www.bbc.com/russian/features-64716917.

19 Vladislav Surkov, "Odinochestvo polukrovki," *Rossiya v global'noy politike*, no. 2 (April 11, 2018), https://globalaffairs.ru/articles/odinochestvo-polukrovki-14-2/.

20 See Malia, *Russia under Western Eyes*, op. cit., 36–9.

21 Ibid., 23–7.

Index